MULTICULTURAL EDUCATION SERIES

James A. Banks, Series Editor

(continued)

MULTICULTURAL EDUCATION SERIES, *continued*

Americans by Heart

Undocumented Latino Students and the Promise of Higher Education

William Pérez

Teachers College
Columbia University
New York and London

Published by Teachers College Press, 1234 Amsterdam Avenue,
New York, NY 10027

Library of Congress Cataloging-in-Publication Data

Pérez, William, 1974–
  Americans by heart : undocumented Latino students and the promise of higher
education / William Pérez.
    p. cm. — (Multicultural education series)
  Includes bibliographical references and index.
    ISBN 978-0-8077-5283-8 (pbk. : alk. paper) — ISBN 978-0-8077-5284-5
(hardcover : alk. paper)
  1. Hispanic Americans—Education (Higher) 2. Hispanic Americans—Education
(Higher)—Social aspects. 3. Hispanic Americans—Social conditions. 4. Illegal
aliens—Education (Higher)—United States. I. Title.
  LC2670.6.P47 2011
  378.1'98268073—dc23

                                                          2011041485

ISBN 978-0-8077-5283-8 (paperback)
ISBN 978-0-8077-5284-5 (hardcover)

Printed on acid-free paper

Manufactured in the United States of America

19 18 17 16 15 14 13 12   8 7 6 5 4 3 2 1

Para mis padres Isabel Perez y Miguel Ángel Perez.
Les debo todo.

Contents

Series Foreword

This timely and significant study of undocumented Latino high school, community college, and university students is informative and compelling. Pérez vividly and sympathetically describes the challenges, stigmatization, and marginalization of undocumented students. However, he interweaves stories of optimism, resilience, and persistence onto almost every page of this engaging and informative book.

The creative and innovate ways that undocumented students described in this book have used to grapple with and in many cases resolve a myriad of intractable and daunting challenges are important lessons readers will acquire from this book. The students' stories are sources of inspiration and hope, as well as springboards for seriously considering ways to transform American society, schools, colleges, and universities.

Thomas Wolfe's (1934) novel, *You Can't Go Home Again*, suggests that discerning travelers cannot return home because they view their own cultures in different and innovative ways when they become immersed in other cultures. Pérez's book enables readers to vicariously experience the journeys of undocumented immigrant students, to acquire new insights, and to view the United States with fresh perspectives. Readers will acquire a painful understanding of the ways in which the treatment of undocumented students seriously violates human rights as codified in the United Nations Convention of the Rights of the Child, as well as American democratic values conveyed in the U.S. Constitution and the Bill of Rights. Consequently, this ingenious book enables readers to experience the egregious journeys of undocumented students, as well as gives them the opportunity to develop a commitment to take action that will expand educational opportunities for undocumented students. Their civic actions will make the United States more democratic and just for all of its residents. In his "Letter from a Birmingham Jail" on April 16, 1963, Martin Luther King said, "Injustice anywhere is a threat to justice everywhere" (online). Creating equal opportunities for undocumented students will expand democracy and justice for all Americans and enable undocumented students to better actualize their political acumen and agency. One of the most encouraging findings in this book is the high level of civic engagement of undocumented students, which exceeds the level of their peers.

This heartfelt and persuasive book will help practicing educators to respond in culturally responsive ways to the growing ethnic, cultural, and linguistic diversity within U.S. society and schools. American classrooms are experiencing the largest influx of immigrant students since the beginning of the 20th century. About a million immigrants are making the United States their home each year (Martin & Midgley, 2006). Between 1997 and 2006, 9,105,162 immigrants entered the United States (U.S. Department of Homeland Security, 2007). Only 15% came from nations in Europe. Most came from nations in Asia, from Mexico, and from nations in Latin America, Central America, and the Caribbean (U.S. Department of Homeland Security, 2007). A large but undetermined number of undocumented immigrants also enter the United States each year. In 2007, *The New York Times* estimated that there were 12 million undocumented immigrants in the United States (Immigration Sabotage, 2007). Pérez points out that 3.2 million children and young adults are among the 12 million undocumented immigrants in the United States, where most of them grew up. The influence of an increasingly ethnically diverse population on U.S. schools, colleges, and universities is and will continue to be enormous.

Schools in the United States are more diverse today than they have been since the early 1900s when a multitude of immigrants entered the country from Southern, Central, and Eastern Europe. In the 34-year period between 1973 and 2007, the percentage of students of color in U.S. public schools increased from 22% to 44.3% (Dillon, 2006; Sable & Plotts, 2010). If current trends continue, students of color will equal or exceed the percentage of White students in U.S. public schools within one or two decades. In the 2007–2008 school year, students of color exceeded the number of White students in 11 states: Arizona, California, Florida, Georgia, Hawaii, Louisiana, Maryland, Mississippi, New Mexico, Nevada, and Texas (National Center for Education Statistics, 2008a, 2008b, & 2008c). Pérez points out that in 2009, children of undocumented immigrants made up 6.8% of students in grades kindergarten through 12 in the United States.

Language and religious diversity is also increasing in the U.S. student population. In 2000, about 20% of the school-age population spoke a language at home other than English (U.S. Census Bureau, 2003). The Progressive Policy Institute (2008) estimated that 50 million Americans (out of 300 million) spoke a language at home other than English in 2008. Harvard professor Diana L. Eck (2001) calls the United States the "most religiously diverse nation on earth" (p. 4). Islam is now the fastest-growing religion in the United States, as well as in several European nations such as France, the

United Kingdom, and The Netherlands (Banks, 2009; Cesari, 2004). Most teachers now in the classroom and in teacher education programs are likely to have students from diverse ethnic, racial, linguistic, and religious groups in their classrooms during their careers. This is true for both inner-city and suburban teachers in the United States, as well as in many other Western nations, such as Canada and the United Kingdom (Banks, 2009).

The major purpose of the Multicultural Education Series is to provide preservice educators, practicing educators, graduate students, scholars, and policymakers with an interrelated and comprehensive set of books that summarizes and analyzes important research, theory, and practice related to the education of ethnic, racial, cultural, and linguistic groups in the United States and the education of mainstream students about diversity. The dimensions of multicultural education, developed by Banks (Banks, 2004) and described in the *Handbook of Research on Multicultural Education*, provide the conceptual framework for the development of the publications in the Series. They are: content integration, the knowledge construction process, prejudice reduction, an equity pedagogy, and an empowering institutional culture and social structure.

The books in the Series provide research, theoretical, and practical knowledge about the behaviors and learning characteristics of students of color, language-minority students, and low-income students. They also provide knowledge about ways to improve academic achievement and race relations in educational settings. Multicultural education is consequently as important for middle-class White suburban students as it is for students of color who live in the inner city. Multicultural education fosters the public good and the overarching goals of the commonwealth.

This needed, informative, and engaging book inspires and enlightens, as well as challenges its readers to develop a commitment to act to create equal educational opportunities for undocumented students and to make it possible for them to participate fully in the nation's civic and public life. Their full participation in American society will enrich the United States and enable it to narrow the gap between the commitment to democracy it proclaims around the world and the marginalization and invisibility that many people who live within its borders experience.

James A. Banks

REFERENCES

Banks, J. A. (2004). Multicultural education: Historical development, dimensions, and practice. In J. A. Banks & C. A. M. Banks (Eds.), *Handbook of research on multicultural education* (2nd ed., pp. 3–29). San Francisco: Jossey-Bass.

Banks, J. A. (Ed.). (2009). *The Routledge international companion to multicultural education.* New York & London: Routledge.

Cesari, J. (2004). *When Islam and democracy meet: Muslims in Europe and the United States.* New York: Pelgrave Macmillan.

Dillon, S. (2006, August 27). In schools across U.S., the melting pot overflows. *The New York Times,* vol. CLV [155] (no. 53,684), pp. A7 & A16.

Eck, D. L. (2001). *A new religious America: How a "Christian country" has become the world's most religiously diverse nation.* New York: HarperSanFrancisco.

Immigration sabotage [Editorial]. (2007, June 4). *New York Times,* p. A22.

King, M. L. (1963, April 16). *Letter from a Birmingham jail.* African American Studies Center, University of Pennsylvania. Retrieved from http://www.africa.upenn.edu/Articles_Gen/Letter_Birmingham.html

Martin, P., & Midgley, E. (2006). Immigration to the United States. *Population Bulletin, 54*(2), 1–44. Washington, DC: Population Reference Bureau.

National Center for Education Statistics. (2008a). *The condition of education 2008.* Washington, DC: U.S. Department of Education. Retrieved from http://nces.ed.gov/pubsearch/pubsinfo.asp?pubid=2008031

National Center for Education Statistics. (2008b). *Public elementary/secondary school universe survey, 2007–2008. Common Core of Data.* Retrieved from http://nces.ed.gov/ccd

National Center for Education Statistics. (2008c). *State nonfiscal survey of public elementary/secondary education, 2007–2008. Common Core of Data.* Retrieved from http://nces.ed.gov/ccd

Progressive Policy Institute. (2008). *50 million Americans speak languages other than English at home.* Retrieved from http://www.ppionline.org/ppi_ci.cfm?knlgAreaID=108&subsecID=900003&contentID=254619

Sable, J., & Plotts, C. (2010). *Documentation to the NCES common core of data public elementary/secondary school universe survey: School year 2008–09* (NCES 2010-350 rev). Washington, DC: National Center for Education Statistics. Retrieved from http://nces.ed.gov/pubsearch/pubs.info.asp?pubid=2010350

U.S. Census Bureau. (2003, October). Language use and English-speaking ability: 2000. Retrieved from http://www.census.gov/prod/2003pubs/c2kbr-29.pdf

U.S. Department of Homeland Security. (2007). *Yearbook of immigration statistics, 2006.* Washington, DC: Office of Immigration Statistics, Author. Retrieved from http://www.dhs.gov/files/statistics/publications/yearbook.shtm

Wolfe, T. (1934). *You can't go home again.* New York: Harper and Row.

Acknowledgments

I am greatly indebted to the academic mentors that have supported my scholarship. In particular I would like to thank Ray Buriel, Amado Padilla, Guadalupe Valdés, Danny Solórzano, and Daryl Smith. I would also like to thank all the scholars that have encouraged my undocumented student research and provided thoughtful words of advice and guidance. I specifically would like to express my appreciation to Patricia Gándara, Kris Gutiérrez, Eugene García, Laura Rendón, Amaury Nora, Bill Tierney, Richard Duran, Marjorie Faulstich-Orellana, Janna Shadduck-Hernandez, Raul Hinojosa, Chon Noriega, Vilma Ortiz, Min Zhou, Kent Wong, Victor Narro, Estela Bensimon, Robert Teranishi, Anthony Antonio, H. Sammy Alim, Eamonn Callan, Evelyn Hu-DeHart, Bruce Fuller, Manuel Pastor, John Rogers, Cynthia García Coll, Michael Olivas, Frances Contreras, Gil Conchas, Alexandra Filindra, Alejandra Rincon, Jessica Retis, Jose Luis Benavides, Miguel Ceja, Anne Marie Nunez, Elsa Billings, Michelle Espino, Alejandro Gradilla, James Rodriguez, Marybeth Gasman, Ben Kirshner, Zenaida Aguirre-Nunez, Miguel Gallardo, Vickie Mays, Andrew Fuligni, Estela Zarate, Miguel Tinker-Salas, Susana Chavez-Silverman, Ricardo Stanton-Salazar, Jennifer Najera, Edward Olivos, Jose Calderon, and Edith Morris-Vasquez.

The work in this book was also enriched by conversations with graduate students, recent doctoral graduates, and emerging scholars that have begun to expand on the small but growing body of research on undocumented students. These include Patricia Perez, Veronica Terriquez, Corina Benavides Lopez, Angela Chen, Edelina Burciaga, Stella Flores, Susana Munoz, Wil Del Pilar, Kara Cebulko, Leisy Abrego, Lisa Garcia, Ignacio Hernandez, Susana Hernandez, Alex Hinojosa, Lindsay Perez Huber, Adriana Maestas, Jessica Duran, and Noe Ortega.

I also want to thank the Claremont Graduate University School of Educational Studies (SES) for their unwavering support and assistance. In particular, I want to thank President Deborah Freund, former Provost Yi Feng, SES Dean Margaret Grogan, and my SES faculty colleagues: Deb Smith, Jacob Adams, Scott Thomas, Gail Thompson, Linda Perkins, David Drew, Susan Paik, Phil Drier, Charles Kerchner, Mary Poplin, Barbara DeHart, Carl Cohen, Sue Robb, Delacey Ganley, Anita Quintanar, Jack Shuster,

Bruce Matsui, and Tom Luschei. Special thanks to Rod Leveque, Esther Wiley, Nick Johnson, Cathy Griffin, Robert Hernandez-Sandoval, and Inma Carbajal for the outstanding assistance with publicity and media relations, and to Raymundo "Aryer Graphics" Hernandez for graciously sharing his artwork to inspire the design of the book cover.

Thank you to all the students, educators, and community leaders that provided important insights to help me develop a better understanding of key issues. I am particularly grateful to Lizbeth Mateo, Carlos Amador, Nancy Guarneros, Luis A. Perez, Matias Ramos, Alma Mirell, Mohammad Abdollahi, Antonia Rivera, Erick Huerta, Francisco Bravo, John Puschila, Alfred Herrera, Antonio Jose Camacho, Eloisa Amador, Melissa Perez, Citlalli Chavez, Fabiola Inzunza, Nancy Meza, Yahaira Carrillo, Yenni Diaz, Cyndi Bendezu, Vanessa Castillo, Ana Grande, Andrea Ortega, Carol Belisa, Carol's Belsai, Diana Ortiz, Maria Gomez, Victor Zuniga, Christian Escareno, Pedro Ramirez, Iliana Perez, Katharine Gin, Claudia Bazan, Efrain Trujillo, Ernesto Zumaya, Facundo Ramos, Fermin Vasquez, Gabriel Belmonte, Steve Rabson, Grace Diaz, Jessica Valenzuela, Jonathan Bibriesca, Jorge Gutierrez, Jose Ortiz, Juana Vizcarra, Kyle de Beausset, Laura Flores, Paz Oliverez, Lizbeth Navarro, Yeimi Lopez, Malou Chavez, Maria Duque, Maria Rodriguez, Martha Melendrez, Maria Melendrez, Uriel Rivera, Perla Flores, Marilyn Corrales, Marla Ramirez, Melissa Rivera, Michelle DePlante, Minerva Gomez, Neidi Dominguez, Nora Preciado, Oliver Lopez, Noemi Degante, Adrian Gonzalez, Oscar Espino, Sofia Campos, Susan Melgarejo, Tolu Olumbunmi, David Cho, Jeff Kim, Mario Lopez, Andrea Chavez, Mayra Soriano, Martha Solorzano, Valeria Ramirez, Eder Gaona, Maria Torres, Jenny Lopez, Silvia Rodriguez, Alonzo Campos, Ana Miriam Barragan, Jacky Acosta, Johanna Perez, Jose Luis Ramirez, Julio Salgado, Oday Guerrero, Russell Jauregui, Andrea Gaspar Cobian, Giovanna Miranda, Carlos Garcia, Carlos Vaquerano, Marta Martinez, Crystal Guerra, Antonio Albizures-Lopez, Balmore Membreno, Ju Hong, Jonathan Perez, Vanessa Tejada, and Aurea Martinez. Thank you Tam Tran and Cynthia Felix for showing me the true meaning of academic excellence and civic engagement. May you both rest in peace.

I greatly appreciate the trust from all the undocumented students who put their apprehensions aside to participate in the research study. I am eternally grateful to the best research crew in the world, Karina Ramos, Richard Cortes, and Heidi Coronado, who gave their heart and soul to this project and were relentless in their efforts to recruit participants. I also owe a debt of gratitude to Roberta Espinoza for lending her expertise in qualitative methods as well as for the countless hours of editorial support. Thank you Brian Ellerbeck and Marie Ellen Larcada for helping this project find a home at TCP. Thank you Aureliano Vazquez and your editorial production staff. Lastly, thank you Professor James Banks, for providing me with the opportunity to publish my research under the "Multicultural Education" series. It is both an honor and privilege.

Americans by Heart

Exceptional Students, Marginal Lives

"I feel American. I can't feel Mexican when I don't know anything about Mexico."

Jacqueline was 2 years old when her parents brought her to the United States from Mexico. She has no memories of the country where she was born. Her mother is now a U.S. legal resident while her father's application for residency was recently denied. Her father has a 6th-grade education and her mother continued her studies after she arrived in the United States, ultimately earning a GED. Jacqueline, her sister, and parents have always lived in a tiny guesthouse located behind the main house where her aunt and her cousins live.

As early as elementary school, Jacqueline excelled in academics, and received numerous awards, particularly in math, her favorite subject. "There was never a semester where I didn't receive anything," she remembers. In elementary school, she developed an interest in planes—flying and designing them. She was identified as "gifted" in 6th grade and was subsequently enrolled in GATE (Gifted and Talented Education) and Honors classes. In middle school, she participated in various academic competitions where she was often the only Latina on a team of predominantly White and Asian students. In high school, she was involved in student council as class secretary, the math club, and joined the soccer team. She graduated in the top 15% of her class. Throughout her education, Jacqueline's parents constantly reminded her about the importance of education. For that reason, her father always forbade her from getting a job because he wanted her to focus solely on school.

It was not until the 11th grade that Jacqueline learned that her undocumented status was going to be an obstacle in achieving her educational and professional goals. Before learning about her limitations, she wanted to attend a nearby university with a nationally recognized aerospace engineering program. She aspires to someday work for NASA as an engineer. Since she was not eligible for any type of government-sponsored financial aid due to her undocumented status, and her parents worked minimum-wage jobs, she could not afford the tuition at her dream school. Her teachers and counselors advised her instead to enroll at the local community college. Making the best of her circumstances, Jacqueline joined her school's Honors program and shortly thereafter was admitted into the National Community College Honor Society. During her first year at the community college, she earned a perfect 4.0 GPA. She also assumed a leadership position in a student group that advocates for the rights of undocumented students and provides information about scholarship opportunities and how to navigate higher education as an undocumented student. In addition to her academic and leadership activities, Jacqueline volunteers at a local elementary school, tutoring young students. Despite her many accomplishments, Jacqueline often feels she "has to work twice as hard as everyone else" to demonstrate her "dedication and worthiness." She also worries about not being able to use her college degree after she graduates.

Jacqueline's story broadly illustrates the types of accomplishments and achievements of all the students surveyed and interviewed for this book, undocumented students who have lived most of their life in the United States and came when they were very young but who face an uncertain future as they transition into higher education and early adulthood. The book also captures the frustrations, anguish, and occasional hopelessness experienced by undocumented Latino students who dedicate themselves to school in pursuit of academic excellence and to eventually earn a college degree only to find their dreams shattered by the limitations they face due to their legal status. *Americans by Heart* presents a detailed analysis of the high academic achievement and civic engagement found among the most unlikely group, low-income Latino undocumented students from homes with low levels of parental education and high levels of economic and social hardship. The book provides an examination of the factors that facilitate positive academic engagement outcomes in the face of overwhelming adversity. In each chapter, I present a different facet of the life experiences, legal challenges, and psychosocial risks that are common to undocumented students. I also demonstrate the principal ways in which these marginalized youth cope with life's challenges and the sources of their social support. Using survey, in-depth interview, and ethnographic data, the book documents the numerous constraints that prevent undocumented Latino students from realizing their true potential while highlighting the need to reform current immigration and education policies that prevent these talented individuals from becoming fully integrated into American society, the only place they have ever known as home.

UNDOCUMENTED IMMIGRANTS

Failed immigration policies as well as economic push and pull factors have played a central role in increasing the undocumented population in the United States to approximately 11.2 million as of 2010 (Passel & Cohn, 2011). About half of the nation's undocumented immigrants live in just four states: California, Florida, New York, and Texas, with populations ranging from 630,000 to 2.6 million. In another group of four states—Arizona, Georgia, Illinois, and New Jersey—the populations of unauthorized immigrants hover at around half a million per state. Overall, the top eight states are home to more than two-thirds of undocumented immigrants (Passel & Cohn, 2011).

About three-quarters (71%) of the nation's undocumented immigrant population are from Latin America. The majority (58%) are from Mexico, numbering 6.5 million. This 58% share has remained roughly constant over the past 3 decades. Significant regional sources of undocumented immigrants include Central and South America (23%) and Asia (11%). Undocumented immigrants are spread more broadly than in the past, and have migrated into states where relatively few had settled just 2 decades ago. This is especially true in Georgia, North Carolina, and other southeastern states. Despite the expanding immigrant Diaspora, long-time immigrant destinations, including Florida, Illinois, New Jersey, New York, and Texas, have retained their appeal to undocumented migrants. California is home to the largest number of undocumented immigrants—2.6 million, or 23% of the total U.S. undocumented immigrant population.

Seventy percent of the undocumented population consists of Mexicans, Salvadorans, and Guatemalans (De Genova, 2004; Passel, 2005). These three groups also have the lowest levels of educational attainment among the foreign born; 66% of Guatemalans and Salvadorans as well as 69% of Mexican foreign-born individuals have not completed high school and are often confined to the lowest end of the socioeconomic spectrum and face additional struggles with institutional and socioeconomic barriers (Hamilton & Chinchilla, 2001).

Socio-Political and Historical Context

Over those last 100 years, a series of adjustments and transformations in immigration laws and labor recruitment practices have shaped the nature of immigrant communities and economic mobility of immigrants from Latin America in the United States (Barrera, 1979; Camarillo, 1979; Chavez, 1998; Galarza, 1977; Gonzalez & Fernandez, 2003; Romo, 1979; Ruiz, 1998). These changes have taken place within the historical contexts of U.S. labor shortages and the massive recruitment of low-wage workers to fill gaps in the labor force on one hand, and few employment opportunities for workers in Mexico and Central America, on the other. As a result, these countries have experienced sustained labor flows across the United States–Mexico border.

Although the relationship between Mexico and the United States spans well over a hundred years, the last 3 decades have brought massive dislocations on both sides of the border. The economic inequalities generated by NAFTA have impacted already disadvantaged sectors of Mexican society and have resulted in the loss of hundreds of thousands of agricultural jobs in Mexico, displacing many farm workers who have made their way to assembly plants along the border and into the United States to work in the agricultural, construction, meat-packing, and service industries.

Today's undocumented immigrants experience increasingly harsh circumstances: poverty-level wages, ICE (immigration and customs enforcement) raids at home and at work, deportations, and rising occurrences of hate crimes. In February 2011, two men from Shenandoah, Pennsylvania, were sentenced to 9 years in prison for beating and kicking an undocumented Mexican young man, who died of his injuries (Associated Press, 2011). In the absence of national legislation, local municipalities and various states have attempted to pass and enforce ordinances and state laws that further restrict and criminalize undocumented persons. Furthermore, anti-immigrant politicians, talk show hosts, and vigilante groups fan the flames of growing nativist hysteria. Some of these nativist myths include the notion that undocumented persons immigrate to the United States to take advantage of free social services. Research, however, clearly shows otherwise. For example, studies using pre-migration survey data from the Mexican Migration Project, a large-scale longitudinal study of both documented and undocumented immigrants from Mexico, find that less than 1% of surveyed immigrants move to the United States primarily for social services (Massey, Durand, & Malone, 2002). Furthermore, confusion about eligibility and fear of deportation deters most immigrants, both documented and undocumented, from using public resources (Bohrman & Murakawa, 2005).

Contradictory Immigration and Economic Policies

Meanwhile, contradictions between the demand for low-skilled labor and the United States' economic and immigration policies have created a growing number of undocumented immigrants. These policy and economic inconsistencies have given rise to an increased number of low-wage laborers to meet the needs of the economy, but without the protections of legal status. These sociopolitical processes have also precipitated the growth of a significant number of immigrant children, like the ones described in this book, for whom legal status, poor schools, and poverty make social and economic mobility extremely difficult.

A major obstacle in the lives of undocumented families is the extreme backlog in the processing of immigration applications. A petition for permanent legal residency can take decades to be processed (Yale-Loehr & Koehler, 2005). Even more important, for many undocumented immigrants, current immigration policy makes it impossible to become legalized if one enters the country "without authorization." For example, according to the visa bulletin published by the U.S. Department of State Bureau of Consular Affairs, if a Mexican-born 8-year-old child arrives in the United States with his or her parents and the family files a petition for permanent legal residency on the basis of one parent having a sibling who is an American citizen, the petition would take 18 years to be processed, at which time the child would be 26, and no longer eligible for benefits since he/she is not a child under 21. This is considered "aging-out." Although the parents can finally become permanent residents after almost 20 years, the young child, who was brought to the United States through no choice of his/her own, remains undocumented. The parents, after becoming permanent residents, could petition for their child, but it would again take many years.

UNDOCUMENTED CHILDREN AND YOUNG ADULTS

The undocumented population includes approximately 3.2 million children and young adults under the age of 24, about one-fourth of the total undocumented population (Hoefer, Rytina, & Baker, 2009), that were brought by their parents when they were very young, often before schooling age. The number of undocumented children under the age of 18 decreased from 1.5 million in 2005 to 1 million in 2010. In 2009, children of unauthorized immigrants made up 6.8% of students enrolled in kindergarten through grade 12. That share grew from 5.4% in 2003. Enrollment levels of children of unauthorized immigrants, however, vary considerably from state to state. In five states—Arizona, California, Colorado, Nevada, and Texas—at least one in ten students in grades kindergarten through 12 have parents who are unauthorized immigrants. But in more than a dozen states, mainly those that have experienced little growth in immigration, less than 2% live with parents who are unauthorized immigrants. Before 1982, various school districts across the country tried to bar undocumented children from attending public schools.

The Context of Education for Undocumented Students

Plyler v. Doe. Undocumented students initially received legal access to K–12 public education as a result of the 1982 Supreme Court case of *Plyler v. Doe*. The Court ruled that undocumented children must be provided access to a free public education because citizens and/or potential citizens cannot achieve any meaningful degree of individual equality without it. The Court held that while undocumented children are present in the United States, they should not forfeit their education because of their parents' decision to immigrate illegally. Furthermore, the Court indicated that denying education to children who cannot affect their parents' conduct or their own status would impose a lifetime hardship on them. The Court also stated that educating children, regardless of their immigration status, is essential for creating individuals who can function in society and contribute to the development of the United States.

Undocumented high school graduates. Presently, however, court-mandated equal access to education ends when undocumented students graduate from high school. Each year, between 65,000 and 80,000 undocumented students who have lived in the United States for at least 5 years become high school graduates, joining the ranks of an estimated 1.7 million undocumented young adults between the ages of 18 and 24. Upon graduating, and after extensive public educational investment, higher education becomes an elusive dream for these young adults, with an estimated 26% of 18- to 24-year-olds enrolling in college (Fortuny, Capps, & Passel, 2007).

Despite the efforts of advocates and immigration reform proponents, the federal government has not been able to agree on legislation that would address the legal limbo of undocumented students, particularly the financial hardship they face if they want to pursue a college education. Under current law, they are not eligible to receive state or federal financial aid. Instead, in most states they are required to pay international student tuition rates despite having all their schooling in the same state. The tuition fees these undocumented in-state high school graduates have to pay if they want to attend a state public university can be three to ten times higher than resident tuition fees of their fellow U.S.-born high school graduates. In high immigration areas such as California, with 40% of the total undocumented student population in the nation, undocumented youth may constitute half of senior and graduating classes (Johnston, 2000; Leovy, 2001).

Federal laws prohibiting access to financial aid. Fourteen years after *Plyler v. Doe*, the passage of two bills greatly curtailed undocumented student access to higher education: the 1996 Personal Responsibility and Work Opportunity Reconciliation Act (PRWORA) and the 1996 Illegal Immigration Reform and Immigrant Responsibility Act (IIRAIRA). PRWORA barred students from access to financial aid for a postsecondary education. IIRAIRA also reaffirmed a no-access policy regarding any type of public financial aid for undocumented students for higher education. Although the IIRAIRA does not bar undocumented students from attending a postsecondary institution, policymakers are unclear if the law allows for in-state tuition charges to undocumented students. In-state tuition charges have a significant impact on whether undocumented students enroll in a postsecondary institution (Flores, 2010).

Barriers to higher education. Undocumented students are far *less* likely than their native-born peers to go on to college (Passel, 2006). A recent study of college attendance by Passell and Cohn (2009) finds that among all undocumented young adults between the ages of 18 and 24, only half (49%) are in college or have attended college. The comparable figure for U.S.-born residents is 71%. Among unauthorized immigrants ages 18–24, a large share has not completed high school (40%)—much more than among legal immigrants (15%) or U.S.-born residents (8%). However, a younger age of arrival in the United States increases the likelihood of higher educational attainment. Of those who arrived at age 14 or older, 46% have not completed high school, compared with 28% of those who arrived before age 14. Among high school graduates ages 18–24 who are unauthorized immigrants, 49% are in college or have attended college. But among those who arrived at age 14 or older, 42% are in college or have attended college. Among those who arrived before age 14, 61% are in college or have attended college. Although this "college continuation rate" is higher for unauthorized immigrants who arrive as young children, it is still considerably lower than the rate for legal immigrants (76%) or U.S.-born residents (71%) (Passell & Cohn, 2009). While unauthorized status and poverty are not the only factors that limit undocumented students' postsecondary access, given the size and potential for vulnerability of this population, these numbers beg the attention of scholars and policymakers alike.

In-state tuition legislation. To address the lack of higher education access to a growing number of undocumented high school graduates, starting in 2001, Texas, followed by California, Illinois, Kansas, New Mexico, Nebraska, New York, Oklahoma, Utah, Washington, Wisconsin, Maryland, and Connecticut took matters into their own hands and passed in-state tuition policies that began to open the doors of higher education. Two states— Texas and New Mexico—provide expanded access in that they also make students eligible for various grants under their state financial aid programs. As of 2011, California is seeking to be the third state to also provide state financial aid (Moulds, 2011, para. 1). Although undocumented immigrants in these states are allowed to attend public colleges and universities at in-state tuition rates, they are still not able to work, due to their undocumented status, even if they earn a college degree. The plight of undocumented students has slowly moved to the forefront of the national debate over legislation concerning the thousands of undocumented high school graduates.

The DREAM Act. As a result of the efforts of various organizations across the country that began pressing Congress to introduce federal legislation that would provide a path for undocumented students to obtain legal resident status, the Development, Relief, and Education of Alien Minors (DREAM) Act was introduced in 2001. The bill would benefit undocumented students who meet the following requirements:

- Entry into the United States before age 16;
- Continuous presence in the United States for 5 years prior to the bill's enactment;
- Receipt of a high school diploma or its equivalent (i.e., a GED); and
- Demonstration of good moral character.

If passed, the DREAM Act would enable undocumented high school graduates to apply for conditional status, which would authorize them for up to 6 years of legal residence. During the 6-year period, the student would be required to attend college and graduate, or serve in the U.S. military for at least 2 years. Students that meet these requirements would be granted permanent residency at the end of the 6-year period (Yates, 2004). Despite a decade of efforts by immigration advocates, as of 2011, the DREAM Act has not been passed into law and thus undocumented students remain in limbo. Most recently, in December 2010, undocumented students agonized for days before being greatly disappointed when the DREAM Act fell five votes short of passing in the U.S. Senate, after having narrowly passed in the House of Representatives (Mascaro & Muskal, 2010). The students' ongoing marginalization continues to be chronicled by countless newspaper stories that describe the impressive academic accomplishments and numerous community service activities of undocumented Latino youths who are unable to continue on to college. What are the educational, social, and psychological characteristics of these students? More specifically, what motivates these marginalized individuals to excel academically and become civically engaged in their schools and communities? What is our responsibility as a nation to them after investing time and resources to nurture their talents only to have them reach early adulthood with virtually no possibilities to fully realize their potential, become fully integrated into American society, and contribute to its civic and economic vitality?

Undocumented Students' Social and Emotional Hardships

Migration stressors. Migration is one of the most radical transitions and life changes that an individual or family can endure. For immigrant children, the migration experience fundamentally reshapes their lives as familiar patterns and ways of relating to other people dramatically change. Some potential stressors related to migration include loss of close relationships, housing problems, a sense of isolation, obtaining legal documentation, going through the acculturation process, learning the English language, negotiating their ethnic identity, changing family roles, and adjusting to the schooling experience (Garza, Reyes, & Trueba, 2004; Igoa, 1995; Portes & Rumbaut, 2001; Suarez-Orozco & Suarez-Orozco, 2001; Zhou, 1997). With respect to Latino immigrant youth, research suggests a host of sociocultural experiences related to the acculturation process that are extremely stressful (Cervantes & Castro, 1985). Using the Hispanic Children's Stress Inventory, researchers have identified several potentially stressful events for Hispanic children and adolescents, which include separation from relatives and friends, feeling pressured to speak only Spanish at home, living in a home with many people, and feeling that other kids make fun of the way they speak English (Padilla, 1986; Padilla, Cervantes, Maldonado, & Garcia, 1988).

Potochnik and Perreira (2010) found that mental health stressors were prevalent in the lives of first-generation Latino immigrants. In their study, three-quarters of immigrant adolescents had been separated from their primary caregiver prior to their migration, and the average separation period lasted 3 years. During their journey to the United States, nearly a quarter (24%) experienced a stressful migration event. Moreover, almost half (42%) of immigrant Latino adolescents experienced discrimination in their lives. The researchers also found that social supports such as familism and teacher support reduced the odds of depressive symptoms but had no impact on anxiety symptoms. Personal motivation reduced the risk of both symptoms of depression and anxiety. After controlling for the presence of multiple stressors, the researchers also found that experiencing discrimination was significantly associated with an increased likelihood of depressive symptoms.

Fear, depression, and anxiety due to undocumented status. Although there is a growing body of research on first- and second-generation immigrant youth, there is a dearth of research on undocumented immigrant students. After migration, undocumented status is a common stressor among first-generation Latino youth. Compared with documented adolescents, undocumented adolescents are at greater risk of anxiety, and children in mixed-status families (where some family members have legal status while others do not) are at greater risk of both anxiety and depressive symptoms (Potochnik & Perreira, 2010). Emotional concerns for undocumented college students include fear of deportation, loneliness, and depression (De Leon, 2005; Dozier, 1993). Undocumented students' fear of deportation is so central to their daily existence that it influences almost every aspect of their lives. Some students are afraid of going to hospitals because they worry that their immigration status will be questioned (Dozier, 1993). Since their legal status makes it impossible to obtain work authorization, they are sometimes forced to stay in bad working conditions because they fear not being able to find another job. Additionally, undocumented students are often reluctant to develop close, emotional relationships with others for fear of their undocumented status being discovered (Dozier, 1993). Despite these stressors, undocumented students manage to accumulate the necessary academic record to be accepted into college. How do they manage such accomplishments in the face of the many obstacles they encounter on a regular basis?

Sources of stress and support. For undocumented college male students, relationships with school counselors and teachers can be both important sources of information and guidance as well as negative treatment (De Leon, 2005). Similarly, undocumented female college students also report both positive and negative experiences with teachers and other school agents. In college, support from faculty and staff plays a key role (Munoz, 2008). Ethnic identity formation, dealing with negative stereotypes, and negotiating gender role expectations with their parents are also significant stressors (Munoz, 2008). Although college students experience frustration, helplessness, shame, and fear due to their undocumented status, getting involved on campus in extracurricular activities is a way to feel a sense of belonging. Despite high levels of economic hardship, parental involvement and support for school, particularly from mothers, seems to play an important positive role in their academic success (Munoz, 2008).

Key interventions from teachers play a significant role in the educational experiences of undocumented students who grow up in low socioeconomic conditions, single-parent households, or with parents who speak little or no English and have low levels of education. Interventions come in a variety of forms such as recommending students for the Honors track or encouraging them to apply to highly selective universities (Gonzalez, Plata, Garcia, Torres, & Urrieta, 2003). Unfortunately, these same high-achieving students, who are often at the top of their class, can also experience a dramatic drop in their academic performance, and may completely disengage from school and discontinue their extracurricular activities, when they first learn that they are undocumented. They often fear the same fate as their older siblings who excelled in school but ended up in undesirable jobs with few options due to their undocumented status. Although some are able to regain their motivation, many became disillusioned and lower their life aspirations (Abrego, 2006; Gonzalez et al., 2003). Length of time in the United States also appears to play a role in the academic success of undocumented students (Oliverez, 2006; Passel & Cohn, 2009). On the one hand, high school students who have spent more time in the United States have lower GPAs than those who had been in the United States for less time (Oliverez, 2006). On the other hand, a younger age of arrival in the United States increases the likelihood of higher educational attainment, such as high school completion and college attendance (Passel & Cohn, 2009). Educators, particularly school counselors, can also act as gatekeepers for undocumented students by questioning their academic abilities and/or refusing to place them in academically rigorous courses (Gonzalez et al., 2003).

Socioeconomic hardships. Undocumented students often grow up in neighborhoods where they regularly experience or witness incidents of violence near their homes and schools. They also attend low-performing and poorly funded schools with extremely low college-going rates (Abrego, 2006). Despite high motivation levels, the high-poverty home environments of undocumented Latino high school seniors are not always conducive to college preparation, even though families support students' aspirations to attend college (Oliverez, 2006). In addition to caring for younger siblings, the often crowded nature of their family's small rented apartment means that students often do their homework away from home, find a secluded corner of the apartment for themselves, or wait until everyone is asleep to get their work done. Most often, students do not have a separate room in their homes where they can find adequate quiet space to study. For example, Oliverez (2006) found that 60% of the undocumented Latino high school seniors in her study lived in crowded homes with six or more people, and 90% lived in single-bedroom or studio apartments where everyone slept in the same room. Beginning as early as high school, students often struggle to complete their academic work because they also have jobs that sometimes leave them too tired to focus on school. As many as 60% of high school undocumented students may work a job after school or on the weekends, ranging between 16 and 40 hours per week (Oliverez, 2006).

Optimism. Although undocumented students recognize the obstacles they will face due to their undocumented status, several studies note that they find ways to maintain high levels of optimism and perseverance. In spite of their parents' limited education and familiarity with the U.S. educational system, undocumented students often report that their parents' hard work and sacrifices motivate them to pursue higher education (De Leon, 2005; Morales, Herrera, & Murry, 2009; Munoz, 2008; Oliverez, 2006). Despite their legal status, undocumented students firmly believed in pursuing "the American Dream" through schooling and often remain positive and optimistic about their future outlook by reframing their negative experiences in positive terms (Morales, Herrera, & Murry, 2009; Perez, 2009). Furthermore, although students are often frustrated by the numerous restrictions they encounter due to their undocumented status, several studies report that many students, particularly college students, dedicate their efforts to mentor or help other undocumented students and/or become involved in activism focused on the DREAM Act and immigrant rights (Morales, Herrera, & Murry, 2009; Munoz, 2008; Oliverez, 2006; Perez, Espinoza, Ramos, Coronado, & Cortés, 2010). Students report feeling a sense of empowerment as a result of their activism (Morales, Herrera, & Murry, 2009).

Overall, the few studies focusing on undocumented Latino students suggest that undocumented status translates into additional layers of stress and hardship. Sometimes students have supportive teachers that help them overcome various challenges and forge ahead; other times, they must contend with teachers who discourage and demoralize them. Undocumented students must also cope with socioeconomic difficulties associated with poverty (Gandara & Contreras, 2009). While previous studies provide important insights into the educational experiences of undocumented Latino students, the psychological and academic effects of legal marginalization have not been fully studied nor addressed by researchers.

THE STUDY

From the beginning, the goal of this study was to gain a deeper understanding of the factors that shaped the pathway to college for undocumented Latino students. I came to know the participants in this study personally over the course of 2 years and interacted with them in various settings, including community meetings and school events. I listened to their stories of struggle and carefully observed their efforts to make better lives for themselves and their families. I also spent time with teachers, counselors, community members, university faculty and staff, and elected officials, trying to understand the broader social and political contexts and the relationships from which they derive support and assistance.

The fieldwork gave me the opportunity to compare what interview and survey respondents told me about their families and school experiences with what I could see from day-to-day interactions. This kind of triangulation allowed me to move beyond the role of mere observer and recorder of their stories, and to become actively engaged in an investigation of the intersections of the law, community institutions, schools, and their lives. This approach helped me to develop a "thick description" of the ways in which their lives are shaped by broader structures and contexts, and how they, in turn, actively influence that larger world (Geertz, 1973). The rich qualitative and quantitative data accumulated over the course of the 2 years are the basis for this book. Figure 1.1 provides an overview of the study's conceptual framework.

Figure 1.1. Conceptual Framework of Undocumented Student Achievement and Higher Education Access

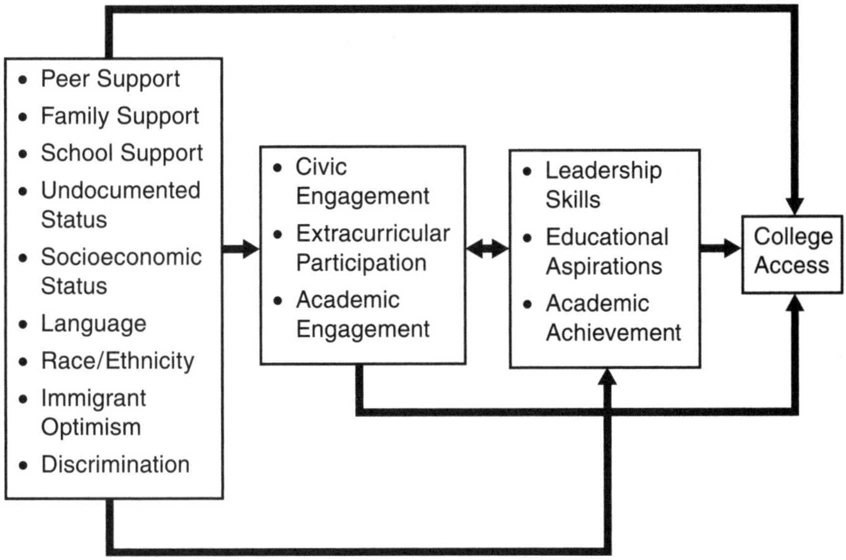

Methods

Survey and in-depth interview data collection occurred over an 8-month period. Participants were recruited via email and flyer advertisements to various student organizations across the country as well as on high school and college campuses. At the completion of their participation, students were asked to share the recruitment flyers with other undocumented students they knew personally. The recruitment flyers and emails invited students to participate in a research study that focused on "the educational experiences of undocumented students." This is the only detail that participants initially received regarding the purpose of the study. Emails and printed flyer announcements contained a link to an online survey.

The online survey included measures of academic achievement, civic engagement, extracurricular participation, leadership positions, and enrollment in advanced-level academic courses. It also consisted of school background and demographic information along with various scales designed to assess distress, bilingualism, student valuing of school, parental valuing of school, and friends' valuing of school. The survey did not collect names, emails, school names, or any other type of identifying information in order to protect the identity of participants.

The third component of the study consisted of in-depth, semi-structured interviews. An advantage of the interview process is that it allows subjects to put forth personal explanations for their behavior rather than requiring them to choose from prepackaged responses. A team of trained researchers, including the author, conducted all interviews. The team consisted of four immigrant bilingual (Spanish, English) Latino interviewers: two male and two female. All interviewers had graduate and undergraduate training in psychology and several years of social science research experience. Interviewers were trained by conducting several practice interviews that were reviewed and analyzed by the principal investigator, who has extensive experience in qualitative in-depth and focus group interview methods. Questions were developed according to the literature on extracurricular participation and civic engagement (Hodgkinson & Weitzman, 1997; Nolin, Chaney, Chapman, & Chandler, 1997; Youniss, McClellan, & Mazer, 2001). The initial set of questions was developed by conducting several pilot-test interviews. At the conclusion of the testing phase, the final set of interview questions was selected.

Interview participants contacted the researchers by email or phone after completing their online survey to schedule the interview. The interviews were conducted in various places, including high school, college, and university campuses, coffee shops, and some by telephone. In the interview, students were asked to reflect on their social and educational experiences beginning in elementary school up to college and to describe any challenges they encountered due to their undocumented status. All interviews were recorded, fully transcribed, and coded for analysis. After the interviews were transcribed, all audio files were permanently destroyed to protect the identity of the participants.

Transcripts were read numerous times and coded using a process of open coding (Strauss & Corbin, 1990) to generate themes. Procedures used to code data employed reliability checks and tests of internal and external validity (MacQueen, McLellan, Kay, & Millstein, 1998; Miles & Huberman, 1994). Four raters first read through each interview and created narrative summaries that condensed the interview material. Each narrative summary was read independently by the data analysts, who looked for themes in the summaries. A theme retained for further analysis had to be identified as a theme by at least two of the three raters, independently. Together, the ethnographic, interview, and survey data provide both a deeper and broader perspective on the experiences of high-achieving undocumented students.

Background Characteristics

One hundred ten undocumented Latino high school, community college, and university students from across the United States participated in this study. Overall, 73% resided in California, 17% in Texas, and 4% in Virginia, while the remaining 6% resided in Georgia, Missouri, New York, Washington, and Washington, DC. In terms of country of origin, 87% were born in Mexico, 7% were born in Central America, while the remaining 6% were born in South America. The average age of participants was 19.97 years. Sixty-two percent of the participants were female. The male to female ratio in the college group in this study is similar to the 61% female college enrollment rate reported for Latinos in previous studies, including the 63% female ratio reported for Mexican students (Hurtado, Saenz, Santos, & Cabrera, 2008). The high school group was gender balanced with 50% female.

Table 1.1 indicates that students, on average, arrived in the United States at 7 years of age and have lived in the United States for over 13 years. Sixty-five percent had started school in their country of origin. Those that had attended school in their country of origin averaged 4.77 years of schooling before immigrating. As a result of their early arrival age, 99% of participants reported speaking, reading, writing, and understanding English either "well" or "very well." There was also a very high level of bilingualism among respondents, with 88% reporting speaking, reading, writing, and understanding Spanish either "well" or "very well." Eighteen percent of participants were high school seniors, 34% were community college students, and 48% were students at a B.A.-granting university.

Table 1.1 also indicates that students grew up in homes where the parents had low levels of education. Participant mothers had an 8th-grade education ($M = 8.35$) while fathers had a 10th-grade education ($M = 9.71$). Eighty-three percent of mothers and 73% of fathers had less than a high school education, with only 4% of mothers and 10% of fathers having the equivalent of a university degree. Respondents also reported that both their mothers and fathers had low levels of English language proficiency. Only 20% of mothers and 32% of fathers spoke English either "well" or "very well." Most students did enjoy the support of both parents at home, with 65% of students growing up with both parents. On average, participants had 2.66 siblings, with almost half (47%) having three or more siblings.

Although students reported having to help in household tasks such as taking care of younger siblings and doing chores, only 19% reported having to do so either "almost every day," or "once or twice a week." They did, however, report working a high number of hours per week at a job during high school. On average, students worked 12.10 hours per week. Forty percent of participants reported working 20 hours or more per week, including 11% who reported working 30 hours or more per week during high school. In college, the average number of hours worked per week increased significantly to 25.22. The average was slightly higher for male students at 28.74 hours per week, compared with female participants who reported working 23.08 hours per week. Overall, 66% of students reported working 20 hours or more per week during college, including 41% who reported working 30 hours or more per week.

Table 1.1. Background and Psychosocial Variables by Gender

	Male (n = 42)		Female (n = 68)		Total (N = 110)	
	%	M	%	M	%	M
Background						
Age		20.00		19.95		19.97
Years in the U.S.		13.03		13.90		13.55
Age when immigrated to the U.S.		7.25		6.79		6.97
English proficiency [a]	100	3.81	98	3.77	99	3.78
Spanish proficiency [a]	92	3.63	87	3.63	88	3.63
Family						
Mother's years of schooling		8.30		8.39		8.35
% Mother with a high school diploma or less	81		84		83	
Mother's English proficiency [a]	21	1.89	19	1.98	20	1.95
Father's years of schooling		9.21		10.05		9.71
% Father with a high school diploma or less	79		70		73	
Father's English proficiency [a]	36	2.14	30	2.19	32	2.17
Household responsibilities [b]	18	2.86	20	2.89	19	2.88
Hours worked per week in high school		13.98		11.31		12.74
% Working more than 20 hrs/wk in high school	49		37		42	
% Working more than 30 hrs/wk in high school	15		9		11	
Hours worked per week in college		28.74		23.08		25.22
% Working more than 20 hrs/wk in college	71		63		66	
% Working more than 30 hrs/wk in college	45		39		41	
Psychosocial						
Rejection due to undocumented status [c]	38	4.28	38	4.18	38	4.22
Lifetime discrimination [d]	3	3.06	0	3.08	1	3.07
Distress [e]	5	1.92	14	2.18	21	2.09
Dual frame of reference [f]	72	5.94	77	6.09	75	6.03

[a] Scale ranged from 1 (not at all), 2 (not very well), 3 (well), 4 (very well). Percent reflects responses 3–4 combined.

[b] Scale ranged from 1 (never), 2 (almost never), 3 (once in a while), 4 (once or twice a week), 5 (almost every day). Percent reflects responses 4–5 combined.

[c] Scale ranged from 1 (never), 2 (almost never), 3 (seldom), 4 (sometimes), 5 (often), 6 (almost always), 7 (always). Percent reflects responses 5–7 combined.

[d] Scale ranged from 1 (never), 2 (once), 3 (a few times), 4 (many times), 5 (very frequently), 6 (always). Percent reflects responses 5–6 combined.

[e] Scale ranged from 1 (never), 2 (sometimes), 3 (often), 4 (all the time). Percent reflects responses 3–4 combined.

[f] Scale range: 1 (strongly disagree)–7 (strongly agree). Percent reflects responses 6–7 combined.

When asked to rate their feelings of marginalization due to their undocumented status, 38% reported feeling that way either "always," "almost always," or "often." However, when asked about their experiences with overt prejudice and discrimination, only 1% reported such instances either "very frequently" or "always." On average, students reported experiencing discrimination "a few times" ($M = 3.07$). Overall, students also reported low levels of psychological distress, with only 11% reporting feeling stressed either "often" or "all the time." Finally, reflecting the immigrant optimism that has been documented in previous research (Suarez-Orozco, 1989; Suarez-Orozco & Suarez-Orozco, 1995) when asked to report how much they felt that their life was better in the United States compared to in their country of origin, 88% reported either "agree" or "strongly agree."

Fifty-four survey participants agreed to be interviewed. The background characteristics of interview participants did not vary much from the overall survey sample. The average age for interview participants was 19.83, and 72% were female. Table 1.2 indicates that these participants had lived in the United States about 15 years, and had immigrated to the United States before schooling age, similar to the overall survey sample. Sixty-three percent of respondents came from two-parent households. The average level of education for interview respondents' mothers was about 9 years of schooling, while for fathers it was about 10 years. Finally, 30% of interviewees were university students, 37% were community college students, and 33% were high school students.

Overall, the students in this study arrived in the United States before schooling age, are highly bilingual, and grew up in homes with low levels of parental education and parental English proficiency. Although students do not report high levels of household chores and responsibilities, they do report working a high number of hours during high school and college. Surprisingly, even though four out of ten students felt strong feelings of rejection due to their undocumented status, very few reported specific incidents with prejudice and discrimination. Along the same lines, students report low levels of distress despite their legal marginality. A potential psychological resource for undocumented students might be their strong dual frame of reference (Suarez-Orozco, 1989; Suarez-Orozco & Suarez-Orozco, 1995) given that most students felt that their life in the United States was much better than in their country of origin.

The process set in motion by the 1982 federal ruling calling for a national guarantee of basic education to all students regardless of immigration status continues to fuel debates on state policies around educational access for undocumented students. As a generation of undocumented students has come of age, graduating from U.S. high schools, they are seeking the next level of opportunity. Presently, however, court-mandated equal access to education ends when undocumented students graduate from high school, despite the fact that most have been in the United States since before

Table 1.2. Interview Participant Background Information

Pseudonym	Gender	School Level	Age	Yrs. in U.S.	Mother's Years of Education	Father's Years of Education	Raised by Both Parents	Civic Engagement
Angelica	Female	University	20	12	17	17	No	Yes
Janet	Female	University	21	17	13	15	No	Yes
Jimena	Female	University	21	17	6	11	No	Yes
Liz	Female	University	24	18	6	--	No	Yes
Olivia	Female	University	22	10	16	16	No	Yes
Sasha	Female	University	19	14	17	16	Yes	Yes
Ulises	Male	University	23	11	16	15	No	No
Adriana	Female	University	25	16	12	12	Yes	Yes
Alejandra	Female	University	20	18	12	12	No	Yes
Alix	Female	University	20	6	17	17	No	Yes
Alma	Female	University	20	17	14	12	Yes	Yes
Eduardo	Male	University	18	17	10	11	No	Yes
Jennifer	Female	University	20	8	--	--	Yes	No
Judith	Female	University	18	15	12	12	Yes	Yes
Liliana	Female	University	18	17	1	5	Yes	Yes
Lourdes	Female	University	22	13	12	14	Yes	Yes
Beatriz	Female	Community College	22	11	7	9	Yes	Yes
Esperanza	Female	Community College	21	18	6	6	No	Yes
Diego	Male	Community College	19	15	4	11	Yes	Yes

Pseudonym	Gender	School Level	Age	Yrs. in U.S.	Mother's Years of Education	Father's Years of Education	Raised by Both Parents	Civic Engagement
Lisa	Female	Community College	19	9	4	5	Yes	Yes
Nailea	Female	Community College	21	18	12	8	No	Yes
Juana	Female	Community College	28	16	7	9	Yes	Yes
Carla	Female	Community College	23	19	4	5	Yes	Yes
Daniela	Female	Community College	19	--	2	--	Yes	Yes
Isabel	Female	Community College	21	19	14	8	Yes	Yes
Jacinto	Male	Community College	22	19	8	12	No	Yes
Jack	Male	Community College	20	16	3	3	Yes	Yes
Jacqueline	Female	Community College	19	18	12	6	Yes	Yes
Jairo	Male	Community College	19	18	5	7	Yes	Yes
Jazmin	Female	Community College	20	20	16	16	Yes	Yes
Karen	Female	Community College	18	--	12	--	No	Yes
Linda	Female	Community College	20	12	8	6	Yes	Yes
Lucila	Female	Community College	19	18	6	15	Yes	Yes
Paulina	Female	Community College	34	27	2	3	Yes	Yes
Rosa	Female	Community College	26	--	4	4	Yes	Yes
Thalia	Female	Community College	19	17	5	6	Yes	Yes
Mia	Female	High School	17	17	12	10	Yes	Yes
Adolfo	Male	High School	17	6	--	--	No	Yes

(continued)

Table 1.2. (continued)

Pseudonym	Gender	School Level	Age	Yrs. in U.S.	Mother's Years of Education	Father's Years of Education	Raised by Both Parents	Civic Engagement
Jason	Male	High School	17	16	8	3	Yes	Yes
Jenny	Female	High School	18	11	9	13	No	Yes
Leslie	Female	High School	17	16	7	10	Yes	No
Leticia	Female	High School	17	12	7	12	No	No
Lilia	Female	High School	16	6	11	7	No	Yes
Jaime	Male	High School	17	14	11	11	Yes	No
James	Male	High School	17	16	8	3	Yes	Yes
Jeronimo	Male	High School	18	17	8	6	Yes	Yes
Noemi	Female	High School	17	14	--	--	Yes	Yes
Penelope	Female	High School	17	9	5	5	Yes	Yes
Selena	Female	High School	18	11	4	--	No	Yes
Viviana	Female	High School	17	12	12	12	Yes	Yes
Mauricio	Male	High School	17	12	--	--	No	Yes
Maximiliano	Male	High School	18	17	2	5	Yes	Yes
Pedro	Male	High School	18	17	--	12	Yes	Yes
Rolando	Male	High School	18	15	2	4	No	Yes
Total	72% female		19.83	14.78	8.73	9.5	63% Yes	91% Yes

schooling age and are often unaware of their status until they reach high school. They have been socialized by school and community influences to view themselves as Americans, equal to other citizens in every way. They have lived in the United States for most of their lives, and as a result, they express an "American" identity with English as their dominant language. Their immigrant optimism further drives their desire to embrace the ideals of civic participation. All these add up to form a set of compelling reasons to engage in serious discussions about the merits of formally integrating them into American society through legalization and higher education access.

ORGANIZATION OF THE BOOK

This book closely examines the pre-college educational experiences and higher education access of undocumented Latino students. Chapter 1 provides the historical, political, legal, and educational context for undocumented children and young adults in the United States. Chapter 2 examines the wide range of educational, social, and institutional challenges that undocumented students face on a regular basis due to their lack of legal status. Despite obstacles, students demonstrate tenacious optimism, drive, and perseverance in the face of societal marginalization. Chapter 3 examines their academic engagement. Results indicate high levels of academic performance across various educational outcome measures along with high levels of extracurricular participation and leadership activities. Chapter 4 focuses on their civic engagement. Results also suggest that these marginalized noncitizens are, in fact, "model citizens" in terms of their high levels of civic engagement activities, which supersede the levels of their "citizen" counterparts. Although community colleges have a mixed history as a path toward a bachelor's degree, Chapter 5 explores the pivotal role they play in providing undocumented students with primary access to higher education due to their low-cost tuition. Although community colleges are often the gateway to higher education for undocumented students, students still encounter a variety of institutional barriers. Chapter 6 explores the experiences of undocumented youths that have graduated from college and discusses the policy implications of the lack of legal incorporation of these college-educated individuals. Focusing on the impact of legalization for college-educated undocumented youths, this chapter also examines the lives of young adults who lived most of their lives undocumented but whose educational and life trajectories, as well as their educational and professional accomplishments, changed dramatically when they gained legal status. The Conclusion provides a discussion of the policy implications of the ongoing legal marginality and higher education obstacles for undocumented Latino students. It also provides a new framework for developing better immigration and education policies that recognize the extensive work and civic dedication of undocumented Latino students.

2

Growing up American and Undocumented

Many studies have demonstrated that parents' social class background has profound implications for their children's educational achievement. One of the best predictors of whether a child will one day graduate from college is whether his or her parents are college graduates (U.S. Department of Education, 1995). Even before kindergarten, children of highly educated parents are much more likely to exhibit "educational readiness" skills such as knowing their letters, identifying colors, counting up to 20, and being able to write their first names (Entwisle, Alexander, & Olson, 1997). There are, of course, low-SES students who attend college, and their enrollment in postsecondary education represents success in overcoming many social and economic obstacles. In the 4-year period following high school, however, they are less likely to persist to a bachelor's degree or to have graduate degree aspirations (Bowen & Bok, 1998; Bowles & Gintis, 1976; Brint & Karabel, 1989; Karabel, 1972; Karen, 1991). With only limited sources of support, less than 43% of Latino high school students are qualified to enroll in 4-year institutions annually. In 2000, the percent of 25- to 29-year-olds completing a bachelor's degree or higher was 10% for Latinos, compared to 34% for Whites. This chapter describes the many ways in which undocumented Latino students dedicate themselves to schooling in the context of the challenges associated with their socioeconomic background and undocumented status.

SOCIOECONOMIC CHARACTERISTICS OF UNDOCUMENTED FAMILIES

Although undocumented children are more likely to live in two-parent families (80%) than immigrant children with legal status and children with U.S.-born parents (71%), they are also more likely to grow up in homes with low levels of parental education. Nearly three in ten adult undocumented immigrants (29%) have less than a 9th-grade education, and an additional 18% have some high school education but have not completed high school (Passel & Cohn, 2009). Overall, the proportion of unauthorized immigrants with either less than a 9th-grade education is roughly double the share of legal foreign-born residents with those education levels. It is far greater than the share of U.S.-born adults—only 2% of those ages 25–64 have less than a 9th-grade education, and only 6% have additional years in high school, but no diploma. Among undocumented adults ages 25–64, 27% have finished high school and gone no further. There are also very large differences in college education rates. Most U.S.-born adults ages 25–64 (61%) and legal immigrants (54%) have attended college or graduated from college, compared with only 25% of unauthorized immigrants (Passel & Cohn, 2009).

Poverty

Many undocumented children grow up in poverty, with all of the associated stresses and dangers. Nearly 40% of undocumented children live below the federal poverty level (compared with 17% of native-born children), while the average income of undocumented immigrant families is 40% lower than that of either native-born families or legal immigrant families (Passel, 2005). Low levels of education and low-skilled occupations lead to lower household incomes among undocumented immigrants, compared with immigrants with legal status and U.S.-born Americans. In 2007, the median annual household income of undocumented immigrants was $36,000, compared with $50,000 for people born in the United States. These differences in household income are particularly notable because undocumented immigrant households have more workers per household on average (1.75) than U.S.-born households (1.23). Mexican-born undocumented immigrants are less educated and have lower incomes than other undocumented immigrants. Among adults ages 25–64, only 4% hold a college degree, compared with 30% of all other undocumented immigrants. In addition, 64% have not completed high school, compared with 25% of other undocumented immigrants. The median household income for Mexican undocumented immigrants was $32,000 in 2007, compared with $45,000 for all other undocumented immigrants (Passell & Cohn, 2009).

Lack of Access to Social Services

Their undocumented condition keeps families in the shadows, avoiding many of the very institutions that have traditionally benefited immigrant families. Growing up in undocumented families means having little contact with institutions and receiving poor services overall. Due to legal status barriers for most services and families' apprehension to utilize services for which they are eligible, undocumented families receive little assistance to pull them out of poverty. Further, family income places them in cramped, overcrowded dwellings in increasingly overcrowded and segregated neighborhoods. This places children in large school districts and in schools with high student-to-teacher ratios. With limited access to teachers and counselors, many students quickly fall through the cracks (Gandara & Contreras, 2009; Waters, 1999). Without question, the childhood experience of undocumented children is distinctively shaped by the low socioeconomic status of their families. In addition, they must also contend with negative public perception regarding their undocumented status.

SOCIAL AND EDUCATIONAL CONSTRAINTS

Learning about their undocumented status and the countless limitations they have already begun to face affected students' psychological well-being. Angelica, for example, said, "I was really depressed because I was outstanding in school and I was like, okay, I can't go to college." Sasha felt similarly dejected, saying, "I was very apathetic toward the end. I felt that even though I worked extremely hard I would have to work twice as hard to go beyond high school." For most students, learning about their undocumented status and the limitations they would face was devastating. Alejandra did not find out she was undocumented until she tried to enroll in an academic outreach program. She said, "That's when I found out I was undocumented when I was filling out this form that asked for a social security number so I asked my mom and she said you don't have one. I was devastated."

Most students did not learn about their status until they reached high school and began to get involved in activities that would prepare them for college. For undocumented students, the end of high school represents a crucial transition in their lives, when they realize the limitations of their status and that they are, in fact, different from their peers. Certain school trips were off-limits and other activities that required state-issued identification were similarly prevented. Further, undocumented students faced the embarrassment of having to justify to peers why they could not get a driver's license or attend a first-choice college because they were ineligible for financial aid.

In the United States, getting a driver's license, securing a first job, starting college, going to bars and clubs, and voting mark one's entry into adulthood. For those who do not have legal status, these important milestones are out of reach. For them, the transition to adulthood is a transition to a state of increased salience of their undocumented status. During childhood and early adolescence, school provides a legal buffer that gives children the opportunity to develop without legal restrictions. Although legal status is not a defining feature of childhood, it becomes so during emerging adulthood. In order to participate in most facets of adult life, legal status is a requirement. Without it, driving, working, voting, traveling, and many forms of everyday socializing are restricted.

At every turn, undocumented students face constraints on their ability to participate in civic life. Because of such limitations, accomplishing the most simple of tasks often means taking uncertain risks. For example, buying a cell phone, obtaining a library card, or even renting a movie all involve difficulty and possible embarrassment. Since undocumented students cannot work legally to cover their educational costs, they must take jobs in the informal economy. At every turn, they risk deportation, because any of these pursuits can place them face-to-face with immigration authorities. Although not all undocumented students are directly exposed to the effects of deportation involving family or immigration agents imposing on their lives, they are all aware of such realities through stories in the news or from family members (Contreras, 2009).

As their day-to-day adult lives become increasingly plagued with legal limitations, accomplishing the simplest of tasks becomes arduous. As a consequence, many of these young adults are constantly on guard, worried about the possibility of getting caught. Often, they avoid certain situations or people as fear becomes a part of daily life and is often manifested in stress and other symptoms. The transition to an undocumented adulthood happens alongside the transition to adulthood by U.S.-born peers and siblings. The emerging contrast between their lives and the lives of their peers, friends, classmates, and family members is all the more difficult. Undocumented young adults experience divergence, not because of ability or achievement, but because of their legal status.

Decreased Expectations

Having spent their lives attending U.S. schools, being told that if they work hard, a college education and career opportunities will follow, undocumented college students are forced to face a harsh reality when they start college and realize that this is not the case. This realization appears to strongly influence the decision of many students to leave school, or to quit applying themselves if they stay (Abrego, 2006; Dozier, 2001; Norrid-Lacey & Spencer, 1999). Furthermore, undocumented students work long hours with little time for studying, have limited access to needed resources such as computers, have restricted financial support, and report persistent stress linked to worrying about future employment (Dozier, 2001; Oliverez, 2006).

Social Stigma

Goffman's (1963) theory of social stigma provides a social and psychological framework for understanding and describing how people deal with socially discrediting attributes such as being undocumented. Stigmatized individuals possess, or are believed to possess, some attribute or characteristic that conveys a social identity that is devalued in a particular social context (Crocker, Major, & Steele, 1998; Goffman, 1963). People are stigmatized to the extent that they possess characteristics that lead others to avoid, shun, reject, or ostracize them (Leary & Schreindorfer, 1998). Undocumented status, because it is tantamount to a lack of legal status, is a social stigma that renders immigrants suspect in the eyes of the rest of society. Aside from the denial of basic rights and protections, undocumented status can also be internalized to affect a person's sense of self. Undocumented youths may perceive their status as a stigma in defining their sense of identity and may only discuss it with other undocumented friends and only when it involves discussions about college or future job possibilities (Chavez, 2009). Youth are careful about disclosing their status to others and will only ask trusted friends questions about legalization to minimize any effects their undocumented status may have on their friendships. Recent studies suggest that, increasingly, undocumented youth actively attempt to construct an identity that empowers them to believe in their self-worth by comparing and viewing themselves as similar to their peers (Abrego, 2008; Chavez, 2009; Seif, 2004; S.I.N. Collective, 2007).

Stigmatized individuals interpret and cope with their stigmatization in a variety of ways, which, in turn, affect their own well-being (Crocker et al., 1998). Siegel, Lune, and Meyer (1998) describe stigma management strategies along a "reactive-proactive continuum." While reactive strategies include concealment, avoidance or withdrawal, and selective disclosure, proactive strategies include preemptive disclosure, public education, and social activism. For the most part, most stigmatized individuals attempt to pass as normal and do what they can to keep their stigmatized status a secret from others (Goffman, 1963; Herman, 1993; Jones, Farina, Hastorf, Markus, Miller, & Scott, 1984; Link, Mirotznik, & Cullen, 1991). While the costs of disclosure range from disapproval, exclusion, and constant worry, there are certain benefits that come with disclosure, such as not having to worry about hiding their stigma, finding others who can help or express approval, and promoting a sense of personal power (Corrigan & Lundin, 2001).

As with most types of stigmas that are not visibly apparent, the undocumented young adults in this study had to make decisions about whether or not to conceal their status. For college-going undocumented students, the school setting produced trusting relationships in which they felt comfortable sharing their fears about their future with teachers or counselors. As a result, many received financial assistance, guidance, and referrals to others who could assist them. For the most part, respondents revealed their status when it worked in their favor, and concealed it in situations where they felt it could be used against them. Often, what governed the decision to conceal or reveal their identity was whether or not they felt contexts were favorable or hostile. Because of past experiences, however, many of the respondents were wary to assume the former.

Managing a Stigmatized Identity

Most undocumented students spent late adolescence concealing their status from teachers, counselors, and even friends. For their families, staying in the shadows and not trusting people outside of their very immediate social networks is justified. Years of survival have conditioned them to conceal a great deal more than they reveal. However, as these students moved on to college and work, the impetus for concealing or revealing their status took on a greater magnitude. Although friends and peers may be trustworthy, many students refrained from revealing their status because of the stigma attached to it. Many were reluctant to jeopardize friendships and feared the repercussions of their disclosure. Although undocumented students were often unable to share their most significant obstacle due to fear of being betrayed or having it used against them, many developed strategies of survival. They shared information with each other, and sharpened their ability to assess people and situations, deciding who to trust and to whom they could disclose their status. Over time, they learned ways to cope with the stigma, frustration, fear, and anxiety that is a part of their daily lives. As they spent their formative years learning English and acculturating to American society and culture, their early adulthood is spent developing various survival techniques that they employ on a daily basis living undocumented.

Missed Educational Opportunities

One of the biggest obstacles undocumented students face in pursuing their education is not being able to take advantage of opportunities to enhance their professional and educational experiences. Most expressed their disappointment about not being able to apply for jobs, internships, study abroad programs, JROTC (Junior Reserve Officers' Training Corps), and the military because of their undocumented status. Jeronimo's disappointment started in high school when he could not go abroad and fully reap the rewards of being at the top of his class. He explained, "In my French class they would take the top students on trips to France during the summer and I knew I couldn't go because I can't get a passport and it was just horrible. You feel restricted from so many things." Sasha listed various internship programs that she has not been able to pursue because of her legal status:

I have had my counselor tell me, "Oh my gosh, your GPA is great! You would love this program, and look, you meet the requirements." So I've filled out the application and I get a call that says, "Yes, but you forgot to mention this so I'm sorry, you don't qualify." I've missed out on a lot of opportunities because of my situation.

Similarly, despite his high test scores on the military entrance exam, Jaime's biggest disappointment was not being able to follow his dream of attending the Naval Academy at Annapolis after high school:

At the end of my junior year I was trying to get into one of the military schools, but I realize that without citizenship it is impossible. . . . I had such a high rank on the test that the administrator . . . told me that I could easily enroll in any military school in the nation. . . . I wanted to go to Annapolis.

Undocumented students are forced to reconcile their deep belief in a meritocracy with the limitations they faced in sharp contrast to their U.S.-born classmates. Seeing the opportunities available to their classmates but not to them was difficult to cope with, as Sasha explained, "I know students that have terrible grades but they are still getting assistance and I'm not, even though I have good grades and I work hard." Penelope had the same realization at the beginning of her senior year of high school when she began planning for college: "At the beginning of the year I was just freaking out. I was thinking, 'Oh my god, I AM not going to get good educational opportunities!' Compared to my friends, my opportunities were pretty low." As she continued to plan for college and compared her options with those of her U.S. citizen friends, she noted, "You don't have a choice. It's what you can afford, not what you want." In high school, when Jeronimo was planning for college, he felt like doors were opening up for other students and closing on him: "They come in showing the PowerPoint about federal aid and Cal Grants and it says, 'Undocumented students cannot apply,' and you feel horrible. Everyone has this great opportunity and you feel like you don't have anything."

Missed Career Opportunities

In addition to a lack of academic options, students often must decline important employment opportunities. On one occasion, Jeronimo was offered a job as an assistant manager at a computer store, but had to decline it because of his status:

I was offered an assistant manager job because I know about computers and I've taken computer courses and they know I know all the programs, so they wanted me to start at $9/hour but of course I can't because, you know, I have no documents.

Similarly, Lilia also had to pass up a highly coveted job she landed:

> Last summer I applied for this job at a bank. They only pick one student out of the entire class and they only offer it to the English Honors class. I had to interview and I had to write an essay. I went through all of that and I got the job. It had a really flexible schedule and it looks really good on a resume to work at a bank at such a young age. The pay was really good, too. During my second day of training and orientation they called me in and . . . I lost my job.

Lack of Financial Aid

Although well-positioned for academic success, these students face a series of obstacles while in college. By far, the largest challenge that college-ready undocumented students confront is the limited access to financial support to pay for their college education. This results from their ineligibility for federal and state aid, their limited scholarship opportunities, and the employment restrictions they confront. Without the ability to compete for federal financial aid, the rising costs of postsecondary education place a substantial and increasing burden on their ability to pay for college. Although undocumented students also have the option of applying for some private scholarships, only a few are available since most others require a social security number and/or legal resident status (Chavez, Soriano, & Oliverez, 2007). Although some students enter college with private scholarships, this funding typically runs out during their time in college, forcing them to scramble to raise enough funds to cover the rest of their education. In order to do so, many take on extra jobs and take time off from school to save money. They may also host fund-raisers, or seek out private donations (Chavez, Soriano, & Oliverez, 2007; Rangel, 2001). Despite their restricted access to government-sponsored state and federal financial aid, undocumented students demonstrate great perseverance in their efforts to secure funds to support their college education.

After enrolling in college, undocumented students face a number of challenges. In addition to studying, homework, exams, and other anxieties that college students face, undocumented students worry about work, continued funding, and fear of legal consequences, such as deportation (Chavez, Soriano, & Oliverez, 2007; De Genova, 2002; Dozier, 2001; Drachman, 2006; Jauregui, Slate, & Stallone, 2008; Rangel, 2001). Because undocumented students faced such heavy burdens, Dozier (2001) found that they were 10 times more likely to be placed on academic probation than documented immigrants. Due to a lack of money, students, like Isabel, experienced several interruptions in college enrollment: "Something that would have taken 2 years, it's taking me forever, but I'm still here, I haven't given up, and I know it's a long process, but I'll get through it." Ulises had to abandon his studies at his dream school because he could not afford the tuition:

> I transferred to Berkeley but I didn't finish. I was there for less than one semester. I thought I could pull it off economically. I thought I would be able to afford it. I thought somehow, I was going for a dream. But then I had to come back because the money was running out. I felt horrible.

As the number of undocumented students enrolled in public colleges and universities have increased over the years, these students have begun to develop their own student organizations and support networks to fund-raise, advocate for students' rights, and increase their access to resources (Chavez, Soriano, & Oliverez, 2007; Seif, 2004).

Balancing Work and School

Balancing school and work becomes very difficult for students who must take on full-time jobs to earn enough money to pay for their tuition. As Paulina describes, "Intellectually and academically, I am just as good as anybody else. In some cases I think I'm better. It's just financial. Everything is so much harder." Carla also lamented the financial hardships she faces in college:

> The biggest challenge is the money. I have disciplined myself enough to do well with my studies, with my homework, but I'm not making enough at work. I have to be very careful where I spend my money because I need it for school.

Balancing work and school was made more difficult by the students' inability to drive, since they are not able to apply for a driver's license and instead, they have to depend on unreliable public transportation or walk to work. Carla explained the long hours she worked beginning in high school to assist her family financially:

> It was really hard. I had to work right after high school. I used to work at Sears, but I had to walk there. In the summers, it was just a drag. I was sweaty and I had to go there and change and get up on the floor and do whatever I had to do, and then I had to walk back home at night, which was pretty stressful. It used to take about an hour to get back home and then I still had to get up early and go to school and make sure my homework was done.

Liliana also worked throughout high school: "I would work around 20 hours per week during my freshman and sophomore year. During my junior year I worked around 30 hours, right after school, and the whole day Saturday and Sunday." When Jennifer explained her hectic school-work schedule, she lamented that the time she worked could be spent focusing more on school: "It is time that you can be doing something else. I have to study late at night and stay up until 2:00 or 3:00, and then I have to wake up at 5:00 in the morning."

SOCIAL AND PSYCHOLOGICAL RESOURCES

Undocumented youth demonstrate high motivation and aspirations. They often receive encouraging cues from parents and teachers who help frame their future possibilities through educational achievements. The concept of hope was a central theme in the narratives of the students in this study. They hoped for a better future for themselves and for their families (Suárez-Orozco & Suárez-Orozco, 2001). While hope may give immigrant children an advantage to succeed, it may be what is allowing undocumented youth to survive the added stresses of their undocumented status.

Dual Frame of Reference

By comparing their social and economic circumstances to those students and their parents left behind in their country of origin, the dual frame of reference can help immigrant students to reframe their challenges and use them as a source of motivation (Suarez-Orozco, 1989; Suarez-Orozco & Suarez-Orozco, 1995). Lilia provided one of the clearest examples of the dual frame of reference and how it helped her to maintain a positive outlook:

> I feel that I don't take things for granted. I remember when I first came here in the 5th grade I would get free lunch. Back in Mexico you have to buy your own stuff because nothing is for free. I remember that I had friends in Mexico that would faint in school because they didn't have anything to eat. It's really that bad. Some people can't go to school because they have to work. One of my friends from 4th grade in Mexico, he had to work so he kept repeating the same grade and his mom was illiterate. My friend one time came to school without doing her homework and the teacher asked her why and she said it was because they didn't have any light. It is those drastic things that make you realize you're lucky just to have a roof over your head.

Sasha also described how she doesn't take her educational opportunities for granted, even if those opportunities are few due to her legal status: "My situation has really made me appreciate my education. It makes me grateful for what I have. It incited a passion for government. It has allowed me to participate." As a testament to the high levels of positive reframing and self-affirmation among undocumented students, Alix, along with many other students, declared that she probably would not work as hard if she had legal status:

> I would probably be less dedicated to my work because if we had papers my brothers and sisters would qualify for financial aid and we could all go to school. I would be less worried. I would not have pushed myself that hard because the government is paying for it. . . . I would be less dedicated.

Belief in the American Dream

Student commitment to education was largely intertwined with an optimistic belief in the American Dream, consistent with previous research on immigrant students (Gandara & Contreras, 2009; Suárez-Orozco, Suárez-Orozco, & Todorova, 2008). Undocumented students believed that they could achieve success, assist their families financially, and provide leadership in their communities. Undoubtedly, undocumented youth manifested a strong sense of optimism and motivation when thinking about their future—whether it was aspiring to go to college, as in most cases, or simply helping their families move forward. Underlying their positive outlook, however, were dissonant feelings toward their status as a result of the conflicting intersection of illegality and aspirations.

Decriminalization and Agency

Undocumented youth perceived their life as limited in relation to the lives of others, yet when they reflected about their own aspirations and motivations, they minimized fears or barriers that could disrupt their journey. In fact, they were inspired by the idea that they could prove themselves to society and the government. School was the principal space in which they found a sense of belonging in society that helped them cope with their fears of persecution and inspired them to establish educational goals. Although they acknowledged their lack of legal status, they actively found ways of challenging the anti-immigrant rhetoric that frames them as "lawbreakers." In constructing their status, youth saw themselves as law-abiding individuals. Their self-decriminalization helped them cope with societal perception of the criminality of undocumented immigrants (Contreras, 2009). Despite their lack of legal status, they wanted to be part of American society and have the same opportunities for an education as their peers. They saw the conditions in which they migrated to the United States as compelling enough to give legitimacy to their perceived non-criminal circumstances.

In many ways, youth actively tried to minimize the salience of their undocumented status, perhaps as a coping mechanism to feel secure. Although they recognized that the experience of undocumented immigrants in society involves discrimination and persecution, they did not want to allow these circumstances to control their lives, even if it still threatens their sense of safety and their aspirations. If they were to see their reality solely through the lens of an "undocumented" individual, they would risk giving up any sense of agency. Agency allowed respondents to counteract a perceived limiting condition and reframe it into opportunity and self-determination to inspire themselves to achieve. Contreras (2009) notes that this is what separated undocumented youth in her study from other native co-ethnics—the fact that they actively sought ways to minimize the salience of their undocumented status in their lives. Her respondents were less likely to blame their situation on undocumented status alone, as they also believed in proving themselves through individual achievements. Chavez (2009) also reports various strategies employed by undocumented youth to minimize the salience of their status. As one of her respondents remarked, "You can do everything just in a different way" (p. 90). The undocumented young man insisted that undocumented youth were not that different from anybody. Although my respondents recognized limitations that they had that their legal peers did not experience, they firmly believed that they could achieve the same dreams as anyone else, even though it may involve taking a different road. Clearly, undocumented youth refused to experience their world solely through their undocumented status. Doing so would force them to live in fear and strip their sense of agency. They preferred to be motivated by their own perceived potential.

Undocumented youth also acquire communication tactics to both cope with and evade the issue of illegality altogether. They have developed ways to address their illegality without necessarily denying their situation. Some undocumented youth used racialized humor to address their status to their peers. Chavez (2009), for example, reports that one of his respondents joked with her friends when asked about her immigrant status by responding with the following remarks, "Yeah, didn't you know? We just hopped the border yesterday" (p. 59). This student felt that joking about her undocumented status made it easier for her and her undocumented friends because they did not have to explain it to people or have to think about it in a serious way and stress about it. For this student, humor not only helped to avoid the discussion of undocumented status, but it also served as a way to cope with illegality collectively with others. As another respondent noted, "I can't change the fact that I don't have papers . . . but I'm not going to let that control me" (Chavez, 2009, p. 59).

Self-Affirmation

Although social stigma (Goffman, 1963) and resilience theories (Alva, 1991) provide some explanations about how social and personal factors function to protect students in conditions that place them at risk for academic failure and psychological distress, self-affirmation theory (Steele, 1988) may also help to explain the sense of agency that helps undocumented students persevere. According to this theory, we all strive to maintain a self-image of being morally and adaptively adequate, being stable, competent, and good. When one feels her or his integrity or adequacy is threatened, self-affirmation is activated. This self-system functions by creating explanations and rationalizations designed to protect the self from perceived threats.

Steele posits that an individual may affirm their self-value in a domain not related to the domain being threatened (Steele, 1988). In the case of undocumented students, since they are not able to change their legal status directly, they may affirm their self-worth in a different area, such as doing well in school, through activism, or through other forms of civic engagement. As a result, undocumented students can eliminate the need to activate the typical defense mechanisms of rationalization and denial. This approach is not necessarily designed to resolve the threat to their self-concept brought about by their legal marginality, but rather to function as an ego-protector to maintain an overall sense of self-integrity. In other words, rather than dwell on their daily constraints and inability to change their legal status, undocumented students might focus on engaging in community service to maintain their sense of being morally and adaptively adequate and restore their positive self-view, esteem, and identity.

In helping to maintain a positive self-regard, self-affirmation works as a process by which "resilience" is achieved. The inconsistency remains, and they're still undocumented; yet in the context of other valued self-concepts, it poses less threat to global self-integrity and thus becomes more tolerable. Herein lies their resilience. Indeed, for undocumented students, this may be the only adaptation possible. For example, in a study of breast cancer victims who are unable to eliminate the threat they are under, Taylor (1983) found that participants adapted by changing their lives to affirm their basic values, such as quitting a boring job and beginning to write short stories. In another study focusing on the effects of name-calling on helping behavior, Steele (1988) found that regardless of whether it was related to their self-concept, women who experienced negative name-calling exhibited more helping behavior compared with women who received positive affirmation or no affirmation. He concluded that women in the negative name conditions helped more in order to reaffirm their general goodness and worth after their goodness had been threatened. He argues that the name-calling induced helping in that study by arousing a general ego-protective system, one function of which is to affirm an overall self-concept of worth after it has been threatened. Thus, in ego defense, people are concerned with the big picture: They regulate their defensive adaptations to maintain very general conceptions of self-integrity rather than to remedy specific threats. Based on this fact, people have considerable flexibility in coping with threats to self-integrity. They can try to adapt to the threat itself by trying to directly diminish or eliminate the treat, by diminishing the perception of the threat, or by diminishing the perception that the threat jeopardizes self-integrity. Steele's research suggests that undocumented students may adapt to a threat with behavioral and cognitive changes not directly toward the threat itself but toward affirming the perception of global self-integrity. This last category of adaptations may give them an extra degree of coping flexibility and resilience, particularly when it comes to schooling.

Social Support

Support from educators. In addition to self-affirmation strategies, students identified various teachers, counselors, tutors, coaches, and other educators as important sources of encouragement and support. Although there is a great range of diversity among the small but growing number of undocumented students making the difficult transition from high school to college, a general pattern has emerged. For college-going undocumented students, support networks help them navigate the process of higher education (Abrego, 2008; Diaz-Strong & Meiners, 2007). At this important juncture, relationships are of paramount importance. Adolescents are at a developmental stage where they are gaining independence, but still require a great deal of guidance and support. Most adolescents, whether documented or undocumented, require adults to shepherd them through important transitions. School provides students with the first opportunities to form important relationships outside their families. The development of these relationships is critical to gaining guidance and support. Positive school-based relationships help students to excel in school by providing them access to information about college, much-needed support, and assistance applying for college.

For undocumented students, these relationships were crucial. Adults served as role models, set high expectations for what they can accomplish, built their confidence by believing in their capabilities, encouraged them to apply to college, and helped them find resources to pay for college. Liz, for example, had a supportive 3rd-grade teacher who often reached out to her parents. Liz said, "He was very supportive of my schooling. He would talk to my mother, telling her that I was doing very well." Lucila recalled a female teacher who inspired her: "She was the greatest teacher I ever had. She always told me I could do whatever I wanted, always emphasized that there is no level that a woman cannot reach." Daniela recalled a Latino teacher in 7th grade who connected with her culturally as a role model and mentor:

> He was just the best teacher I ever had. He was not like everybody else. He was this Latino teacher that came from an area just like the one I came from, but had graduated from a big university, had gotten his degree. . . . He always told me, "You know, I'm going to be there for your high school graduation and then when you go to college, I'm going to be there," and I guess that's something that I needed.

Penelope's aspirations to go to college also grew out of an encouraging relationship she had with a Latino teacher in high school:

> He got a guy from a California university to do college awareness with us. He actually got him to come to our classroom and tell us about college opportunities. That really had an impact on me. I started thinking about going to college rather than just finishing high school and getting a job. He had guest speakers. Most of them were college-educated people. Some of them were community leaders.

Influential teachers not only set high expectations for their students, but also built students' confidence. Jeronimo recalls his science teacher as someone influential who gave him the confidence to succeed:

> I was involved in soil science and we had to go to a regional competition. I was not confident about it but he just pulled me aside and he said, "I know that you're not comfortable. I know you're feeling like you don't know this, but you do, you studied it," and he just filled me with confidence that day and I came home with a silver medal and I was proud that day . . . he inspired me.

Eduardo reported that his most influential teacher encouraged him to participate in activities that made him a competitive applicant for college:

> He started the National Honor Society, so he's the one who advised me, "Oh, you should run for president. You should do it because I know you can do it." He wrote my letters of recommendation and he told me to read them too because he just didn't want to send them out, so I read what he had to say and he'd always tell me, "Oh, you know, you're Harvard material and you're this and that."

Students aspired to attend college, but did not know if it would be possible due to their legal status. Some teachers and counselors helped them apply to college and find funding. Judith, for example, had a teacher in high school who advised her on applying to college as an undocumented student: "My math teacher, Mr. P, helped me with the college applications and he advised me on what to do and how to apply. He also helped me with scholarships for undocumented students." Beatriz's faculty advisor was also a key supporter:

> My advisor . . . She has always been there for me, I could always go up to her and tell her anything. And she understands where I come from and she knows my situation. . . . Three days ago she gave me a list of scholarships. She said that you don't have to be an Honors student to get them. There is information out there but all we have to do is just go get it.

High school counselors also played a supportive role in helping students navigate the college application process. Adolfo's high school counselor was an important resource for him when applying to college:

> Nobody in my family has been to college, so no one knows, so I would just go ask her all those questions. She probably got tired of me. She really helped me, telling me about fee waivers, about scholarships, about Websites where you go to apply for college.

Through relationships with teachers, undocumented students formed the trust necessary to disclose personal information about family circumstances and their immigrant status. With this information, teachers were able to intervene and provide students with early academic assistance and planning.

Although school-based adults were the most cited sources of support, some students also received support from other adults. Olivia, for example, had a tutor in high school who was very influential. Additionally, Nailea's role model was a Latina tutor she met in an afterschool program. As she explained, "I admired the fact that she was a Latina and she would talk about many different things that I had never heard about in school like minorities succeeding. I had never been pushed to be the best because I was a Latina." Adolfo found support from someone at a community nonprofit organization, "He already went through college and got his master's so he's showing me the way. He's like my mentor and also a friend. He helped me a lot, like if I needed a letter of recommendation." Key relationships with teachers, school personnel, and other adult mentors enabled the undocumented students in this study to access important resources and information necessary to move from high school to college. When asked about how they found out about the process, students mentioned high school counselors, teachers, and college fairs.

Contreras (2009) found that undocumented students in Washington state reported campus experiences that were often discriminatory on the one hand, but exposed them to resources and supportive individuals to trust to help them navigate college on the other. The different levels of guidance and support brought about differing approaches in how these students were able to enroll in their respective colleges and pay for school. Solorio (2009) also noted that guidance from educators, mentors, and role models played a significant role in providing the necessary information on the college application process for undocumented students. She found that 80% of participants in her study reported receiving guidance from advisors, mentors, and role models. The majority were from their respective high school, although some received support from organizations and college prep programs outside of school. Many advisors and mentors from these respective programs were aware of the challenges undocumented students face. School staff, though, had varying responses to undocumented students. Several students remarked that their counselors did not know how to help undocumented students. Solorio (2009) also found that 61% of students described some type of institutional support from the colleges and universities, which included financial aid, student groups, or academic and career advising.

Support from peers. Peers also played a significant role. Within the stratified structure of schools, undocumented students who were in the college, Honors, or Advanced Placement track had unique access to teachers and counselors. These classes also provided them with a circle of high-achieving peers, with whom they competed for grades, shared information, formed study groups, and received support. As a result, they developed college readiness and leadership skills; they participated in clubs, extracurricular activities, and community service activities; and developed into leaders on their high school campuses. This positive environment also helped undocumented students feel more comfortable about revealing their status to teachers and counselors, the very people who could help them. These exceptionally high-achieving students took these skills and talents with them to their college and university campuses.

Some colleges had supportive student groups on-campus for undocumented students. The student groups provided more in-depth information in learning how to navigate through college, fund-raise, and raise awareness for other students on campus (Solorio, 2009). Chavez, Soriano, and Oliverez (2007), for example, noted the growing number of undocumented student groups on college campuses. Some undocumented students, however, were restrained from making the student group public on-campus due to issues of safety and conservative climates. In this situation, university administrators informed undocumented students about support groups available to them upon admission.

Support from parents. Most children from undocumented households do not have parents who went to college and, as a result, parents are often not able to assist with the process of transitioning to college. Due to their lack of knowledge of the U.S. educational system, parents cannot assist their children in selecting an institution, completing the paperwork, or navigating their undocumented status. Several students mentioned that they had to educate their parents about the process of getting into college. Although the families were unable to assist them with the process of attending college, their emotional and verbal support played a critical role in the lives of students (Portes & Rumbaut, 2001). Solorio (2009) reports that 74% of participants in her study stated that they received encouragement to do well in school and continue from their parents. Level of involvement, however, varied. Some participants described a lack of parental support for their postsecondary inspirations. Although students received varied parental support, all students lacked guidance on the college application process from parents.

Most students described their parents' support and encouragement as an important factor in their educational success. They reported that their parents always emphasized the value of obtaining a good education and going to college. Making school a top priority was often enforced by parents. Janet's parents, for example, insisted that she always put her best effort into school: "My mother and father would tell me that I had to be the best that I could in school. I just kept hearing that." Angelica recalls her parents' support for a college education while she was growing up, even though they did not actually know what was required to get there:

> It was always a given that I was going to go to the university, they just didn't explain how I was going to pay for it, how I was going to get in, or anything else. They would say, "when you grow up, you're going to go to university."

Alma's parents raised her with a similar message, but they also reminded her that doing well in school would indicate to others that she is deserving of legalization:

> I always remember my parents in the back of my mind saying you have to go to college. Since I was very little my parents told me that if you do well in school somehow the government will know that you are a good student and you are a good citizen and they are going to grant you that opportunity to be a citizen. . . . I think that is what always pushed me to do well in school and I always try because I think that if I do that I may have the opportunity to become a legal resident.

One of the most important ways in which parents motivated students was to highlight their own lack of opportunity to get an education to inspire their children to be dedicated students. Jimena's mother took her to work so she could see firsthand the kind of job she would have if she did not do well in school. During her sophomore year in high school, she recalled that her mother sat her down and said to her, "Do you really want to clean bathrooms like me?"

Parents also made various financial sacrifices to support students. Jason recalled an instance when his parents worked overtime to buy him a computer for school:

> I remember during 6th grade, I had to do my first typed essay and we did it on a computer and my parents worked overtime every day in order to have enough money to buy a computer so I could type my assignments and receive good grades. That meant a lot to me. At first, I didn't realize the hard work, but afterward I thought about it and I realized they really cared about me and they want me to succeed and become somebody in this country.

Students reported that their parents worked extremely hard so that they could focus on school. Jaime feels his father has made many sacrifices to provide him with educational opportunities: "He sacrificed himself so I could have an education and I don't want his hard work and sacrifice to go to waste."

For a majority of students, mothers played a vital role in their educational success. It was often mothers who were actively involved in activities both inside and outside of school that nurtured the participants' desire to focus on school. Janet's mother was very active in her schooling growing up: "My mother would always come, she would always come to parent conferences, open house." Alejandra's mother also made an effort to be involved: "She was part of the PTA. She volunteered in everything possible. In elementary school she was there, involved in my education." Eduardo remembers his mom always bringing stuff to his classes. He credits her for his academic success: "I'm extremely grateful for all her motivation and pushing and critiques and everything because she's the one who's actually pushed me and made me strive for more. . . . I guess I can say that all my accomplishments are thanks to her." Adriana's mother always helped her with homework and studying: "She would walk me to the bus stop in the mornings and we would recite together the times tables, and she would quiz me. She would help me out when I had tests." Mia's mother was an important source of support and encouragement, especially when others doubted her:

> She was always there for me. When I was applying for college, she would always go to meetings for me so that she could get information since I am a first-generation student. Even though a lot of people used to tell her and tell me that I wasn't going to be able to go to college because of my situation, she just ignored them and she turned around and looked at me and said not to listen to that.

CONCLUSION

Although undocumented students dedicate themselves to school and doing well academically, they soon learn that the opportunities promised to them if they work hard preclude them. Despite their academic achievement, undocumented students are not able to participate in a variety of programs that require citizenship or a social security number. Although their academic credentials make them eligible for summer jobs, internships, study abroad programs, academic enrichment programs, and scholarships, they are not able to reap the benefits of their hard work. At the college level, the challenges further increase. Ineligible for any form of public funding, students have to work long hours to be able to afford their tuition. Furthermore, since they are not eligible to apply for a driver's license, they have to depend on unreliable public transportation to commute to and from school. Due to the high cost of a college education, undocumented students who have been accepted at highly selective colleges and universities have to forego their admission and instead attend the local community college due to cost with the goal of transferring in 2 years or in hopes that a law will pass that will help them legalize their status.

Undocumented students are regularly reminded about their limitations as they see their classmates, who, despite less impressive academic accomplishments, are able to participate in various academic programs and pursue a college education, because they have access to financial resources that are not available to undocumented students. Students report moments of despair when they feel that their dreams, and all that they have worked for, will not come true. Nevertheless, many find ways to reframe their circumstances in positive terms. They compare their opportunities with what they might have had in their country of origin and use that perspective to remain committed to school and their educational goals. They find ways to see the upside of their circumstances. Whereas many report various types of negative experiences with teachers and counselors, key teachers and counselors, along with their parents, particularly mothers, and peers, are an important source of strength for undocumented Latino students.

Undocumented students highlighted the support and encouragement they have received from caring teachers during their elementary school years who not only served as role models, but also helped them find ways to continue with their education. The teachers went above and beyond their duties to ensure that students continued on to college. Students also credited their parents, particularly mothers, for helping them through difficult times. Many parents took on additional jobs to help pay for school-related costs and provided constant reminders about the importance of getting a college education. It's hard to imagine how young adults could manage such uncertainty and distress without the support of caring adults.

Given the critical transitions taking place in the adolescent lives of un-documented high school students, adult guidance is crucial in the mid- to late high school years. Without such assistance, students are left to cope with stigma and negotiate barriers on their own. The transition from high school to college is an important one for undocumented youth to make, as it allows them to move from one institution where they can legally participate to another where they can continue to participate. Having key mentors to help them access resources and information is of paramount importance. With proper assistance, students can successfully transition from high school to college. The ability to make this transition, and obtain financial support in the process, can preserve a positive outlook on educational attainment and future career goals.

3

Academic Engagement

Undocumented Latino students demonstrate a positive orientation toward school, a theme extensively documented in the immigrant student research literature (Suarez-Orozco, 1989; Suarez-Orozco & Suarez-Orozco, 1995). Despite the frequent challenges they face due to their legal status, they aspire to do well in their classes and hope to attend college. The analyses in this chapter integrate resilience and extracurricular participation theories to examine the ways in which marginalized youth remain engaged in schooling.

ACADEMIC RESILIENCE

Researchers argue that resilience is the process (Olsson, Bond, Burns, Vella-Brodrick, & Sawyer, 2003) of overcoming the negative effects of risk exposure, coping successfully with traumatic experiences, and avoiding the negative trajectories associated with those risks (Garmezy, Masten, & Tellegen, 1984; Luthar, Cicchetti, & Becker, 2000; Masten & Powell, 2003; Rutter, 1985). A key requirement of resilience is the presence of both risk and protective factors that either help bring about a positive outcome or reduce/avoid a negative one. Although resilience theory is concerned with risk exposure among adolescents, it is focused more on strengths rather than deficits and understanding healthy development in spite of high risk exposure. Personality characteristics and environmental social resources are thought to moderate the negative effects of stress and promote positive outcomes despite risks (Benard, 1995; Kirby & Fraser, 1997; Masten, 1994; Werner & Smith, 1992).

Risk Factors

In addition to social and psychological outcomes, resilience research has also examined academic success and persistence despite stressful events and conditions during childhood and adolescence (Alva, 1991; Wang, Haertel, & Walberg, 1994). Well-established academic risk factors include being a minority student attending an inner-city school, or coming from a low-income home where English is not the primary language. Undocumented students report many of these challenges, one of the biggest being learning English. For Lilia, the language barrier made her adjustment to the American school system difficult academically:

> It was a really hard year for me. It was mostly the language barrier.
> In 5th grade, they didn't have bilingual classes and my teacher only
> spoke English. Sometimes for 2 weeks straight I was really lost in class.
> I would try to get information from the people who sat next to me,
> but they really didn't know how to explain things to me so I got really
> stressed out.

Another major obstacle students face in school is having their academic capabilities questioned by school personnel. Many students reported having an experience with a teacher or academic counselor who questioned their ability to do well in school. Sasha explained a situation she experienced in elementary school shortly after she arrived in the United States:

> In 3rd grade I had a teacher that was actually incredibly mean and
> intolerant. She would discriminate against a lot of the students based on
> their ethnicity. She would pick on me a lot. She would tell me things like,
> "You'll never get an A in my class because you are a dirty Mexican,"
> stuff like that. She would ask the students to raise their hands if they
> wanted to be president and she would put my hand down and say, "You
> will never be president, you should focus on other things."

Low teacher expectations were a persistent risk factor for undocumented students. These negative attitudes from school personnel often shaped students' views about themselves. Just learning about the bad experiences of other students or siblings was enough to impact students adversely, as in the case of Lucila:

> In high school, I had a counselor, it was the same counselor my sister
> had, and this counselor told my sister that she wasn't going to be able
> to do it. My sister told her she wanted to be a lawyer and she told her,
> "Oh no, your people are better off doing housework." She put her down
> so I didn't even want to go to my counselor and ask her for help. I just
> felt so discriminated against.

High-achieving undocumented students were often one of only a few minority students in the academically rigorous advanced classes such as Honors or AP (Advanced Placement). As such, they report frequently feeling like an "outsider." Being one of the few Latinas in her advanced courses,

Paulina felt isolated. Her peers often made her feel as though she did not deserve to be in those classes, even though she was one of the most dedicated students:

> They were like, "What are you doing here?" But joking. Nobody said it in a serious tone, but sometimes it did feel like that. . . . It was really upsetting. That's why I felt like I couldn't do a lot of what I wanted to do.

Similarly, Rubi had to challenge school personnel to get into AP classes that she knew she needed to take to prepare for college:

> I had to fight them to let me into the AP program because I was in ESL. I had straight A's all the way through high school. I told them that I wasn't being challenged. Everybody would talk about APs and I didn't know what that meant but I wanted to be in it. I had one AP class but it was Spanish. Then my teacher in Spanish said, "Hey, you should take my AP literature class." So I took that, but they wouldn't let me take AP chemistry or any honors English classes. I had to fight with the counselors to get in.

According to resilience theory, although there are many students in high-risk environments who perform poorly academically, there are others who manage to do well in school (Dauber, Alexander, & Entwisle, 1996; Jimerson, Egeland, & Teo, 1999). Two types of protective factors have consistently been identified as evident among academically invulnerable children: personal and environmental resources (Garmezy, 1981, 1983; Garmezy & Rutter, 1983; Werner, Bierman, & French, 1971; Werner & Smith, 1982).

Personal Protective Factors

Personal characteristics such as social competence, problem-solving skills, autonomy, sense of purpose and future, and high positive expectations play an important role in resilience (Bernard, 1995). The more resources young people have to draw on during times of stress, the better their chances are of dealing with difficulties more effectively (Luthar & Zelazo, 2003). Resilient children exhibit good communication skills, a sense of responsibility, achievement orientation, caring attitudes, an internal locus of control, a positive self-concept, and a belief in self-help (Werner & Smith, 1992). Gender has been frequently confirmed as a correlate of resilience. Longitudinal studies find that women are generally more skilled in accessing and using social supports and resources (Werner, 1989). Women also report more extraversion, trust, gregariousness, and nurturance, which are hypothesized to be important personal protective factors (Feingold, 1994).

Motivation to prove others wrong. Students who do well in the classroom show a positive self-evaluation of their academic status at school and
a sense of control over their academic success and failure (Dweck & Licht,
1980; Dweck & Wortman, 1982; Stipek & Weisz, 1981; Willig, Harnisch,
Hill, & Maehr, 1983; Wylie, 1979). Faith in their own cognitive skills has
been found to be one of the main differences between resilient and non-resil-
ient Latino students in an urban school environment. High academic achievers excel because they believe in their own capabilities to achieve (Gordon,
1996). This was the case for Lucila when her 7th-grade math teacher openly
questioned her ability to win a speech competition:

> When I was practicing for my competition I asked him, "You know,
> this might take a little bit of time from your classes, can I take that
> time?" And he said, "Well, you can go ahead and take all the time that
> you want. I don't even know why you're competing. . . . " I remember
> hearing that and being so angry and going back and writing my speech
> and at the very last state competition he showed up with his wife and
> I just remember laughing because I had the highest grade in his math
> class, and I was a 7th-grader and I won the state speech championship
> and I beat out seniors in high school.

Jimena also encountered a similar negative experience with a school counselor when she moved to a new school. When she requested to be enrolled
in physics and other natural science courses, he tried to discourage her: "He
told me that I might have been the valedictorian of another high school but
that here it was a little bit different. And that's when I decided I wanted to
prove him wrong. He put me down but I guess that anger, I used it against
him." If it would not have been for an elementary school teacher that doubted Sasha's academic ability, she might not have been identified as gifted early
on and enrolled in an accelerated magnet program. Sasha recalled:

> It was the best thing she could have done for me because it got me to
> the point where I decided that if she wasn't going to give me that A, I
> was going to become the best students I could possibly be to show
> her that I had the capacity and that my status in no way equated to
> my capacity. Thanks to her, we had the state department of education
> come down and conduct an IQ test because she said I was mentally
> challenged. It was a really good thing because that is what put me in
> the magnet program. It really gave me a lot of strength to continue and
> to not listen to individuals that were so closed-minded.

Academic identities. Overall, the undocumented students in this study
had a variety of personal resources that helped them overcome challenges they encountered. When asked to indicate whether doing well

in school was important for their self-image, 78% indicated that they "agree" or "strongly agree." Academic self-concept[1] was highest among female students, with 83% reporting "agree" or "strongly agree," compared with 69% of males. Students also indicated high levels of academic self-confidence or self-efficacy.[2] Seventy-five percent either "agree" or "strongly agree" with scale items that measured their academic self-efficacy. Similarly, students preferred new challenges in their academic work rather than avoiding difficult academic tasks.[3] Only 2% indicated that they "agree" or "strongly agree" when asked about whether they prefer to avoid unfamiliar academic work. On the other hand, 82% indicated that they "agree" or "strongly agree" when asked whether they value schooling.[4] This rate was higher for females at 86% compared with 74% for males.

Optimism. Students described various personal resources that they drew from to confront regular educational challenges to excel academically. In addition to high levels of optimism, they were also competitive, determined, and tenacious, or in the words of the students themselves, "stubborn." Students demonstrated a remarkable ability to draw motivation from being able to prove unsupportive educators wrong, aspired to be different from academically unsuccessful peers, and had the desire to do well academically for the sake of their families. When Paulina was asked why she has been so successful, she responded, "My optimism, without that I would not have done anything. Seriously, I would have given up a long time ago." Similarly, Penelope explained, "I know for a fact my success is because of my relentless determination . . . what makes the difference is that I have a positive attitude and most other students don't." Jacinto recalled that growing up he was admired for his optimism:

> My ability to look on the bright side of things. I always thought that the glass was always half full. If I wasn't allowed to go to college, well I did my best in high school and I got a lot out of high school and I am going to work to get ahead. We got evicted and I thought maybe we just needed to get out of this neighborhood and look for a different neighborhood. If I lost a job, I thought I would get a better job.

Competitiveness. The students I interviewed also described being competitive with their classmates, always striving to be the best student in class. As Samantha explained, "I remember wanting to be at the top of my class, always trying to see who I was competing against, who had the highest grade." Jairo also recounted his competitiveness with his peers: "I would say that I'm a competitive person. Like when I get grades, it always felt good for me to be higher than other people."

Tenacity. Another characteristic of undocumented students that seemed to be associated with their academic achievement was their persistent drive and determination to succeed. Jacqueline explained:

> I think because I'm determined to do what I want. I have my goals set, and I just know that I need do whatever I can to obtain them. I think that I'm very persistent, I just won't give up. Even if I have the biggest obstacle in front of me, I'll just try to jump right over it.

Similarly, Jacinto expressed strong determination not to let anything stand in the way of his dreams of going to college:

> I remember just trying to do the best. I love learning and I love school. In high school, I decided I wanted to do more for my education so I would study really hard and get good grades. I was on the honor roll my 4 years. I remember really wanting to go to college. I knew that if you were in clubs and you had good grades, then you had a higher chance of getting into college. So that's what I did.

Undocumented students reported high levels of tenacity, or as Jimena and others described it, "I guess I am stubborn. When people put me down, like my counselor or my mom saying that I am not going to college, I don't listen to them." Alejandra also credited her persistence or "stubbornness" for her success:

> I am stubborn so I fight to get something I want or the grade I want. I push for the higher grade. I remember in my sociology class, the first paper I ever got, I got a B- and I didn't like it so I went to the professor's office hours and I kept asking for pointers and for help until finally he gave me an A- on my other papers.

Karen also considered her stubbornness an asset in her academic pursuits: "I'm very stubborn. I decide something, I pursue it. Once I decided that I was going to go to college and finish high school, I went with it and I stuck with it and nobody moved me out of that place."

Motivation to avoid the same negative fate as peers. The unfortunate reality in the communities where undocumented students grew up was elevated high school dropout rates, low college-going percentages, and other types of social challenges. Some students were motivated by not wanting to be like many of their peers who did not continue with school. Penelope, for example, described her desire to do well in school to avoid the same fate as the neighborhood kids she grew up with, "Where I live most of the kids give up on their education. I don't want to think that education is something that is impossible for me." Similarly, Daniella did not want to share the same fate as her cousins and friends who became pregnant at a young age, even if those around her did not believe that her future would be different:

> A lot of my friends have gotten pregnant at an early age, have not continued to go to school, and most of my family members also didn't finish high school . . . a lot of my cousins got pregnant and people always point at me and say, "You're next. You're next," and for me I thought, "No, I'm not going to do that. I have dreams, I have goals . . . I'm going to achieve them. Even if it takes me longer, I will."

Obligation to be a role model. Other students persisted in school because they wanted to be role models for younger siblings and other Latino students. Isabel was motivated to do well in school and pursue higher education to set a good example for her younger siblings:

> As the oldest, I want not only more for myself, but also for my siblings. I want them to know this is not just the only life, that there's more in the world that they can go and accomplish. So yeah, I just want to set a positive example for them and that, it's hard, but not impossible.

Jairo also shared Isabel's sentiment: "I feel that I'm paving the way for my brothers and sisters because I'm older. I am the first to go to college and I want to make sure that my brothers go to college, too." Sasha wanted to be a role model for other undocumented students to show them that college is possible regardless of their legal status: "I see those students that are in high school and it is my job to show them that it can be done."

Family obligation. As previously noted by research that examines immigrant students' sense of family obligation (Fuligni, 1997), undocumented students report being motivated to do well in school to be able to take care of their parents, which was also indicated by 92% of participants in this study who reported that it was either "somewhat true" or "very true"[5] for them. For example, Jason was motivated to continue his education to take care of his parents and to set a good example for his younger siblings:

> I want to help them. I want to buy them a house or whatever they need when they're older and I want to be there for them. Not only for my parents, I want my younger sister and my brother to know that there's high opportunities out there, especially since they're American citizens. At my high school graduation I told my sister, "You have to graduate higher than me, possibly valedictorian or salutatorian, go to a good college and get a good life, and since you're an American citizen, get a lot of financial aid so you can pay for college, unlike me."

Overall, undocumented students reported an extensive array of personal resources that allowed them to excel academically. A complementary set of environmental resources provided an overall rich support structure that enabled them to persist in their educational endeavors.

Environmental Protective Factors

Parental support. Resilience is also an ecological phenomenon in that environments may contribute to a person's risk of various problems, but can also provide protection to enhance the likelihood of positive outcomes (Greene, 2002; Jozefowicz-Simbeni & Allen-Meares, 2002; Richman & Fraser, 2001). Resources are positive factors that are external to the individual and help overcome risk, such as parental support, adult mentoring, or community organizations that promote positive youth development. Academically successful students also appear to have a supportive network of family members, friends, neighbors, and teachers on whom they rely for advice in difficult or stressful situations. Mexican-American parents, in particular, are mentioned by successful students as an important source of support and encouragement (Alva, 1991; Arellano & Padilla, 1996; Gandara, 1982). For example, in her study of successful Mexican-American professionals, Gandara (1982) found that 93% reported that the educational support they received from their parents during childhood and adolescence was the single most important factor affecting their high academic goals and expectations. Thus, family is a very important factor in the development of resiliency in immigrant students (Siantz, 1997). In a study of low-income Mexican adolescents and their families, Stanton-Salazar (2001) found that immigrant parents articulated high aspirations for their children even though many did not have the opportunity to attend school in their own country, and were not able to help their children with academic material or navigating the educational system in the United States. Supportive relationships, particularly encouragement from teachers, school personnel, and other adults, are also a key protective factor in the development of resilience among immigrant students (Bernard, 1995). In the only previous study to examine resilience among undocumented students, Perez and his colleagues (2009) found that despite various risk factors, undocumented students who had high levels of personal and environmental protective factors, such as supportive parents, friends, and participation in school activities, reported higher levels of academic success than students with similar risk factors but lower levels of personal and environmental resources. In this study, students reported high levels of peer and parental support for their academic pursuits. When asked how much their parents valued schooling, 88% reported that it was "important" or "very important." Similarly, when asked how important schooling was for

their friends, 68% reported that it was either "important" or "very important." Students were motivated to do well in school because their friends
also valued school, as reported by 53% who reported "somewhat true" or
"very true," that they wanted to do well in school because of their friends.[6]

Academic enrichment programs. Despite undocumented students' difficulties learning English and unsupportive teachers, the in-depth interviews
revealed that several students were identified early in their schooling as high
academic achievers. Over a third of students surveyed reported participating in GATE (Gifted and Talented Education). According to Table 3.1, 39%
of male students and 34% of female students participated in GATE. On
average, females enrolled in GATE in earlier grades than males, with male
students identified for GATE in 7th grade (M= 7.21) and female participants identified in 6th grade (M= 5.87). The GATE participation rate is
noteworthy given that, as a comparison, GATE participation was 8.4% in
the state of California during the 2007–2008 academic year. The Latino
GATE participation rate was even lower, at 5.11% that same year. Thus,
undocumented students in this study had a GATE participation rate that
was almost seven times higher than the California statewide rate for Latinos
(California Department of Education, 2009). Thalia was one of the students
who was identified as "gifted" in early elementary school:

> By 2nd grade . . . I was considered gifted. They tested me and
> then they changed my classes. At the beginning I hated it, but
> then I really liked it. They put all the smart kids in one class and
> we were labeled "gifted."

Other students were placed in accelerated magnet programs. Sasha, for
example, joined a magnet program in 3rd grade: "The year after I arrived I
joined the magnet program . . . I really enjoyed it because the groups were
smaller and because they really pushed critical thinking. They created an
environment that was very friendly and incited the students to learn." Those
students identified as gifted early in their schooling seem to have developed
a strong academic confidence that served them well in confronting the challenges they faced later in their educational careers.

ACADEMIC ENGAGEMENT

Although most students struggled to learn English when they first arrived
in the United States, most mastered it quickly and were recruited into accelerated programs. For Ulises, moving from English as a Second Language
(ESL) to AP courses was a source of pride: "My greatest accomplishment in

Table 3.1. Academic Engagement by Gender

	Male (*n* = 42)		Female (*n* = 68)		Total (*N* = 110)	
	%	M	%	M	%	M
Academic Preparation						
Grade when enrolled in GATE [a]	39	7.21	34	5.87	36	6.38
Honors and AP courses [b]	67	4.79	73	4.16	71	4.40
Achievement & Academic Recognition						
High school GPA		3.43		3.51		3.48
College GPA		3.13		3.08		3.10
Elementary school awards [b]	55	1.10	75	1.65	67	1.44
Middle school awards [b]	79	1.62	79	1.63	79	1.63
High school awards [b]	83	1.64	85	1.90	85	1.80
College awards [b]	43	.52	46	.66	45	.61
Total academic awards [b]	95	4.88	94	5.84	94	5.47
Psychosocial Academic Orientation						
Educational aspirations [c]	85	5.36	94	5.60	90	5.51
Educational expectations [c]	51	4.59	68	4.94	61	4.81
Academic self-concept [d]	69	6.24	83	6.46	78	6.34
Academic self-efficacy [d]	77	6.26	75	5.99	75	6.09
Effort avoidance [d]	3	2.72	2	2.47	2	2.57
Valuing of schooling [e]	74	6.07	86	6.51	82	6.34
Parent-derived achievement motivation [f]	97	3.63	90	3.59	92	3.60
Friend-derived achievement motivation [f]	49	2.82	56	2.85	53	2.84
Social Support for Academics						
Parental valuing of schooling [g]	92	3.60	84	3.50	88	3.54
Friends' valuing of schooling [g]	59	2.93	73	3.16	68	3.07

[a] Percentage reflects participation rate.

[b] Percentage reporting 1 or more.

[c] Scale range: 1 (graduate from high school), 2 (some college), 3 (A.A. degree), 4 (B.A. degree), 5 (M.A. degree), 6 (J.D./Ph.D./M.D. degree). Percent reflects responses 5–6 combined.

[d] Scale range: 1 (strongly disagree)–7 (strongly agree). Percent reflects responses 6–7 combined.

[e] Scale range: 1 (not important at all)– 7 (very important). Percent reflects responses 6–7 combined.

[f] Scale range: 1 (very false), 2 (somewhat false), 3 (somewhat true), 4 (very true). Percent reflects responses 3–4 combined.

[g] Scale range: 1 (not important), 2 (somewhat important), 3 (important), 4 (very important). Percent reflects responses 3–4 combined.

high school was going all the way from ESL 3 in 9th grade to AP English in the 12th grade." Similarly, Janet was placed in a class with older, advanced students: "I was the only 9th-grader in the Honors Biology class. Everyone else was either in the 10th grade or 11th grade. They didn't believe that I was in the 9th grade, and I did very well." And Alma was an outstanding student in high school. As she described:

I graduated in the top 10 of my class. I received the Target Scholarship for volunteering and from the California Scholarship Federation, I got a gold tassel for my volunteer work and doing well academically. I was also MVP for my basketball team at school and was an Academic-Athlete Scholar. That is when you play sports and your GPA is above a 3.5.

Most students were enrolled in academically rigorous courses. In all, two-thirds (67%) of male students and three-fourths (73%) of female students had taken at least one AP/Honors course during high school. On average, male students took a total of five (M=4.79) academically rigorous Advanced Placement (AP) and Honors courses, while female students took a total of four (M= 4.16). Comparing only the AP course-taking of undocumented Latino students with the AP course-taking rate of California students during the 2006–2007 academic year indicates that whereas 53% of the Latino undocumented students in this study had taken at least one AP course, the percentage of California high school students taking at least one AP course was less than half the percentage of the students in this study, at 22.47% (California Department of Education, 2009).

Along with rigorous academic coursework, students reported high levels of academic achievement. Their average high school GPA was 3.47, while for college students, the average college GPA was 3.11. Due to his achievement record, Eduardo qualified for membership in academic clubs such as the National Honor Society (NHS) and California Scholarship Federation (CSF). Miranda was also a member of academic organizations:

Something I'm really proud of was being in the Honor Society for 3 years. You had to have 80 hours of community service total. I also received this one certificate where if you have a 3.5 GPA or above for all 4 years you get a special golden scholar award.

Students also reported various academic accomplishments in high school. Many had graduated at the top of their senior class. Jennifer graduated with 4.0 GPA and was the valedictorian. Samantha and Raul also graduated as class valedictorians. Others had graduated in the top 5% to 10% of their senior class, like Ismael, who was ranked in the top 5% of his class of 500 students, and Rubi who graduated ranked 5th out of 900 seniors. Jaime also graduated with a 4.0 GPA and was ranked 6th out of a class of 300 seniors, while Jeronimo had a 4.02 GPA and was ranked 17th out of a graduating class of 500 students.

Academic Recognitions

Students received various academic recognitions throughout their schooling, particularly in elementary school. On average, about half (55%) of male students and three-fourths (75%) of female students received one or more academic award in elementary school, as Ismael described:

> I had various awards. I got perfect attendance, character awards for responsibility, and I remember in 6th grade I got a president's award. It was an award for people who excelled academically throughout the year. My teacher nominated me. I was really proud of that.

For Sasha, it was a thrill to win a spelling bee competition in 4th grade even though she had only been in the U.S. for 2 years: "I was really proud of it because English was my second language and for many students it was their first language." Almost four-fifths (79%) of students received one or more academic awards in middle school. Eduardo was most proud of his most distinguished academic accomplishment:

> I had a lot of accomplishments in middle school. Eighth grade was my best year. I was salutatorian, so that was awesome. I'm most proud of my salutatorian award because I came out the top two in my class. I also got academic excellence in history, English . . . yeah, tons of other awards.

The average number of awards students received increased slightly in high school. About four-fifths of students received one or more academic awards at this level. The highlight of Jairo's senior year of high school was the senior awards night when he was awarded a prestigious scholarship:

> I got one in front of all the school and all the parents. The whole football stadium was full. There were people standing on the sides, the bleachers were full. My classmates were there and all the teachers. I was really nervous because they called my name in front of all of these people. And then they started reading my whole life in front of all of these strangers. It was really amazing, and I was really nervous. And I was really embarrassed at the same time. . . . I will never forget that.

Daniella never imagined she would even get one scholarship, let alone eight: "I always thought, scholarships, no, I'm not going to get anything. That was my thinking, but I did apply and . . . right out of high school, I got eight scholarships." In all, Daniella received $10,000 worth of scholarship money when she graduated from high school.

Overall, 94% of students received at least one academic award during their schooling. On average, students received 5.36 academic awards sometime during elementary school through college. Table 3.2 presents detailed information regarding the types of awards students received during elementary, middle, high school, and college. Student of the month awards were most common during elementary school (27%). Honor roll distinctions were more common in middle school (30%) and high school (29%). Although students reported receiving awards for spelling bee, writing, and poetry contests, the percentages were very low overall. Only 6% of students received these awards in elementary and middle school, while 2% of students received them in high school and college. Academic subject awards such as math, science, and social studies were highest in high school (26%) and middle school (25%). Over one-third of students had received academic merit and/or achievement awards in both middle school (35%) and high school (40%). Six percent of students were either valedictorian or salutatorian of their graduating high school class, while 12% reported receiving some type of academic scholarship in college. As the next section describes, students were involved in various extracurricular activities for which they also received various awards. For example, Table 3.2 indicates that during their high school years, 17% of students received awards for sports participation, while 5% received leadership awards. During college, 10% received community service awards.

Educational Goals

In many ways, their achievement history, extracurricular experiences, and leadership roles shaped the ambitious educational attainment goals of undocumented Latino students. A majority of students (90%) aspired to earn a master's degree or higher. When students were asked to indicate how far they thought they would actually go in school, their educational expectations decreased, with about two-thirds (60%) expecting to earn a master's degree or higher, perhaps reflecting the myriad of challenges they face. In both educational aspirations and expectations, female students had slightly higher educational goals. Despite the challenges they face, undocumented students felt confident that they would at least be able to earn a college degree, as Angelica described:

> I want to get my Ph.D., just because there are not many Hispanic women who have one, and I just want to set the standard for other women so they can say, "She did it, I can do it, too."

Table 3.2. Percent of Students Receiving School Awards by School Level When Received

Type of Award	Elementary School	Middle School	High School	College
Academic Awards				
Student of the month	27	7	9	--
Honor roll	23	30	29	16
Attendance	31	24	20	--
Spelling bee, writing, poetry	6	6	2	2
Subject (math, science, social studies)	10	25	26	0
Science fair /pentathlon/ decathlon	2	7	6	1
Student of the year	6	5	4	--
Merit, achievement	4	35	40	14
Valedictorian/salutatorian			6	--
Scholarship				12
Extracurricular Participation Awards				
Sports	6	5	17	0
Band, music, choir	2	6	6	1
Community service	5	2	4	10
Citizenship	15	10	6	--
Talent show	3	1	1	0
Student council	2	1	5	6
Art	3	0	1	0

Ivan wanted to "Go to law school and become an attorney, practice law for a while, then I want to get into politics. I would love to be a senator or be a chief justice." Despite lowered educational expectations, most students had big dreams and aspirations, like Angelica: "Despite everything, I think I'm destined for greatness, I think I will do something big, I just need a chance."

EXTRACURRICULAR ACTIVITIES

Almost half of school-age children's time in the United States is spent on leisure activities (Larson & Verma, 1999). During adolescence, much of this leisure time is in organized school-based extracurricular activities such as competitive sports and academic clubs (Carnegie Corporation, 1992; Eccles & Gootman, 2002; Mahoney, Larson, & Eccles, 2005; Mahoney, Larson, Eccles, & Lord, 2005). In 1997, 57% of youth 12–17 years old participated in sports and 60% participated in clubs or organizations during the previous year, while in 2002, 75% of 14-year-olds participated in structured extracurricular activities (Mahoney, Schweder, & Stattin, 2002). In addition, in 2005, 70% of adolescents surveyed indicated that they are currently, or are planning on, participating in school-based extracurricular activities that school year (Feldman & Matjasko, 2005).

Although there are some recent studies that examine civic engagement specifically among immigrant students, few have discussed the extracurricular participation rates of immigrant students. One of the few studies on the topic found that in college, immigrant students were less likely to participate in extracurricular activities due to various barriers they face that likely limit their participation, such as work and family responsibilities (Gray, Rolph, & Melamid, 1996). Despite the increasing number of undocumented students, no studies have examined their extracurricular participation. We know very little about how members of this marginalized population of students become involved despite the myriad of challenges they face on a regular basis.

In early adolescence, youth begin to make their own decisions about how to spend their time after school, and these choices can have important implications for their future developmental trajectories. Establishing relationships with peers and feeling connected take on increasing importance during this period (Lerner & Steinberg, 2004). Involvement in supervised and organized activities during afterschool hours is associated with positive outcomes, while participation in unsupervised and/or unstructured contexts is related to less favorable adjustment (Feldman & Matjasko, 2005; Mahoney & Stattin, 2000). Participating in high-quality organized activities affords youth the opportunity to form supportive and caring relationships with adults in the wider community who can provide them with social capital (Eccles & Gootman, 2002). Extracurricular activities provide a unique context for developing relationships with diverse peers and belonging to a group (Eccles & Gootman, 2002; Patrick, Ryan, Alfeld-Liro, Fredricks, Hruda, & Eccles, 1999).

Undocumented students felt that joining clubs helped them grow and develop a different perspective on important social issues and allowed them to connect with other students. Some students joined clubs to develop leadership skills, contribute to their communities, mentor or counsel those in need, and to learn about their cultural heritage. Jimena and Jazmin both highlighted the benefits of getting involved in school clubs. Jazmin commented, "High school was just the best experience for me. I think it's a great place for kids who grow up in a less fortunate family to get involved in school, to participate, to sow the seeds of what could be done." Some students joined clubs that allowed them to provide support to their peers.

In middle school, Raul was involved in a peer counseling group. So was Jacinto: "Basically, what we would do is take students who got into a lot of conflicts and we would talk to them. And we would make sure that the problem didn't reoccur." In high school, both Rolando and Jeronimo were involved in conflict mediation. Rolando explained it: "You help students solve their problems if they have family issues or problems in school." Other students, including Eduardo, joined JROTC (Junior Reserve Officers' Training Corps) to gain valuable leadership skills: "I was involved in Junior ROTC and I just developed a lot of leadership skills and I became a better public speaker." Other students joined clubs that celebrated their cultural heritage. Jason joined the National Movimiento Estudiantil Chicano deAztlan (MEChA), while Penelope joined the Hispanic heritage club at the suggestion of her history teacher and found the experience very rewarding: "We did a lot of community awareness. We participated in the Cesar Chavez walkathon. A lot of the activities were related to our heritage." These clubs provided a sense of belonging and connection with other students who shared similar backgrounds.

Students also frequently took on leadership roles. More than half of students (55%) participated in extracurricular activities in elementary school, while about 25% held leadership positions. In middle school, 64% participated in extracurricular activities, and about one-third held leadership positions. In high school, 86% reported participating in extracurricular activities and approximately half (56%) held leadership positions. Among the college students, half (53%) had participated in extracurricular activities in college and 36% held leadership positions.

Early participation in extracurricular activities is associated with indicators of positive adjustment at both 8th and 11th grades (Fredrick & Eccles, 2008). Participation in middle school clubs is also related to positive academic adjustment in both middle and high school. The higher grades and perceptions of school value for participants as compared to nonparticipants may be a function of increased social capital and a greater likelihood of associating with peers who value academics (Barber, Eccles, & Stone, 2001; Eccles, Barber, Stone, & Hunt, 2003; Finn, 1989). There may also be some psychological benefits from involvement in organized activities during the middle school years, especially in terms of perceived psychological resiliency. High-quality organized activities offer youth the opportunity to participate in challenging tasks with support for autonomy. This may help youth to develop problem-solving skills, a critical aspect of resiliency (Eccles & Gootman, 2002; Fredrick & Eccles, 2008).

In general, participating in school activities during high school has also been found to be associated with positive adjustment. Participation has been positively linked to academic outcomes, including higher grades, test scores, school value, school engagement, and educational aspirations (Eccles &

Barber, 1999; Fredricks & Eccles, 2005, 2006a; Marsh & Kleitman, 2002), and psychological outcomes such as higher self-esteem, higher psychological resiliency, and lower rates of depression (Eccles & Barber, 1999; Fredricks & Eccles, 2006b; Mahoney, Schweder, & Stattin, 2002). Involvement in extracurricular activities during high school is also related to having more friends who plan to attend college and are doing better in school than adolescents who do not participate (Barber, Eccles, & Stone, 2001; Eccles & Barber 1999; Eccles et al., 2003).

Undocumented students felt that joining academic clubs challenged them intellectually and allowed them to make connections with teachers and school personnel. When asked about the academic clubs she participated in during high school, Penelope listed many: "I did participate in a lot of academic clubs like the math club, the science club, the social science club, speech and debate, academic decathlon." Alejandra's most memorable experience in high school came from her participation in the academic decathlon: "My best experience was participating in academic decathlon. That's where my close friends came from, my best teacher, my mentor. He was my teacher for five classes." Adolfo joined the academic decathlon team his senior year in high school:

> It was a lot of fun, but it was also very challenging academically and it made me change as a person a lot. We used to study for hours. We started during 6th period and then we just studied like until 5:30 PM every day after school. When the competition was nearing, we used to stay even later.

Many students joined clubs at the encouragement of a teacher. Ivan participated in numerous clubs both inside and outside of his school:

> I also joined the JSA, the Junior States of America. It's a debate club. I did MESA competition, which is for mathematics. I also participated in speak easy, which is impromptu speeches. I received third place so I got a medal. I also did chess club for 2 years. Our high school had competitions and I won first place one time. My senior year, I also participated in academic decathlon and in CHIRLA [Coalition for Humane Immigrant Rights of Los Angeles] for 2 years, where we used to discuss things like AB540 students and immigration.

Extracurricular involvement is also related to lower dropout rates, lower delinquency, and less frequent substance use (Mahoney & Cairns, 1997; Youniss, Yates, & Su, 1997). In general, studies suggest that across the majority of outcomes, the effects of organized activity participation are generalizable by race and gender (Eccles & Barber, 1999; Fredricks & Eccles,

2006a; Marsh, 1992; Marsh & Kleitman, 2002). A few studies have documented interactive effects of organized activity participation by socioeconomic status. They suggest that youth from lower-socioeconomic status families may benefit more from extracurricular participation than youth from higher-SES families (Marsh, 1992; Marsh & Kleitman, 2002). For example, adolescents who begin high school significantly at risk for curtailed educational attainments are twice as likely to graduate high school and enroll in college if they engage in positive extracurricular activities more than once a week during 11th grade (Roeser & Peck, 2003). College enrollment rates increase dramatically for vulnerable youth who are involved in both school clubs and organized sports. Vulnerable adolescents' engagement in any one of these positive activities results in a threefold increase in the likelihood that they would subsequently go on to college, compared with youth who are not engaged in these activity patterns (Peck, Roeser, Zarrett, & Eccles, 2008).

Table 3.3 provides information regarding the types of extracurricular activities and leadership positions students held at each level of their education. Participation in student council was a popular activity in elementary school (14%), middle school (15%), and high school (18%), and less so in college (5%). Most students who participated in newspaper/magazine/yearbook did so in high school (15%) or middle school (6%). Cultural dance participation happened most frequently in elementary school (11%), followed by middle and high school (6% each). Participation in clubs was highest in high school (67%) and college (47%). Students who reported participating in an academic club did so most frequently in high school (31%). Only 3% of college students reported being in a fraternity or sorority.

Sports Participation

Like most typical American students, undocumented students joined various sports teams. Involvement in sports was the most frequently reported activity in elementary school (30%), middle school (26%), and high school (41%). Some students participated in school teams while other students joined sports teams outside of school. Students felt that playing sports gave them an outlet to vent as well as build their confidence, especially when they received awards. Alma played basketball and volleyball in high school, Rubi was the captain of her high school basketball team, and Mauricio was selected as the president of his high school golf team. Daniella said playing tennis helped her release stress and gave her a sense of enjoyment: "I was always happy when I was playing tennis. It helped me release a lot of my stress. I got really, really good at it . . . when I was playing, I really didn't think about other things." Many students were scholar athletes like Rolando, who played varsity soccer for 2 years while also earning several academic recognitions:

Table 3.3. Extracurricular Activities & Leadership Positions by School Level When Participated

	Elementary School	Middle School	High School	College	Total	
	%	%	%	%	%	M
Extracurricular Activities						
Student council	14	15	18	5	35	
Sports	30	26	41	6	59	
Band, music, choir	23	19	9	0	37	
Drama	3	3	6	1	12	
Newspaper, magazine, yearbook	1	6	15	3	21	
Cultural dance	11	6	6	2	21	
Clubs	7	22	67	47	80	
Academic club	10	13	31	5	40	
Summer sports activity	0	3	6	0	9	
Summer band camp	0	0	2	0	2	
Fraternity/sorority	0	0	0	3	3	
Total Extracurricular Participation	55	65	86	54	95	4.75
Leadership						
Student council officer	9	14	14	5	29	
Hall monitor	4	0	0	0	4	
Sports team captain	14	8	10	0	26	
Club officer	2	5	40	33	58	
Band chair	1	6	5	1	6	
Yearbook/newspaper editor	0	5	6	3	11	
Student council/class president	5	5	6	0	12	
Club president	0	1	21	15	35	
Summer leadership activity	0	4	6	6	11	
Total Leadership Roles	24	32	57	36	78	2.35

Sophomore year, I played varsity and we won the state regional championship. It was a good feeling just being there. I was also in the top 10 of my class all 4 years. I was in the National Honor Society and the California Scholarship Federation. Last week, we had a banquet and I got the Bank of America award for math.

Arts Participation

Students' participation in band, music, or choir was more prevalent in elementary school (23%) and middle school (19%). Olivia played the violin in the orchestra in 5th grade. Eduardo also joined in elementary school: "I was involved in the orchestra 6th, 7th, and 8th grade. I won the orchestra award for top violinist player in my class, so that was awesome." Jairo was involved in the band and orchestra all 4 years of high school: "I was in marching band for the first half of the year and then I moved to orchestras for the second half." Liz played the guitar in her middle school's mariachi band. Initially, she was resistant to it, but her music teacher insisted:

In 7th grade I took a guitar class and my teacher told me that I was good at it, so he told me to join the mariachi. At first I didn't want to. He told me to join the band because he thought I was really good.

Jaime participated in the band for 2 years in high school: "I played the percussion instruments. My second year, I was the first chair for the percussion section." He also has been involved in running the summer band camp: "Whenever August came around I always went to band camp. I helped run this year's band camp." In addition to the school band, Jaime also plays in a community band: "I play in the community bands and we perform in different venues, we go to shows, anything that we get called for. There are people of all ages in the band."

Leadership Experiences

Some of the features of extracurricular activity settings that may be particularly instrumental in enhancing positive youth development include good structure, positive social norms, and opportunities for skill-building (Eccles & Gootman, 2002). When vulnerable youth are exposed to a broad distribution of extracurricular activity settings that afford them constructive, developmentally appropriate opportunities (e.g., to befriend healthy peers, develop competencies and skills, exercise some autonomy, develop long-term mentoring relationships, and explore their commitment to education more generally), then their chances of being educationally resilient are increased.

For students who reported participating in student council, some held leadership positions as officers. Fourteen percent of students held a student council officer position in middle and high school. Others held the position of class president. Six percent held this position in high school, and 5% in both elementary and middle school. Pedro joined student government in middle school: "We helped out the school and the community. We planned the dances for the school, and the activities. For the staff, we would have a staff day where we provided lunch for them." Sasha participated in student government in high school: "I liked it because I was able to work for my school. Improve it. Also I liked it because it was a good experience. It was a good way to attain leadership skills." Jacinto participated in student council to increase his competitiveness for college: "I remember really wanting to go to college. I knew that if you were in clubs and you had good grades then you had a higher chance of getting into college. So that's what I did. I got good grades and I was on the student council." In the summer during high school, Raul was chosen to participate in the California Boys State program, a prestigious leadership development program for high school students whose distinguished alumni include former president Bill Clinton.

Students who were in clubs also held leadership positions as club officers; 40% did so in high school and 33% in college. Others held the position of club president; 21% held this position in high school and 15% in college. Penelope was club president in high school:

> I am the president for the speech and debate and the social science clubs. I am also the secretary for the science club. I am a member of academic decathlon and I participated in the super quiz, which was televised. Being in the clubs was great.

Eduardo held one of the highest leadership positions in his high school's JROTC: "I was a captain; the top ranks were captain and major."

Undocumented students not only assumed a variety of leadership positions in existing clubs, but they also demonstrated higher-order leadership and initiative by creating new clubs on their school campus. Ivan noted, "I became the president of JSA my 11th-grade year and that continued to the 12th grade. I was the president so I was in charge of raising the money. I also co-founded teen court at my school." Judith demonstrated initiative as well as leadership when she decided to start a new club at her school:

> I was also the president of a club I founded at my school. We raised money to grant the wish of a terminally ill child. . . . I started looking at clubs that other high schools had that we didn't so I just found this club and I decided to start it at my school. A lot of people got involved. It turned out pretty good; we raised $4,000.00.

Samantha also started a club at her school: "I started a community service club to raise money for domestic abuse people in shelters." Likewise, in college Sasha was the founding president of a student organization that supports undocumented students on campus. When asked to elaborate on her duties as president, she modestly replied, "I never really think of it as president. I feel that it is a collective effort. We had to give the title to one of us. And we decided that it would be me. But we all work really hard."

The literature on organized activities suggests that, in general, adolescent participation is related to positive developmental outcomes, including higher educational attainment and achievement, reduced problem behavior, and positive psychosocial adjustment (Barber, Eccles, & Stone, 2001; Feldman & Matjasko, 2005; Holland & Andre, 1987; Mahoney, Schweder, & Stattin, 2002; McNeal, 1998). High school activity participation is also associated with a higher likelihood of college attendance, more favorable mental health, and increased civic engagement (Barber, Eccles, & Stone, 2001; Mahoney, Cairns, & Farmer, 2003; Youniss & Yates, 1997). Finally, extracurricular involvement is associated with lower dropout rates and is linked to reduced problem behavior (Mahoney & Cairns, 1997; McNeal, 1995; Youniss, Yates, & Su, 1997). Overall, 95% of students had participated in extracurricular activities. The average number of extracurricular activities was 4.70. In total, about the same percentage of male students (79%) and female students (78%) reported taking on a leadership position in various clubs and student organizations. Among those who participated in sports, 14% were team captains in elementary school, 8% in middle school, and 10% in high school. Students who were in yearbook and newspaper held the position of editor in middle school (5%), high school (6%), and college (3%). On average, students held 2.40 student leadership positions during their formal schooling years.

CONCLUSION

Learning English was not the only obstacle that undocumented Latino students faced after they arrived in the United States and enrolled in school. Beginning in elementary school, they reported various instances of prejudice and discrimination. Many described unsupportive teachers that questioned their academic talents, counselors who suggested that they were not college material, and exclusion by middle-class White peers in their classes, accompanied by a sense of isolation being one of a few or the only Latina/o student in academically rigorous courses. Despite these challenges, students reported drawing on their inner strength, strong commitment to education, and desire to be the best. Many participated in academic enrichment programs that shaped their academic confidence. They had a solid record of achievement dating back to their elementary school years. For some, the culmination of those efforts was graduating as the valedictorian or salutatorian of their senior class.

College-going and college-bound undocumented Latino students are not typical. Despite attending similar schools and sharing similar socioeconomic characteristics, their academic profile is very different compared with the general academic profile of Latino students in the United States. Whereas an increasing number of researchers (e.g., Gandara & Contreras, 2009) highlight the Latino educational crisis, the students in this study were doing well academically despite socioeconomic and demographic backgrounds that would predict otherwise. They had higher than average participation rates in Gifted and Talented Education programs, Advanced Placement course enrollment, high grade point averages, and academic and extracurricular awards. Their strong psychosocial orientation toward schooling was quite possibly a significant factor in their academic success, as noted by the high degree to which doing well in school was an important aspect of their self-image, their high level of academic confidence, their preference for academically challenging material, their strong valuing of schooling, and the high degree to which their parents and friends served as sources of motivation to do well in school. Not surprisingly, students reported that both their friends and family highly value education. All of these sources of support for education most likely shaped their high educational aspirations, academic confidence, and resilience. Most students did not want to settle for just a college degree but aspired to complete at least a master's degree.

The survey data underscore the high rates of extracurricular participation among undocumented Latino students. Among the most popular activities for undocumented students were sports, clubs, student council, band, school newspaper, or yearbook. Extracurricular participation peaked in high school and decreased during college, possibly due to the increased number of hours students had to work to pay for their college expenses as well as the difficulties they faced securing transportation. Starting in elementary school, students reported not only participating in extracurricular activities, but also assuming various leadership positions. The highest rate of leadership participation peaked in high school, where 40% of students reported holding a leadership role.

The interview data suggest that students are motivated to get involved to expand their horizons, develop leadership skills, contribute to communities, and develop a sense of belonging. Students joined and assumed leadership positions in volunteer clubs, JROTC, ethnic affinity clubs, student council, and academic clubs. The academic clubs were noted as important sources of support from encouraging teachers, friends, and peers who similarly valued school and supported the students' educational aspirations. Students positively reflected on the long hours of academic preparation required for academic competitions. In addition to sports participation, many students also reported the sense of accomplishment they felt participating in music programs. A significant component of the extracurricular experience of undocumented students was the volunteer work, community service, and other forms of civic engagement. To gain a deeper understanding on the context of legal marginality and the impact on the civic engagement of undocumented students, the next chapter examines how and why undocumented youth became civically engaged.

NOTES

1. Academic Self-concept was measured using a scale comprised of four statements. Student responses for each statement were averaged to create an academic self-concept index score.

2. Academic Self-efficacy was measured using a scale comprised of five statements. Student responses for each statement were averaged to create an academic self-efficacy index score.

3. Effort Avoidance was measured using a scale comprised of five statements. Student responses for each statement were averaged to create an effort avoidance index score.

4. Valuing of Schooling was measured using a scale comprised of five statements. Student responses for each statement were averaged to create a valuing of schooling index score.

5. Family-derived Achievement Motivation was measured using a scale comprised of two statements. Student responses for each statement were averaged to create a family-derived achievement motivation index score.

6. Friend-derived Achievement Motivation was measured using a scale comprised of three statements. Student responses for each statement were averaged to create a friend-derived achievement motivation index score.

4

Civic Engagement

Numerous studies have documented the connection between participation in voluntary associations and political involvement (Olsen, 1982; Verba, Schlozman, & Brady, 1995). Usually, the explanation for this affiliation is that voluntary associations and extracurricular activities mobilize people to become more politically active. Scholars of political behavior since de Tocqueville have contended that a primary way in which people can become engaged in political participation is through organizational membership (de Tocqueville, 1848. Organizational involvement is hypothesized to be transformed into political activity through a host of interrelated processes. In general, researchers claim that organizational membership affects political attitudes, information about public issues, social networks, norms for participation, and civic skills. Each of these factors can lead to political participation. Several similarities between adult voluntary associations and high school extracurricular activities suggest that they might play similar roles in generating political engagement for students (Hanks & Eckland, 1978).

While the U.S. Supreme Court mandates that undocumented children in public schools be accepted as students, due to current immigration policies, they are not accepted as citizens. Is it possible for noncitizen immigrant youths to participate in American civic life, even as they remain "officially" outside the polity as noncitizens? Although much has been written on the civic and political engagement of immigrants, most of this research is primarily focused on adults (DeSipio, 1996; Ramakrishnan & Espenshade, 2001; Sierra, Carrillo, DeSipio, & Jones-Correa, 2000). Relatively little is known about immigrant youth's civic engagement. The undocumented immigrant population is even less studied, with no research focusing on their civic engagement behaviors. As an integral part of overall school engagement, civic engagement among undocumented students will be discussed in this chapter.

FACTORS THAT SHAPE CIVIC ENGAGEMENT

Research on civic engagement shows that families, educational institutions, and organizations all play an important role in influencing youth to be civically engaged (Andolina, Jenkins, Zukin, & Keeter, 2003; Kelly, 2004; Metz & Youniss, 2003; Torney-Purta, 2002; Youniss, Bales, Christmas-Best, Diversi, McLaughlin, & Silbereisen, 2002). Parents and family members play an important role by setting examples. When parents, siblings, and extended family are civically engaged, youth are more likely to develop civic competence (Youniss et al., 2002). Similarly, youth who come from homes where at least one family member has volunteered are more likely to be involved themselves. Whether it is by joining a club or organization, wearing buttons, or volunteering, they are more active than youth who come from homes where no one volunteers (Andolina et al., 2003). Even among minorities, families play an important role in developing civic engagement behaviors (Kelly, 2004).

Like family influences, educational institutions also play a central role in fostering an interest in civic engagement (Andolina et al., 2003). In classrooms, students learn not only about the importance of being civically engaged, but also the necessary practical skills. Classroom discussions, lectures on the importance of voting, and knowledge about the democratic process all predict later civic engagement among youths. When schools help organize volunteer opportunities and make community service a graduation requirement, students are more likely to continue to be civically engaged after graduation. The types of clubs they have available for students to join are also predictive of later civic engagement. Furthermore, when students are members of political clubs on campus, they are more likely to be civically engaged after graduation, compared with students who never joined political clubs at all (Andolina et al., 2003; Torney-Purta, 2002; Youniss et al., 2002).

Through schooling, students inherit a set of civic resources and opportunities as they experience political socialization and have opportunities to forge friendships (Jarvis, Montoya, & Mulvoy, 2005). College students accumulate political resources such as political sophistication, knowledge about politics, political skills, and a broader understanding of political life; psychological resources such as the motivation to appreciate democratic governance and to develop democratic values; and social resources such as the opportunity to spend time with other students and to join organizations that increase participation in civic life.

Over the last decade, a new body of research has documented how school-based experiences contribute to civic knowledge, commitments, and engagement. Galston (2004) notes that students develop such knowledge and beliefs most powerfully when schools offer an array of civic learning opportunities. Clearly, some of these opportunities center on the class-room—for example, instruction in the history and principles of American democracy and classroom discussion of current events that make a direct and tangible difference in young people's lives. Equally important are other opportunities that students encounter in the broader school context: com-munity service, participation in extracurricular organizations, and partici-pation in public forums and democratic governance in school (Kahne & Westheimer, 2003).

Immigrant Student Civic Engagement

Attention to civic development and engagement has been missing in the immigrant student literature despite the need for such studies given the on-going national political debate about immigration, citizenship, and what it means to be "American." On virtually a daily basis, American news media feature stories about immigrants' civil rights and responsibilities, and the nature of their commitment to the United States and American values. There has also been an increase in media coverage about immigrants entering into the public debate through various forms of civic engagement, ranging from public marches to local community projects to student walkouts. The civic potential of young immigrants became evident in early 2006 when rallies were held across the United States in support of immigration policy reform. Students held rallies or walked out of school to express their support for immigrant workers (Bada, Fox, & Selee, 2006). Whereas the recent immi-gration policy reform debate in Congress has focused on economic, security, and legal issues, the debate has largely ignored the civic engagement of im-migrant youth.

A recent study that examines immigrant generational differences in civ-ic engagement finds that 80% of first-generation, 90% of 1.5-generation, 89% of second-generation college freshmen in South Florida volunteered or had done community service in the past 12 months, compared with 87% of non-immigrant students (Stepick, Stepick, & Labissiere, 2008). The rates for the 1.5- and second-generation students were higher than the 82.6% reported for freshmen nationwide in 2001 (Sax, Lindholm, Astin, Korn, & Mahoney, 2001). Even the first-generation immigrants compare favorably with the approximately 75% of high school seniors nationwide who did volunteer or community service in high school (Lopez, 2003).

On the other hand, a different study finds that among young adults between the ages of 15 and 25, when compared on a wide range of civic engagement measures, immigrant youth were less engaged than the children of immigrants or natives (Lopez & Marcelo, 2008). However, many of the differences observed between immigrant youth and natives were mitigated after controlling for demographic factors, suggesting that differences in engagement are explained by factors such as socioeconomic background and other structural barriers to engagement that young immigrants face, rather than a desire not to get involved.

A recent study also notes that some immigrant young adults are motivated to tutor, help others, and take part in politics out of concern for the needs and accomplishments of their immigrant and cultural communities, as well as with the representation and respect afforded these communities within the larger polity (Jensen, 2008). The study found that immigrant adolescents were civically engaged more so at the community than political level. The 88% participation rate among these immigrant adolescents was higher than the 75% of high school seniors who reported community service or volunteering within the past 12 months in a recent national survey (Lopez, 2003).

Undocumented Student Civic Engagement

In *Plyler v. Doe*, the Supreme Court considered how access of undocumented youth to public schools was related to the democratic purposes of public education. In considering this issue, the Court made two related arguments. First, it reasoned that there was no way of knowing with certainty whether a particular undocumented youth would later attain legal residency or citizenship status. Denying undocumented students access to public education risked undermining the civic education of future legal residents and citizens who would later be called upon to exercise civic responsibilities. Second, the Court articulated the country's interest in ensuring educational access for those youth who would *not* later attain legal status. Public education enables such youth to function within civic institutions. Conversely, denying these students access to public schools would "foreclose any realistic possibility that they will contribute in even the smallest way to the progress of our nation."

The importance placed by the Supreme Court in *Plyler v. Doe* on the health of democracy and the quality of civic engagement by undocumented students has experienced renewed attention given the size of the undocumented student population. Furthermore, in recent years, policymakers and scholars in political science and education have addressed the need for youth to understand the purpose and function of government and to develop the skills and commitments needed to participate robustly in electoral politics, public institutions, civic organizations, and (where necessary) protest activities (Carpini & Keeter, 1996; Niemi & Junn, 1998). A broad consensus has emerged that public schools are uniquely positioned to support these ends.

Do undocumented youth develop civic knowledge, skills, and commitments through their participation in public schools? Few studies have tried to address this question (Perez, Espinoza, Ramos, Coronado, & Cortés, 2010; Rogers, Saunders, Terriquez, & Velez, 2008). Rogers, Saunders, Terriquez, and Velez argue that guaranteeing access to public schools promotes the civic participation of both undocumented youth and adults, and in so doing, enhances the quality of democratic life. Public schools teach about, and provide practice in, civic engagement. Undocumented immigrant students and parents develop knowledge, skills, and commitments for civic engagement by participating in school activities, school-based social networks, and school governance.

Using case study analyses, Rogers and colleagues (2008) noted that taking several social studies courses that highlighted the origins, meaning, and practice of democratic government encouraged students to participate in school activities, recognize the value of diversity, and perform community service. In their study, undocumented students expressed an appreciation for courses that connected the broad principles of democracy to their everyday concerns inside and outside school. One of the students described in Rogers and colleagues' study was so taken with class discussions about "how the government works" that she decided to study political science in college.

Extracurricular activities, even when they do not directly address civic concerns, afford students opportunities to practice civic skills such as communicating political ideas, negotiating differences within diverse communities, and identifying and acting upon shared interests. Rogers and colleagues (2008) described a student who participated in "Diverse Democracy," a student- and faculty-led program that convened students of various ethnic backgrounds to identify stereotypes and discuss common interests across groups. She later became a facilitator for the program due to her leadership skills and commitment. She was also active in MEChA, where she played a leadership role in the club's activities, which included bringing attention to the low enrollment rates of Latino students in her school's college preparatory, Honors, and Advanced Placement courses.

Previous research suggests that undocumented students are no strangers to political activity and civic engagement (Abrego, 2008; Gonzales, 2008; Seif, 2004). Many of the leadership skills and organizing experiences that these young people possessed were incubated on high school and university campuses. Through community service activities such as tutoring classmates after school in math and science, coordinating the tutoring program at their school, and volunteering at church, students developed a service ethic. Members of undocumented student advocacy groups became involved in numerous clubs and organizations as early as high school. Students participated in student government elections. In California undocumented students joined a campaign against Proposition 21—a California ballot measure that sought to move many youth offenders into the adult criminal justice system (Rogers et al., 2008).Through participation in school-based extracurricular activities, civically engaged undocumented youth developed important organizational skills, and an awareness of community issues.

Having gained early leadership skills and community service experience in high school, many of these students went on to higher levels of participation in college. Several students held leadership positions in campus clubs or other community groups. In college, however, they also had to contend with the limitations of their unauthorized status as it began to become increasingly more salient in their day-to-day lives. Unable to secure financial aid for school and uncertain of their futures, civically engaged youths turned to immigrant rights groups and activities as a way to advocate for themselves and their families. Previous research finds that undocumented youth participate in activities such as voter drives, organizing for driver's license bills, and immigration reform activism (Abrego, 2008; Gonzales, 2008; Seif, 2004).

In order to measure the extent to which the students in this study engaged in various service and volunteer activities, four main civic engagement indicators were formulated based on the research literature on civic engagement (Hodgkinson, & Weitzman, 1997; Nolin, Chaney, Chapman, & Chandler, 1997; Youniss, McClellan, & Mazer, 2001): (1) providing a social service, (2) working for a cause/political activism, (3) tutoring, and (4) functionary work. Providing a social service entailed volunteer work that requires interaction with people in need. For example, any volunteer work that included visiting, feeding, or caring for the homeless, poor, sick, elderly, or handicapped was considered social service. Working for a cause and political activism were activities focused on a particular social issue or cause such as the environment, a political party, human rights, or other causes that do not entail direct interaction with the needy. For example, activities that focused on immigrant rights were coded as working for a cause/political activism. Tutoring was defined as coaching, child care, or academic tutoring. For example, math tutoring or providing free child care through an educational or community-based organization was coded as tutoring. The fourth dimension of civic engagement described in the research literature is functionary work. This type of volunteer work is characterized by cleaning, maintenance, and administrative tasks and activities. Examples of functionary work include beach and graffiti cleanup.

As Table 4.1 shows that, on average, during elementary school, 34% of participants volunteered at least 1–10 hours per year. The time spent on civic engagement increased with age as 46% reported spending at least 1–10 hours volunteering in middle school, 67% in high school, and 58% in college. It was during high school when students spent the most amount of time on civic engagement, with as many as 35% reporting spending more than 41 hours per year volunteering. The most popular types of civic engagement in elementary school, middle school, high school, and college were functionary work followed by tutoring. Providing a social service and activism became more prevalent during college. Male and female students differed somewhat in their civic engagement activities. Females (23%) were more

Table 4.1. Civic Engagement by School Level when Activity Was Performed and by Gender

	Elementary School		Middle School		High School		College		Male (n = 42)		Female (n = 68)		Total (n = 110)	
	%	M	%	M	%	M	%	M	%	M	%	M	%	M
Volunteer Hrs/Yr														
None	66		54		33		42		14		12		13	
1–10	13		20		12		11		21		10		15	
11–20	6		11		4		6		14		9		11	
21–30	6		3		8		10		24		19		21	
31–40	1		6		9		5		14		25		21	
41+	8		7		35		26		12		25		20	
Civic Engagement Types														
Social service	2		1		7		9		5	.05	23	.28	16	.19
Activism	1		2		5		22		9	.17	28	.37	21	.29
Tutoring	22		18		34		21		38	.60	69	1.16	57	.95
Functionary work	23		25		56		36		79	1.31	78	1.44	78	1.39
Total Civic Engagement	38		40		73		55		86	3.60	93	5.06	90	4.50
Civic Engagement Award	5	.05	2	.02	4	.04	10	.10	7	.07	22	.28	16	.20

likely to provide social services than males (5%). They were also more likely to be involved in activism (28% for females compared with 9% for males), and tutoring (69% female versus 38% male). Overall, 93% of females had engaged in some form of civic engagement, compared with 86% of males. Since more female students had engaged in civic engagement activities, it was not surprising that female students were more likely to have received an award for their volunteerism (22%), compared with their male counterparts (7%).

Civic engagement triggers. In addition to individual motives, various "trigger events" or specific circumstances in the external environment can facilitate civic engagement. The trigger events can include school clubs or church activities. Personal motivations include creativity/self-expression, friendship, helping other people, pleasure/new experience, professional satisfaction, religious/spiritual fulfillment, recognition from others, social justice/equality, working for peace/reconciliation, sense of satisfaction from helping others, duty to correct societal problems, meeting people, acquiring career skills, religious beliefs, or repayment for services previously received (Serow, 1991).

The majority of students indicated the critical role that school clubs, and to a lesser extent, church programs played in facilitating volunteer activities. Many students belonged to their school's honor society, which required community service involvement. For example, Alejandra, Jack, and Viviana joined their school's Key Club chapter, a national community service student group, where they volunteered at convalescent homes and read to children at the local public library. Daniella's passion for civic engagement increased when she enrolled in a class that helped students develop their own volunteer programs:

> It opened my eyes to what was going on with my community and how I could help. I mean, I always had this passion for community service. I always saw things that other people did not. People my age usually don't worry about poverty, why people can't go to school, those sort of things, and I can't ignore that because that's in front of me and I always feel that I have the ability to do something.

Other students were driven to volunteer in part by their desire "to belong" in American society. Shortly after Hurricane Katrina, Lucila took a semester off from school to go to Louisiana to help with the relief efforts:

> We were watching everything that was happening during the disaster and I remember my mom saying, "You know, somebody needs to go help them," and I was like, "You know what? I'm going to go down and

see if I can answer phones or help locally." When I got there they asked me, "Do you want to work here or do you want to be deployed to the area to help?" And I said, "Well, I can help anywhere you guys want to put me." They called me a couple of days later and told me, "Call this number. Your plane leaves this day."

In addition to a sense of accomplishment, Lucila described her experience as a "life-changing" event because she had the opportunity to show her fellow "American" volunteers that she was just like them and cared about the same issues they did:

There were people from all over the country who came to volunteer. I was very open with them in telling them, "Yeah, I am an illegal immigrant," and everybody was kind of in shock. I remember some people from Missouri and North Dakota just looking at me like, "You're what? You're an immigrant?" and I said to them, "Yeah, I'm just a college student trying to get by." They had a new image of what an immigrant was like and I think that was the biggest impact that I've ever had because I told them, "Look, we don't come here to take your money. I'm just trying to get an education and succeed in life." They were in shock that I was so young and out there willing to do stuff.

Lucila was pleased that "regular Americans" were beginning to see her as similar to them rather than different. Despite her dedication to the relief efforts and her life-changing experience, when Lucila came back home, she felt a renewed sense of frustration because she still could not do many of the things she wanted to do because she was undocumented: "It's kind of hard because it's like I'm doing all these things. I've done volunteer work, I've gone with the Red Cross, I'm willing to go out there," but her status still kept her marginalized with limited options. Both Lucila and Daniella, like many students in this study, articulated an obligation and responsibility to directly effect change. For many, this was done through student activism and/or working for a social cause.

Providing social services. During high school, Alejandra volunteered at a local hospital: "We did things like blood drives, that's how I started donating blood; we went to the local hospital and played bingo with the patients that had no arms and feet, and we held activities for kids." Janet dedicated 12 hours per week during high school volunteering at a rehabilitation center for people with brain trauma and other injuries. She even took the bus to get there since she was unable to drive due to her undocumented status. Similarly, Liz dedicated many hours volunteering for the local chapter of the United Farm Workers as well as for a drug and alcohol prevention program for kids in her neighborhood. Through her church, Karen spent countless hours providing various types of community services. She explained:

> I've been to shelters, feeding the homeless. We go to the shelter to donate clothing and general accessories. We have also gone to the pregnancy center where we host a dinner for wealthy people who donate their money to fund a program for women who are suffering through pregnancy. They're young or they're in a bad relationship and so that program helps them. Also, if there's a family in need in our community, we help to gather whatever is needed, either money or clothing, and we give it to them. Then we also have the Christmas and Thanksgiving baskets, which go to people who are in need.

Students demonstrated high levels of civic engagement despite other demands on their time, including time-intensive and academically rigorous courses. In addition, they were involved in various extracurricular activities and had afterschool jobs, working an average of 12 hours per week during high school and 25 hours per week during college.

Tutoring. Another major theme among the civic engagement activities of undocumented immigrant youths was working with children and students in educational settings. During 9th and 10th grade, Adolfo worked as a tutor: "I just tutor elementary students, helping them with their homework, math, English, and twice a week I read to them in Spanish and also in English." Students also tutored outside of school settings. James worked as a mentor at a local community center: "I became a mentor at a local art center. They started a program this year that would help kids with reading or their homework so they could get ahead in school and I helped them out with that." Thalia worked with at-risk middle school students:

> We worked with kids who were on probation or about to get kicked out of school. I was in high school and the kids were in middle school. We would just mentor them. We would help them with their homework. At the beginning, they had a hard time opening up but at the end, they thanked us. They changed their attitude. They wanted to go to school. I think we made a big difference in their lives. It made me feel great. It feels good to make someone else feel good about themselves.

Thalia's comment about feeling good making a difference was also noted by other students interviewed. In addition to reflecting the students' commitment to ideals such as duty and helpfulness, civic engagement also served as a psychic reward for undocumented youths. There are many personal benefits for being civically engaged, besides the benefit that service has on society as a whole. Civic engagement can act as a type of personal empowerment by allowing the individual to be aware of their competence and ability to make a difference. It makes individuals feel good about themselves as result of the satisfaction obtained by helping others in need (Serow, 1991).

Working for a cause. The students in this study worked on various social causes, even those that painfully reminded them of their societal exclusion. Sasha, for example, worked on voter registration: "During the different elections, even though I can't vote, I help to create awareness within my campus. I encourage students to register to vote." Sasha has also been involved in union activities. Judith, on the other hand, was the president of a club to raise money for terminally ill children when she was in high school. Unlike Judith, Esperanza's selection of a terminal illness as her social cause had a strong personal connection. After her uncle died of AIDS, she began to participate in the yearly AIDS walk:

> I've been participating in the AIDS Walk for about 6 years. Each year in October, I get my sheet with my stickers and I go door-to-door in my community, at my job, at school, or anyone that I see on the street, even at liquor stores. I go and I ask for money and I donate it to the AIDS fund.

Constraints to civic engagement. Civic engagement does not come easy for undocumented students. Since they are legally barred from getting a driver's license, they are limited to unreliable public transportation to get to and from school, work, and volunteer activities. Many students, like Alix, shared their frustrations about not being able to continue to volunteer: "I tried to but it's hard for me because I take the bus everywhere. It's hard when your meeting ends at 8:30 PM or 9:00 PM. . . . I live in a very shady neighborhood so that's my biggest limitation." When Lisa began her first year at the community college, she continued the same high level of civic engagement she maintained in high school. Unfortunately, she had to increase her work hours to save enough money to pay for college. As a result, she had to discontinue all her volunteer activities:

> I can't do it anymore because it's really tough. I have to work and I have to go to school. I would do it every Tuesday or Friday, which are my days off, but I can't now because it's really tough for me. I'm doing finals so right now I'm taking a break from that because I just can't make it. I have to work. I work 31 hours a week and I'm a full-time student, so it's really tough.

The challenges and obstacles students faced often force them to reduce or discontinue their civic engagement activities, particularly in college. Despite the myriad of challenges they encountered, many continue to find ways to volunteer. Sasha's comment highlights the attitudes of many undocumented students in this study: "Even though things are difficult for a lot of us, we really do make an effort to find ways to keep on learning, volunteering, and being a part of different social events."

Civic engagement motives. It is not completely surprising that students in the study had higher civic engagement rates compared to national trends since college and college-going students tend to be more involved in civic engagement activities (Eccles & Barber, 1999). What is surprising is the fact that their high civic engagement rates are also accompanied by various obstacles they face due to their undocumented status, including working many hours per week to pay for school and personal expenses, and in many cases, difficulty finding reliable transportation. As in previous studies (Fitch, 1987; Serow, 1991; Wiehe & Isenhour, 1977), participants explained their motivation to volunteer by referring to ideals such as duty and helpfulness to others or personalizing those concepts by referring to specific individuals or groups (i.e., their community, poor people, immigrants) that they wanted to help. Although previous research suggests that community service rarely produces tangible extrinsic rewards, and is often interpreted as altruistic in its intent (Finch, 1987; Wiehe & Isenhour, 1977), undocumented students generally derived various benefits for themselves as well. This was often expressed in the generalized terminology of psychic rewards such as "it makes me feel good to be able to help someone else" or in concretely stating how they thought service would benefit them (e.g., Latino students, immigrant youth). This pattern was exemplified by students who were involved in political activism and other activities that focused on undocumented students.

For undocumented youth, particularly young women, civic engagement may be motivated not just out of a political interest, but more important, out of a concern for real human needs, including their own. It may offer them a form of personal empowerment in which they not only acquire and display competence, but attempt to extend the benefits of their service to others in their communities. For undocumented students, civic engagement may be an attractive alternative to the frustrating impediments of legal marginality, as it is one of the few public acts they can do to feel like contributing members of society.

Civic engagement as a protective factor. Civic engagement can act as a protector against risky behaviors. Youth civic engagement is positively correlated to good attendance, higher GPA, higher self-esteem, higher academic self-efficacy, involvement in extracurricular activities, and motivation to learn (Eccles & Barber, 1999). Additionally, civic engagement has the power to influence career aspirations and further political involvement (Balsano, 2005). Table 4.2 indicates that civic engagement participants also took part in a greater number of extracurricular activities and had higher GPAs than nonparticipants. Those who had participated in social service activities also had higher levels of extracurricular participation. Students involved in activism reported higher extracurricular participation, higher educational expectations, and a higher sense of rejection due to their undocumented status compared with students who reported no activism. Students who reported functionary work activities also had higher extracurricular participation and higher GPAs compared with those reporting no functionary work. Finally, students who had received an award for their civic engagement reported higher educational expectations, accompanied by a higher sense of rejection due to their status, and higher levels of discrimination. Overall, these analyses indicate that students who reported the highest level of extracurricular participation and higher academic engagement had higher civic engagement rates. A noteworthy finding is the association between activism and sense of rejection.

UNDOCUMENTED STUDENT ACTIVISM

Activism is a significant dimension of civic engagement and has been an important part of African American and Latino history and culture (Barnes, 2006; Bobo & Gilliam, 1990; Brown, 2006; Dixson, 2003; Garcia & Marquez, 2001; Martinez, 2005). While the best-known instance of political organization for African Americans is the success of the civil rights movement, political involvement of Latinos has recently become more prominent as the Latino population has increased in the past few decades. Political issues such as immigration have contributed to the more recent increase in political participation of Latinos (Garcia & Marquez, 2001; Martinez, 2005). Historical racial inequalities that still exist today have motivated members of these groups to become politically involved in order to improve social conditions.

Political involvement not only improves social conditions, but also provides personal benefits to participants themselves. Prior research has found that there is a positive relationship between political involvement, self-esteem, and self-efficacy (Bobo & Gilliam, 1990; Carmines, 1978; Finkel, 1985; Scaturo & Smalley, 1980; Sigel, 1975). The potential for change involved with political participation may lead to an increased sense of empowerment and improve competency in areas such as academic performance. Political involvement may also relate to an overall higher level of interest in social events, which may relate to increased levels of intellectual curiosity and development (Bobo & Gilliam, 1990; Hamilton & Fauri, 2001; Schussman & Soule, 2006).

Table 4.2. Civic Engagement Participation by Demographic, Academic, and Psychosocial Characteristics

	Civic Engagement		Social Service		Activism		Tutoring		Functionary work		Award	
	Yes	No	Yes	No	Yes	No	Yes	No	Yes	No	Yes	No
Employment	16.94	14.00	15.47	16.86	16.36	16.71	15.20	18.58	18.32[a]	10.75[b]	15.89	16.79
Family responsibilities	2.92	2.50	3.17	2.82	2.94	2.86	2.93	2.81	2.93	2.67	3.17	2.82
Extracurricular activities	5.02[a]	2.36[b]	6.33[a]	4.45[b]	5.78[a]	4.48[b]	5.06	4.34	5.20[a]	3.17[b]	5.56	4.60
GPA	3.38+	3.11	3.34	3.35	3.37	3.35	3.43[a]	3.24[b]	3.37	3.28	3.43	3.33
Educational expectations	4.85	4.40	5.00	4.77	5.09+	4.73	4.90	4.68	4.83	4.71	5.17+	4.73
Rejection due to status	4.27	3.73	4.15	4.23	4.70+	4.09	4.28	4.14	4.34	3.76	4.82+	4.10
Discrimination	3.10	2.85	3.07	3.08	3.15	3.05	3.15	2.97	3.11	2.93	3.44+	3.00

Civic Engagement category columns not sharing a superscript are statistically different at the .05 level
+ Denotes $p < .10$

In the face of perceived threats, persecution, discrimination, and exclusion, marginalized groups often forge a reactive identity. It is one mode of ethnic identity formation that highlights the role of a hostile context of reception in accounting for the rise rather than the erosion of ethnicity (Aleinikoff & Rumbaut, 1998; Portes & Rumbaut, 2006; Rumbaut, 2005). Like native minorities, immigrants also become heavily engaged in politically related activities in response to discrimination (Stepick, Stepick, & Labissiere, 2008). The limited previous research indicates that prejudice and discrimination against immigrant youth increases their civic engagement. Latinos in California, for example, experienced an emergence of ethnic consciousness in response to Proposition 187, which sought to deny benefits to undocumented immigrants. In the case of Cuban-origin college students in the Miami area, the Elian Gonzalez case increased perceptions of discrimination and produced heightened ethnic consciousness and engendered some form of civic engagement (Ramakrishnan & Espenshade, 2001; Suarez-Orozco, 1996). Rumbaut (2005) described the case of Stephanie Bernal, a Southern California native and high school senior who joined her friends who were organizing her school's anti–Proposition 187 movement, which served to affirm and strengthen her ethnic identity. Despite the passage of Proposition 187, Stephanie's Mexican ethnic self-identity was "thickened" in the process. The divisive campaign had the unintended consequence of accentuating group differences, heightening group consciousness of those differences, hardening ethnic identity boundaries between "us" and "them," and promoting ethnic group solidarity and political mobilization.

Because they are legally always at risk of being deported, the law plays an explicit and palpable role in the lives of undocumented students. Unlike their adult counterparts who were socialized in their home countries, undocumented youth's legal consciousness is informed by U.S. social values that venerate education and individual merit (Hochschild, 1995; Kaiser & Major, 2006; McNamee & Miller, 2004). Undocumented students believe in meritocracy and the notion that dedication alone should be enough to achieve upward social mobility (Abrego, 2008; Olivas, 1995). Research on policies and programs that provide greater access to colleges and universities in California, Texas, and other states has revealed a variety of complexities associated with undocumented students' participation in college under these policies, including some important areas of student empowerment and mobilization on their own behalf (Abrego, 2008; Diaz-Strong & Meiners, 2007; Drachman, 2008; Flores & Chapa, 2009; Frum, 2007; Gonzales, 2007; Seif, 2004; S.I.N. Collective, 2007). Among undocumented college student leaders in California, activism has served as a vehicle to impact their current status in the policy arena and inform community members of their rights (Gonzales, 2008). Similarly, others have noted that the passage of

California's in-state tuition law AB 540 nurtured and transformed student activism by providing a mechanism for student legitimacy, a sense of confidence, and the fuel for student mobilization efforts on campus and in the community (Abrego, 2008).

Abrego (2008) also found that academically high-achieving undocumented students use the language of "justice" to claim legitimate spaces for themselves in higher education. This allows them to declare themselves worthy members of society, even though, legally, their presence in the United States is in violation of immigration laws. Youth declare themselves as law-abiding to override the immigration laws that they are "breaking." They appeal to a greater sense of common good through which they have *earned* their belonging. By underscoring their actual and potential positive contributions to society, undocumented students claim legitimacy. In their interpretation, although their presence in this country is outside of the law, their civic engagement and their efforts to improve their lives through education redeem them (Abrego, 2008).

Undocumented students interpret the rights granted to them by in-state tuition laws as a formal recognition of their merits, giving them a sense of legitimacy to invoke the law to demand additional rights. Abrego (2008) notes that shortly after the passage of the California's in-state tuition law, also known as AB 540, students were still relatively timid about claiming their rights. However, 4 years later, she found that the same students, who initially dreaded disclosing their status to school staff, were approaching them to claim their rights and expressing a greater sense of entitlement. Such high confidence stood in stark contrast to the stigma they all felt prior to the law. Collectively, they became better organized and informed greater numbers of undocumented students about their rights, and further mobilized to claim legal rights.

These findings suggest that laws have the potential to transform social identities and encourage political mobilization. Although the label "undocumented" or "illegal" continues to be a source of shame for most students, in-state tuition laws like California's AB 540 or the federal DREAM Act have provided new, more neutral, and non-stigmatized social labels. The labels "illegal" and "undocumented" conflict with the students' perceptions of themselves as upstanding and productive members of society. After the passage of AB 540, students in California began to use and prefer the "AB 540 student" label when referring to themselves and their undocumented peers (Abrego, 2008). Similarly, most recently, students across the country have adopted the label "DREAMers." These new labels help students not only conceal their stigmatized status but also reinforce their merits as students. Under these new labels, often identifiable only by their undocumented peers and fellow activist allies, students organize, recruit others, and share resources. Unintentionally, AB 540 and the DREAM Act have become a powerful symbol for undocumented students. To them, these laws not only represent access to higher education and legal status, but they are also a formal recognition of the students' earned belonging in society and signal support for their endeavors and affirmation of their legitimacy.

In efforts to claim rights and a political voice, some undocumented youth have engaged in legislative activities through NGOs (Seif, 2004). In California, undocumented youth have spoken at press conferences, petitioned, educated others by "tabling" at community events, and sent letters to elected officials with their personal stories. Students have also testified in favor in-state tuition laws and have asserted a political voice with the support of Latino elected officials, who often rely on these courageous young adults to humanize the plight of undocumented immigrants and challenge popular stereotypes of the "illegal alien." Their visible engagement makes the frustration and tragedy of growing up undocumented palpable. The presence of these student activists at press conferences and legislative hearings has forced elected officials and voters to look these students in the eye as they make important decisions about their educational access and futures.

As a result of this student activism, there are growing numbers of identified undocumented student groups and statewide networks throughout California and across the United States. The student organizations meet with chancellors, vice-chancellors, vice-provosts, school admissions and registrar's offices, scholarship providers, legislators, community leaders, community organizations, counselors, parents, and other students to increase awareness of policies like in-state tuition laws that help improve access to resources and opportunities that exist (Chavez et al., 2007; Seif, 2004). Social networking sites have nurtured the growth of these student activist groups and have become a powerful tool for undocumented youth activism. Compared with other media, the Internet is dispersed and decentralized, features that increase the ability of ordinary people to create and sustain social movements (Gurak, 1999; Kedzie, 1997; Schwartzman, 1998). It is a domain in which adolescents are not stigmatized by their age or specifically blocked from participation because of status. Over the last few years, these Internet resources have facilitated undocumented student efforts to promote legislation such as the DREAM Act, which has been the central activity for most undocumented student groups. DREAM Act advocacy work gives many of these students a means to participate in the political process on an issue that is directly relevant to them (Rincon, 2008; Seif, 2004). Students have become involved in activities on the ground, including contacting legislators, mobilizing their various communities, and staging public actions such as fasting and vigils that have received broad media coverage (Mena,

2004). Despite the dangers involved in speaking out publicly, many students have become frustrated by the limitations of their status and are finding strength and courage in numbers. For some, the transition to postsecondary education is linked to a growing politicization (Gonzales, 2008; Rincon, 2008).

Among the students I interviewed, political activism activities focused on various issues such as higher education costs, labor rights, and electoral issues. Adolfo was the president of the Coalition of Young Activists (CYA) club at his high school. Although a main component of the club is supporting undocumented students, they also worked on other important political issues:

> CYA stands for the Coalition of Young Activists and it's like a club in my school that supports undocumented students. We do organizing and disseminate information to students about resources available to them. In my senior year, I did some electoral work for the special elections. I did phone banking, just calling registered voters to tell them to vote against propositions 76, 77, and 78. I also did precinct walking where you go to the doors of registered voters and inform them about a proposition and try to persuade them not to vote for those propositions.

Janet participated in protests against multinational corporations and the state public university system for increasing tuition fees, while Liz participated in several marches with the United Farm Workers. Similarly, Isabel was actively involved in an immigrant rights organization and helped to organize rallies and marches. She traveled to the California state capital to lobby on behalf of immigrant rights. She also regularly conducted community education workshops. She explained that her involvement started because "I didn't want to be someone that just complains. If you're going to complain, do something about it, then you can complain. I was tired of just being in that situation, so I decided to do something about it." For Isabel, as well as for other students, political activism became a form of personal empowerment. Juana was involved in a student organization that helped high school students become more politically active:

> We provide support to high school students who are getting involved in the recent walkouts. We were trying to get them organized because some of them didn't have a group at their school where they could actually talk about these things and the issues that were going on. So we held open discussion forums for high school and middle school students who would come and learn about their rights as students and ways they could form clubs at their schools.

The students I interviewed were not just driven to become civically engaged by their commitment to certain political and social ideals, but their engagement served as an antidote to the political and social marginalization they faced as undocumented students. Activism allowed them the opportunity to affirm themselves as good people and model citizens. Researchers have theorized that structured activity participation, especially in service activities, exposes students to the norms and values of organized collective action and creates network ties that integrate teens into normative society (Youniss, McLellan, & Yates, 1997; Youniss & Yates, 1997). Participation in some high school clubs and pro-social activities also introduces youths to political ideas that they might not have been exposed to, offering them the opportunity to learn interpersonal and leadership skills that are likely to inspire continued involvement in civic causes in young adulthood (Glanville, 1999; Hanks & Eckland, 1978).

A New Civil Rights Movement

President Obama's omission of a comprehensive immigration reform agenda in his January 27, 2010, State of the Union Address triggered a vigorous response from undocumented student activists. A few days after the president's speech, an event in historic Olvera Street headlined by Illinois Congressional Representative and strong immigration reform proponent Luis Gutierrez, brought together representatives from a broad array of immigration reform supporters such as the Southern Christian Leadership Conference, labor unions, immigrant advocacy organizations, and most strikingly, undocumented student activist groups. Around the same time, a similar event was unfolding in Chicago, where a student group, the Immigrant Youth Justice League, raised $243,000 to bring 10,000 marchers to Washington, DC, the following month to lobby for immigration reform (Caputo, 2010).

First introduced in 2001, the DREAM Act has been a beacon of hope for undocumented students during the past 10 years. Most recently, that hope has turned into frustration as Congress and the president have waivered in their commitment to immigration reform. In an unprecedented demonstration of their leadership, political savvy, and organizational skills, undocumented student activists and their allies responded with a well-coordinated youth-led national movement to pressure Congress and the president to pass the DREAM Act in 2010. Rather than solely rely on Congress and other immigrant rights advocacy groups to advocate on their behalf, increasingly, undocumented student activists have moved to the forefront of these efforts.

Trail of dreams. The start of the current resurgence of the undocumented youth civil rights movement actually occurred almost 4 weeks before President Obama's State of the Union Address on January 1, 2010. Risking deportation from the only country they have ever known, four undocumented students embarked on a journey from Miami to Washington, DC, to advocate for the passage of the DREAM Act. Walking 18 miles per day, they arrived at the nation's capital in May 2010, having walked more than 1,800 miles on a journey they called the "Trail of Dreams" (Preston, 2010). In addition to bringing increased media coverage to the plight of undocumented students, along the way they also picked up support from various religious and civic groups.

Inspiration from the civil rights movement. The following month, February 2010, was also the beginning of a monthly campaign advocating for the DREAM Act organized by undocumented students across the country through United We Dream, a fast-growing national umbrella organization of undocumented student activist groups (Altschuler, 2011). According to Lisa, an undocumented college senior who is a member of a Los Angeles area undocumented student group:

> Part of the reason for these events is to stress the urgency of the DREAM Act. A lot of times people are sympathetic to undocumented students but they really don't see the urgency and the reason why we need the DREAM Act to pass this year, now, as soon as possible.

The timing of the events has another significance according to Lisa, who has been actively advocating for the DREAM Act for the past 5 years:

> We really see a close connection and a parallel between our movement and the African American movement and their experiences in the United States. As undocumented students, we are constantly being denied certain rights in the United States and within our school campuses. We are fighting for our own humanity. A lot of tactics that we're using as undocumented students are borrowed frameworks that were established in the '60s with the civil rights movement.

Since February is nationally recognized as "African American History Month," undocumented students hoped to highlight parallels between the civil rights movement of the 1960s and their efforts to pass the DREAM Act. As in the 1960s, students are once again at the forefront of civil rights activism, only this time, the movement is led by undocumented students.

Passage of the DREAM Act is the main priority of a growing national network of undocumented student groups. In 2010, they concluded that passage of the DREAM Act by the end of the year was an achievable goal. According to Lisa:

> The most important goal is to reach middle America, to listen to our stories. The majority of people who are against the DREAM Act are so because they haven't met any of these DREAM students, they

haven't heard our stories. We're calling on the United States to reflect on how we're treating our young people and how we're treating our undocumented population in the United States.

Almost a decade has passed since the bill was first introduced in 2001, and the sense of urgency continues to rise. As a result, starting in 2010, undocumented students began taking greater risks by going public with their status in an effort to gain public support, as Lisa states:

> We're willing to take the risk of putting ourselves out there and putting ourselves in danger because for us it's more of a risk to remain silent and not to speak about our realities and the everyday obstacles that we go through. Right now we are not afraid to speak up and to come out because that's what we need to do in order to be heard, in order to create change.

Furthermore, Mary, an undocumented recent college graduate involved with a national undocumented student activist organization, added:

> The DREAM Act is something that different people can relate to regardless of how they feel about our current immigration situation because it speaks to our core values as people and to our sense of fairness. It tugs at your heart when you hear of a student that has been here since he was 6 months old but is in deportation. Nothing about that seems right and so reaching into those communities that have not been as immigrant friendly, we've been able to get support from people that you wouldn't ordinarily expect to be on the side of undocumented immigrants.

Mary's assessment of growing support is certainly affirmed by the increasing ranks of the undocumented student activists network. For example, in March 2010, Princeton University students joined the network by establishing the Princeton DREAM Team. That same month, students decided to risk deportation and potential separation from their families by organizing a series of "coming out" activities across the country to highlight the urgent need for the DREAM Act. This campaign drew inspiration from the tactics previously used by gay and lesbian activists. Their Websites and social network pages prominently displayed quotes by famed gay activist Harvey Milk to encourage undocumented students to disclose their status to advocate for equal rights and the passage of the DREAM Act. To launch the campaign, on March 10, 2010, a group of eight undocumented students held a press conference at the Federal Plaza in Chicago to publicly announce their undocumented status ("Young Illegal Immigrants," 2010).

Protests and acts of civil disobedience continued to increase. In April 2010, the Washington Dream Act Coalition (WDAC), a youth-lead movement, mobilized for a 10,000-strong state rally by reaching out to high schools and colleges; recruiting through political, business, religious, and ethnic clubs; presenting at various churches and classrooms; posting rally flyers around communities throughout the state; and like other youth groups across the country, utilizing social networking sites (Santiago, 2010). After numerous calls and emails, including a petition started on Change.org ("Ask Senator Scott," 2010), and a sit-in at his local Boston office, Harvard College Act on a DREAM and the Student Immigrant Movement, two undocumented student groups, got newly elected Senator Brown to meet with them to discuss the DREAM Act (Sacchetti, 2010). The motto of this new undocumented youth movement has become "Undocumented & Unafraid." Impressively, with the help of other student activist groups, undocumented students have continued to secure public endorsement for the DREAM Act from various college presidents, including Ivy League presidents at Harvard, Brown, and the University of Pennsylvania ("Brown Professors," 2010; Sacchetti, 2009; Zarya, 2010).

As a nod to undocumented students' efforts to link their struggle with the civil rights movement of the 1960s, when the "Trail of Dreams" walkers reached the state of Georgia, members of a local NAACP chapter joined them as they confronted KKK protesters. Juan, one of the student walkers, noted this in his blog entry on that day:

> Ultimately, the success of today was to be able to stand hand in hand with our friends from the NAACP; singing liberation songs together and acknowledging our united struggle for racial justice. We ALL deserve to be treated with dignity and respect. We all deserve to be acknowledged for our humanity (Juan, 2010).

Undocumented student activists have learned from the successes of the civil rights movement and have applied some of the same strategies in their struggle for equality. During the Martin Luther King Jr. national holiday, the "Trail of Dreams" walkers held a press conference in St. Augustine, Florida, a pivotal site for the civil rights movement during 1963–64 ("Community Leaders," 2010). Not only were they marching in the tradition of nonviolent social movements, but they have also linked their struggle with previous civil injustices. The "Trail of Dreams" is also a historical reference to the Trail of Tears, the mass relocation of Native Americans to Oklahoma in the 1800s. Without the DREAM Act, undocumented activists argue, undocumented students will continue to live with the fear of relocation to a country of origin that is virtually unknown to them. Inspired by history and equipped with strategies learned from previous struggles for civil rights, students are becoming increasingly daring in their struggle for justice. Through public disclosure of their undocumented status, they are willing to risk deportation from the only home they have ever known to remind Congress to deliver on the promise first made in 2001 when the DREAM Act was introduced.

A new civil rights movement led by undocumented students certainly seems to be under way. Forty-five years ago, landmark civil rights legislation not only improved the lives of 18 million African Americans, but it also made the country better as a whole. More important, as Mary so eloquently stated:

> The DREAM Act is not a Democrat issue, it's not a Republican issue, it's a human issue, it's a civil rights issue for the students that are trying to go to school. It's about finding a just and humane way for people that are in an untenable situation. It's amazing what the students have been able to achieve even with this obstacle, imagine what they can do without that drawback. These are very passionate, involved, devoted, active, intelligent individuals and it would be a great loss to the country to give up on them. I believe that we're better as a people having DREAMers amongst us and we would be a better country if we passed the DREAM Act. It would affect the lives of hundreds of thousands and we've put everything on the line to get this done and I believe that we'll get it done.

Future Leaders

Social science research offers definitive evidence that schooling powerfully shapes adult participation in civic life (Lake & Huckfeldt, 1998). Study after study over the past 50 years has identified formal education as a critical determinant of democratic political behavior and attitudes in the United States (Nie, Junn, & Stehlik-Barry, 1996). On average, as levels of formal education rise, so, too, do the skills and resources that support robust civic participation (Verba, Schlozman, & Brady, 1995).

Previous research, for example, has found that participation in civil rights activities during the 1960s helped define views of self–society relationships that were evident 25 years later as these volunteers continued to be active politically both at the local and national levels (Fendrich, 1993; McAdam, 1988). Comparisons of participants in Mississippi Freedom Summer with applicants who were selected but unable, for a variety of reasons, to participate found that over the subsequent course of their lives, participants and no-shows manifested separate paths, which were distinguished by the participants' continuing service, political values, and activism (McAdam, 1988). Black college students' participation in the civil rights movement in the South during the 1950s and 1960s has also been found to predict their political interest and activism 10 and 25 years later (Fendrich, 1993).

Similar results have been found with White civil rights participants, who remained distinguishable from nonparticipants in their political and civic behavior 25 years later (DeMartini, 1983; Fendrich, 1993; McAdam, 1988). Although involvement in the civil rights movement was enhanced by being part of a signal moment in history, various activities reported by undocumented students in this study, such as partaking in high school government, also have been associated with political participation in adulthood (Hanks & Eckland, 1978; Otto, 1976; Verba, Schlozman, & Brady, 1995). When service is the formative youth experience, the effects have been equally enduring and broad in effect, producing politically active citizens who, on one hand, vote at exceptionally high rates, but on the other hand, are ready to protest and lead other citizens to take critical stands toward the status quo (Fendrich, 1993; McAdam, 1988).

A recent longitudinal study that followed a cohort of 8th-graders into adulthood also demonstrates the powerful effect of out-of-classroom activities on adult civic participation (Hart, Donnelly, Youniss, & Atkins, 2007). It found that students who participated in high school community service and extracurricular activities in school had higher rates of political participation and volunteering as adults. Community service provides young people with the opportunity to become personally involved with public issues and to think about them concretely (Metz & Youniss, 2005; Youniss & Yates, 1997). Engagement in extracurricular activities enables young people to practice working within social networks and, at times, offers them opportunities to express collective identity or respond to social issues (Crystal & DeBell, 2002).

So, what can be expected in the future of undocumented youth who demonstrate high levels of civic engagement as young adults if they were to become legalized? Research consistently shows that young adults who are civically involved continue to be so as adults (Ladewig & Thomas, 1987). Furthermore, participating in high school government has been linked with political participation in adulthood (Otto, 1976; Hanks & Eckland, 1978; Verba, Schlozman, & Brady, 1995). Thus, these findings suggest that since service has been a formative experience for undocumented youths in our study, they will most likely continue to assume leadership positions in their community and remain civically active throughout their lives. The extent of that involvement, however, remains uncertain as long as their legal status remains the same.

Service Profession Aspirations

Motivation for civic engagement can encompass a mixture of self-regarding forces such as one's identity, exposure to local norms, and personal and social values (Oliner & Oliner, 1988; Serow, 1991). Numerous studies have concluded that altruism may be less important than occupational goals and personal relationships in motivating volunteer activity (Daniels, 1988; Sills, 1957). Just as the research literature on civic engagement suggests (Balsano, 2005; Serow, 1991), volunteer activities seemed to have shaped the professional aspirations of many of the undocumented students in this study. For these students, a career as an educator is seen as an ideal platform for their continued service as adults. Jacqueline shared her hopes to help other people:

> Besides my professional goals I would like to help people with low resources, mainly kids. Everyone wants to make lots of money but it's not about how much money you have, it's about how you use it, so I would like to use it in a good way, just helping those who really need care and that don't have it for some reason or another.

Growing up, Jacqueline experienced frequent financial hardships. Her family lived in a very small backhouse belonging to her aunt. As a result, Jacqueline wants to achieve financial security, but at the same time, she also wants to use some of her desired financial success to help those less fortunate, particularly kids. Esperanza also expressed a similar vision. She has strong ties to her community and wants to use her education to help others:

> This is where my school is, this is where I want to come back and help the people in my community. I live in South Central and I've been living there for 18 years and I see a lot of negative things and I don't want for kids to grow up in violence and drugs.

Many of the participants reported volunteering in elementary school working with younger kids in kindergarten and 1st grade. Many of these same students also reported aspirations of becoming school teachers. Linda's life goals include:

> Finish school, be a teacher, have my own classroom, have my group of kids, and then go back to high schools and encourage Latinos and Hispanics to pursue a higher education and also my family, cousins, my younger cousins, and my little sister.

Like Linda, other participants wanted to become role models for other Latino students and siblings. They expressed a desire to motivate younger students to pursue education as a way to minimize or eliminate the many hardships they personally experienced or observed in their communities. Esperanza draws on her struggles as an undocumented student to define her educational and professional aspirations:

All my undocumented friends have the same opinion as I do, you know,
I do want to go to school, I want to help my parents, and I want to help
my little brother and sister, I want to help my community, I want to affect
change, I want to be a teacher and I want to be able to make LAUSD
[Los Angeles Unified School District] better.

Similarly, Jacinto wanted to become an educator so he can inspire students
and his family members to pursue an education:

I want to be there and tell them not to give up. Just because you're poor
and you have been told that you are dumb doesn't mean that it's true.
All you have to do is try and not let yourself get down. I want to really
encourage and let them know that it is possible to live a life without
living paycheck to paycheck.

Financial hardship was a salient experience for the majority of the study
participants. Another prominent experience in the lives of undocumented
immigrant youths was social and political marginalization. Juana wanted
to become a teacher to help students use education to empower themselves:

I want to teach. I definitely see the need for bilingual teachers. I think
that becoming a teacher would help me get kids to think for themselves
and question what's going on so they'll have the power and ability to
make change for themselves and, I mean, that's what it's all about,
making people aware of what's going on around them and how it affects
what they do.

Undocumented immigrant youths demonstrated a deep commitment to
improving the lives of their younger family members and other Latino youth
in their community through a career in education. A similar pattern emerged
with students who professed an interest in the legal profession. Many undocumented students wanted to become legal professionals to help advocate for
immigrant rights and for the rights of the poor. Janet was one of these students:

I do want to do something with immigration because I feel strongly about
it. So I either want to go to law school and become an immigration rights
lawyer or I want to work for a nonprofit because I really think that it's so
important that everyone know their rights. There are so many violations of
people's rights in this country that I don't think is fair at all.

Sasha also wants to pursue a law career to work as an advocate for
legal rights: "I would love to work for different organizations, like legal aid.
I would like to utilize the knowledge I have to improve the community."

Janet and Sasha expressed a desire to become legal professionals and work in the nonprofit sector. Diego, a community college student, also dreams of someday working on human rights issues: "For me, it would be great to work for a nonprofit organization such as Amnesty International, or working at the UN. My plan is to go to law school and get into human rights, defending people's rights and also fighting poverty."

Interestingly, despite their legal fears, several students expressed an interest in law enforcement. Judith wants to pursue "a career in law enforcement or forensics. I want to work at the local police department." Similarly, Liliana wants to be either "a sheriff, an FBI agent, a detective, or undercover officer, anything that has to do with law enforcement." Students who expressed a desire to work in law enforcement articulated a deep belief in justice and equality for all.

Another professional aspiration for undocumented students was the medical profession. Undocumented immigrant youth wanted to become doctors not because of the financial rewards or the prestige—neither of these was mentioned in any of the interviews—but rather, because they wanted to serve immigrant and poor communities. Jimena explained her reasons for wanting to be a doctor:

> I volunteered at a clinic and I see how many people really need it. And how most of the PAs and doctors don't speak the language. They don't speak Spanish and the patients just weren't very comfortable. When I went in to translate they were just very happy to see me. They really opened up.

Jimena sees that immigrant patients do not always receive adequate or culturally and linguistically appropriate care and she wants to be able to provide that for them.

Undocumented students also aspired to become social work professionals. Lucila, who spent months volunteering for the American Red Cross during the Hurricane Katrina relief efforts, stated, "I love working with kids. I'm looking into social work, probation officer, or even running my own foster home. . . . I would love to be able to just take in kids and take care of them." Consistent with the other students' professional aspirations, those aspiring to become social workers expressed a desire to work with children who have faced a variety of hardships and obstacles.

Perhaps due to their familiarity with the nonprofit sector through their extensive volunteer activities, many students aspired to work in the nonprofit sector or starting their own nonprofit organization. Some students, like Adolfo, expressed a desire to combine their interest in the legal profession with a nonprofit. He stated:

> After college, I want to start my own nonprofit organization dedicated to promoting economic development in underprivileged communities and providing different resources for students and people that don't have the same opportunities as everyone else.

All the students in this study come from poor immigrant backgrounds, and face economic and legal hardships on an everyday basis. Janet, Sasha, Alejandra, and Diego expressed a desire to make a difference in their community by working on these issues that affected them directly. Their experiences of marginality and exclusion informed their desire to work to create change for people like themselves. Adolfo expressed a desire to work on an issue with which he is personally familiar, that of economic hardship. As the students developed their passion for service and continued to develop their career aspirations that will allow them to continue serving, many expressed the central role that their experiences as marginalized youths played in informing their career goals. As Daniella explains:

> It's always been very rewarding for me when I do community service. I feel that I'm giving back. Even though I was not given a lot, there are other people that don't have enough, they're in a worse situation than I am in and I feel that if I know what's going on and other people choose to ignore what's going on in their community or just choose not to help, I choose to help.

In many ways, the undocumented immigrant youth in this study see themselves as being in a better situation than other youth in their community. Since they understand issues of poverty and marginality by virtue of their civic engagement activities, they expressed an obligation to effect change for individuals who may not be able to do it for themselves. They also contrast their orientation toward helping others in their community with the orientation of those their age who do not.

Due to the *Plyler* decision, undocumented students are politically socialized through the educational system and other civic institutions to become actively engaged "citizens." The youth in this study appear to embrace their role as civic participants. Despite their social marginalization, students in this study demonstrated a strong commitment to civic participation. Rather than become completely dejected, hopeless, and apathetic, they invested time in community service, volunteerism, political mobilization, activism, and advocacy. Their unique experiences with legal, political, and social marginalization as well as the economic hardships they faced seemed to influence their civic engagement activities and future professional aspirations.

CONCLUSION

This chapter investigated the extent to which undocumented youth are civically active by focusing on civic activities such as providing social services, working for a cause, political activism, tutoring, and functionary work. An analysis of these measures of civic engagement suggests that undocumented Latino youth are participating in American civic life at very high rates. The findings also both expand on and challenge current notions of civic engagement. The results indicate high levels of civic participation among undocumented students, with 90% of participants reporting civic engagement in the form of providing social services, working for a cause/political activism, tutoring, and functionary work.

By virtue of the extensive civic development efforts of schools, both formal and informal, undocumented students adopt an American social and political identity, prompting them to act and behave according to the democratic and civic ideals they learn in school. Their adherence to American democratic values has been nurtured for years by teachers, extracurricular activities, and the social studies curriculum (Hess, 2005; Ochoa-Becker, 1996; Thornton, 1991). However, as they approach the transition from secondary education to higher education, their legal dilemma comes to the forefront, as the *Plyler* decision no longer guarantees their educational access once they complete high school. As a result of their legal limbo, some youth might develop a weak affection for a system where they feel treated like an outsider and may disengage completely from civic action due to their feelings of marginalization. Others become engaged in collective action with other undocumented youth who share in their sense of disenfranchisement (Flanagan & Gallay, 1995). Such collective efforts have the potential to build a sense of personal efficacy, a belief that social change is possible and that their actions can have an impact on the political process (Campbell, Gurin, & Miller, 1954).

Results of the study suggest that there is no reason to suspect that undocumented Latino youths are not active participants in civic life. Immigrants and noncitizens are impacted by public policy and socioeconomic trends in America just as native-born Latinos and White non-Hispanics are, thus we would expect them to react to the political and social environments rather than withdraw. The findings indicate that despite ongoing concerns about their legal status, participants in this study reported high levels of civic engagement. Nevertheless, the long-term civic benefit to American society is uncertain due to their legal status. The U.S. government does not recognize undocumented immigrant youth as formal members of society despite their various civic contributions and academic accomplishments. These model citizens, therefore, remain in the shadows and with few prospects to fully realize their potential as civic leaders. Results presented in this chapter provide rich detail of the wide array of civic participation of undocumented students and challenge simplistic characterizations of them as "lawbreakers." The data highlight the various ways they make important contributions to our civic society and are active participants in the social and political life.

5

The Primary Gateway to Higher Education

Although most undocumented community college students in the study more than exceed the criteria for admission into 4-year colleges and universities, the affordability of community colleges provided students with the only viable path to a college degree. Among the students surveyed, 80% of community college students reported planning to transfer to a 4-year institution upon completing their general education requirements. This chapter provides an in-depth examination of the role of community colleges in providing undocumented students access to higher education. Even though community colleges provide an opportunity to undocumented students where few exist, students face a variety of challenges and frustrations because community colleges are ill-prepared to serve a student population they hardly understand, and often, are hardly aware of their presence on campus. For many undocumented students who are faced with few or no other alternatives, the community college system provides the primary entry point to higher education.

THE COMMUNITY COLLEGE AS GATEWAY AND GATEKEEPER

Since the community college made its debut more than 100 years ago, its focus has been access, educational opportunity, and workforce preparation (Cohen & Brawer, 2003). Although these institutions have also been charged with preparing students for transfer to baccalaureate programs, they are also expected to be the primary providers of workforce preparation at the postsecondary level. Their low tuition, convenient locations, and wide selection of vocational programs make them an attractive option for a diverse population that might otherwise not be able to attend college (Barry & Barry, 1992; Bauer, 1994; Bernstein, 1986; Fields, 1962; Kintzer, 1970, 1973, 1996; Kintzer & Wattenbarger, 1985; Knoell, 1966; Knoell & Medsker, 1965; Phillippe & Sullivan, 2005; Rifkin, 1996; Witt, Wattenbarger, Gollanttscheck, & Suppiger, 1994). Thus, for many, community colleges seemingly serve as the gateway to the baccalaureate.

Unfortunately, studies dating back to the 1970s indicate sharp declines in transfer rates from 2-year to 4-year colleges, which inevitably result in fewer students achieving the baccalaureate degree when they commence postsecondary studies at community colleges (Brint & Karabel, 1989; California Community Colleges, 1994; Dougherty, 1992, 1994; Fields, 1962; Grubb, 1991; Koltai, 1981; Lombardi, 1979; Pascarella & Terenzini, 1991; Pincus, 1980; Pincus & Archer, 1989; Shaw & London, 2001). Transfer rates fell from 57% in 1970–1971 to 28% in 1984–1985 (Barry & Barry, 1992). Although the transfer rates have been relatively stable for the past 20 years, they have been far from impressive, and such data call into question the characterization of community colleges as accessible paths toward the baccalaureate degree.

As a result of their mixed legacy, community colleges have been characterized as both the gateways and gatekeepers of American higher education. As gateways, they are open-access colleges with minimal enrollment requirements and low tuition. They offer a "something for everyone" curriculum, including occupational certificate programs, general education credits toward the completion of an associate's degree and for transfer to 4-year colleges, developmental (or remedial) education, English language instruction, and noncredit short courses for business training, self-improvement, or leisure (Bragg, 2001; Dougherty, 2002). Currently, they enroll nearly 8 million students and about 40% of all undergraduates (Horn & Nevill, 2006). However, as a route from the lowest rung to the highest rungs of higher education, transfer primarily serves students of middle and high socioeconomic status (SES) (Dowd et al., 2006). Only a very small proportion (7%) of community college students who transferred to highly selective institutions is made up of students from low-SES families. On average, the academic and social characteristics of the eventual transfers closely resembled those of their counterparts who had entered a 4-year college directly after high school. The more socially and academically disadvantaged students, who need to attend the community college due to their academic history but are not empowered by their community college experience, are less likely to transfer. Thus, despite the symbolic and structural emphasis on the gateway role of community colleges, some scholars have argued that the real function of the community college is to act as a gatekeeper (Brint & Karabel, 1989). Latino students are greatly affected by this trend (Nora & Rendón, 1990; Pincus & Archer, 1989).

Immigrant Students at the Community College

There is very little research that focuses particularly on the experience of immigrants in community colleges. City University of New York (CUNY) analysts conducted some research on the experience of immigrants in the university, including some analysis of the differences between 2- and 4-year institutions (City University of New York, 1995). Their report noted that more than one-third of the first-time CUNY freshmen in 1990 were foreign-born, while only about 28% of the city's population was not born in the United States. Native-born children of immigrants—particularly second-generation youth—were found to enroll in college at continually higher rates and were rapidly overtaking the 46% enrollment rate for Whites (Fry, 2002).

As a whole, foreign-born students were *not* any more concentrated in 2-year programs than they were in CUNY in general (Bailey & Weininger, 2002). It is important to note that the foreign-born were not a homogeneous group. Immigrants at CUNY who attended high school outside of the United States were more likely than foreign-born students educated in the United States to enroll in an associate degree program. One of the most striking findings in this study was that immigrant students were actually overrepresented among the CUNY students relative to their share of the population. Although the foreign-born share of the population was just over 40% in 1999, their share of CUNY enrollments was 48% in 1997. Immigrant 2-year entrants did appear to have higher levels of educational achievement than natives who entered the same programs. Irrespective of where they attended high school, immigrants earned more credits and were more likely to complete an associate degree. Additionally, immigrants who went to U.S. high schools were more likely than native-born 2-year entrants to transfer to a bachelor's program (Bailey & Weininger, 2002). Despite these findings, research that focuses specifically on community college immigrant students remains scarce.

Latinos at the Community College

Latinos are disproportionately enrolled in 2-year colleges (Nora, Rendón, & Cuadraz, 1999). In 1996–1997, 70% of Hispanics were enrolled in community colleges, compared with 69% of African Americans, and 60% of Whites. In the fall of 2000, 58% of Latinos enrolled in college were attending 2-year institutions, compared with 42% of African American and 36% of White students (Harvey, 2003). Research also suggests that community colleges have not served as a gateway to a bachelor's degree for large numbers of lower-income and ethnic minority populations (Hoachlander, Sikora, Horn, & Carroll, 2003; Wassmer, Moore, & Shulock, 2004). Approximately 25% of Latino students in the Beginning Postsecondary Students Longitudinal Study who attended a 2-year college initially intended to transfer to a 4-year institution and obtain a bachelor's degree. However, 6 years after first enrolling in community colleges, only 6% had been awarded a bachelor's degree (Hoachlander et al., 2003).

In 2002, only about 10% of Latinos who completed high school continued on to college within a year or 2 of graduation, and these youth were more likely to enroll in community colleges and attend part-time (Fry, 2002). In the fall of 2004, nearly 2 million Latinos were enrolled in degree-granting programs in American colleges and universities (making up 12.5% of all students). Community colleges enrolled more than 972,400 of these students—the largest minority group (15% of all enrollments) in those institutions (NCES, 2006).

Latinos are also much more likely to attend less selective institutions, particularly community colleges, regardless of their socioeconomic background or prior academic preparation and achievement (Fry, 2004). In 2003–2004, only 37.7% of college-bound Latinos enrolled in baccalaureate programs, whereas 39.8% enrolled in associate degree programs (both transfer and applied). In community colleges, they enroll more frequently in occupational programs or non-degree tracks than in programs leading to transfer (Horn, Nevill, & Griffith, 2006). Therefore, although the choice to attend a community college might be positive in providing access at a reasonable cost and an environment where other Latinos are enrolled, there are also drawbacks with regard to less rigorous program choices and likelihood of transfer and degree completion.

Transfer Barriers for Latino Community College Students

Latino community college students experience several significant barriers in transferring to 4-year institutions. First, they and their parents are not familiar with higher education and have little or no knowledge of academic requirements and procedures (Jun, 2001; Martin, 1999; McDonough, 1997; Tornatzky, Cutler, & Lee, 2002). Second, these students typically lack adequate high school preparation (Fry, 2004; Shaw & London, 2001; Swail, Cabrera, & Lee, 2004; Wellman, 2002). They enroll in academic courses or college preparatory courses at lower rates than their White and Black peers (*Latinos in Education*, 1999). Third, many immigrants have limited facility with English, and instruction and tutoring are usually delivered in English (*The High-Quality Learning Conditions*, 2002). Fourth, Latino students work to survive and help support their families, and thus, may prioritize work over school due to economic necessity (Bean & Eaton, 2000; Bean & Metzner, 1985; Hagedorn, Maxwell, Chen, Cypers, & Moon, 2002; *The High-Quality Learning Conditions*, 2002; Salinas & Llanes, 2003). Fifth, many Latino students who transfer experience difficulty in adjusting to colleges that lack racial or ethnic diversity (Laanan, 2001; Lee, 2001; Zamani, 2001). Lastly, numerous institutional barriers impede transfer, including relatively few faculty and staff role models (*The High-Quality Learning Conditions*, 2002; Lee, 2001; Perez, 1999), lack of counseling and orientation

(*The High-Quality Learning Conditions*, 2002; Perez, 1999), prejudice on the part of faculty, and limited transfer programs (*The High-Quality Learning Conditions*, 2002; Lee, 2001).

UNDOCUMENTED STUDENTS AT THE COMMUNITY COLLEGE

There is a need for research on Latino undocumented students at the community college given the rising trend of enrollment noted in both Texas and California (Chavez, Soriano, & Oliverez, 2007; Jauregui, Slate, & Stallone, 2008). In California, the most recent estimates suggest that there are about 30,000 undocumented students enrolled in the community college system, compared with less than 5,000 enrolled in the University of California and California State University systems (Chavez, Soriano, & Oliverez, 2007). Undocumented students have demonstrated a "mixed pattern of attendance," in which students alternate between full-time and part-time enrollment (Dozier, 2001). The discrepancy has been found to be partially related to lack of funds to pay for full-time enrollment and/or added responsibilities at work or home (Chavez, Soriano, & Oliverez, 2007; Dozier, 2001).

Previous studies suggest that community colleges play a key role for undocumented students. They bring down costs by allowing students to enroll full-time or half-time at cheaper costs (Dozier, 2001; Jauregui, Slate, & Stallone, 2008; Oliverez, 2006; Solorio, 2009). For a significant number of students attending community college, it was not their first choice. Many are initially admitted to top 4-year schools, but are forced to decline due to financial constraints (Chavez, Soriano, & Oliverez, 2007; Oliverez, 2006). The community college is often seen as the most economically accessible option. Even after completing their general requirements, some students simply cannot afford to transfer to a 4-year school.

Table 5.1 provides a comparison between community college students and their high school or university counterparts in this study. A comparison of the commitments that students had outside of school revealed that while high school students report a high rate of household responsibilities, community college and university students did not differ in the amount of household responsibilities they had while growing up. However, 57% of community college students reported working 20 hours or more per week, compared with 17% of high school students and 40% of university students. Similarly, 70% of community college students worked 20 hours or more per week, compared with 63% of university students.

Academically, community college students reported lower high school GPAs (M = 3.14) than current high school (M = 3.61) and university students (M = 3.67), but their college GPAs (M = 3.13) did not differ from those of university students (M = 3.08). Community college students also

Table 5.1. Demographic and Academic Profiles of High School, Community College, and University Students

	High School (*n* = 20)		Community College (*n* = 37)		University (*n* = 53)	
	%	M	%	M	%	M
Demographic						
Immigration age<7	58	5.74	56	7.03	43	7.42
Mother's education [a]	89	8.17	85	8.15	79	8.57
Father's education [a]	83	8.89	74	9.29	69	10.33
Grew up with both parents	68		69		61	
Non-academic commitments						
Household responsibilities[b]	75	3.40a	50	2.77ab	51	2.73b
High school hours worked/week [c]	17	7.44	57	15.19	40	11.98
College hours worked/week [c]	--	--	70	30.52a	63	21.65b
Academic						
High school GPA [d]	71	3.61a	32	3.14b	71	3.67a
College GPA [d]	--	--	29	3.13	24	3.08
AP/Honors courses [e]	80	6.3a	57	2.14b	77	5.26a
Academic awards [e]	95	5.40ab	92	4.51b	92	6.17a
GATE[f]	32		29		29	
Involvement						
Civic engagement	85	2.65a	89	4.11ab	89	5.23b
Social service	5	.05	16	.22	16	.23
Activism	5	.10a	14	.14a	13	.47b
Tutoring	55	.80	46	.76	46	1.13
Functionary work	60	.75a	81	1.43b	81	1.60b
Extracurricular participation	85	3.50a	95	4.76ab	94	5.23b
Leadership position	75	1.75	76	2.38	81	2.55
Psychosocial						
Distress [g]	10	1.93	3	1.99	16	2.22
Discrimination [h]	5	2.60a	0	3.06ab	0	3.26b
Rejection due to status [i]	15	3.43a	15	4.49b	24	4.35ab

	High School (n = 20)		Community College (n = 37)		University (n = 53)	
Dual frame of reference [i]	70	6.10	69	5.77	82	6.19
English proficiency [k]	100	3.86	100	3.69	98	3.82
Spanish proficiency [k]	95	3.70	94	3.57	84	3.63
Orientation toward schooling						
Educational aspirations [l]	85	5.40	80	5.37	100	5.65
Educational expectations [l]	55	4.60	51	4.69	71	4.98
Academic self-concept [m]	80	6.40	71	6.22	82	6.48
Academic self-efficacy [m]	80	6.18	73	6.01	75	6.11
Valuing of schooling [n]	85	6.44	79	6.16	82	6.44
Effort avoidance [o]	0	2.48	0	2.46	4	2.68
Parent-derived motivation [p]	90	3.60	100	3.66	92	3.55
Friend-derived motivation [p]	60	2.75	35	2.78	63	2.91
Social support for schooling						
Parents' valuing of schooling [q]	100	3.88a	85	3.28b	86	3.58ab
Friends' valuing of schooling [q]	65	3.03	68	2.98	69	3.15

[a] Percentage represents the proportion of those with 12 years of schooling or less.
[b] Scale ranged from 1 (never), 2 (almost never), 3 (once in a while), 4 (once or twice a week), 5 (almost every day). Percent reflects responses 4–5 combined.
[c] Percentage represents the proportion of those working more than 20 hours per week.
[d] Percentage represents the proportion of those with a 3.5 GPA or above.
[e] Percentage reporting 1 or more
[f] Percentage reflects participation rate.
[g] Scale ranged from 1 (never), 2 (sometimes), 3 (often), 4 (all the time). Percent reflects responses 3–4 combined.
[h] Scale ranged from 1 (never), 2 (once), 3 (a few times), 4 (many times), 5 (very frequently), 6 (always). Percent reflects responses 5–6 combined.
[i] Scale ranged from 1 (never), 2 (almost never), 3 (seldom), 4 (sometimes), 5 (often), 6 (almost always), 7 (always). Percent reflects responses 5–7 combined.
[j] Scale range: 1 (strongly disagree)–7 (strongly agree). Percent reflects responses 6–7 combined.
[k] Scale ranged from 1 (not at all), 2 (not very well), 3 (well), 4 (very well). Percent reflects responses 3–4 combined.
[l] Scale range: 1 (graduate from high school), 2 (some college), 3 (A.A. degree), 4 (B.A. degree), 5 (M.A. degree), 6 (J.D./Ph.D./M.D. degree). Percent reflects responses 5–6 combined.
[m] Scale range: 1 (strongly disagree)–7 (strongly agree). Percent reflects responses 6–7 combined.
[n] Scale range: 1 (not important at all) — 7 (very important). Percent reflects responses 6–7 combined.
[o] Scale range: 1 (strongly disagree)–7 (strongly agree). Percent reflects responses 6–7 combined.
[p] Scale range: 1 (very false), 2 (somewhat false), 3 (somewhat true), 4 (very true). Percent reflects responses 3–4 combined.
[q] Scale range: 1 (not important), 2 (somewhat important), 3 (important), 4 (very important). Percent reflects responses 3–4 combined.

reported taking fewer AP and Honors (M = 2.14) courses and fewer academic awards (M = 4.51), compared with the high school (M = 6.3 and M = 5.40, respectively) and university students (M = 5.26 and M = 6.17, respectively), but there were no differences in the percentage of students who were identified as gifted and talented. Despite their higher work hours, community college students did not differ from their university counterparts in their civic engagement (both 89%) and extracurricular participation rates (95% and 94%, respectively). There was only a slight difference in the rate of leadership positions, with 76% of community college students having had a leadership role, compared with 81% for university students.

Despite the fact that they had lower educational aspirations and expectations as well as a lower academic self-concept than university students, Table 5.1 shows that community college students did not differ from their university counterparts in their academic self-efficacy, valuing of schooling, effort avoidance, and achievement motivation. University students did report being more motivated to do well in school by their friends, compared with the community college group. Finally, students did not differ much in the level of support for school they received from their parents and friends, although high school students reported slightly higher levels.

Affordability

The relative affordability of the community college often provides the only path to higher education for undocumented students, who, regardless of their academic achievement, are generally excluded from higher education because they cannot afford the tuition elsewhere. Daniella explained her situation:

> I felt that going to community college would just give me a little bit more time to just raise more money, to find more resources, and hopefully by the time I graduated from community college I would have saved some money to pay for the university.

Some community colleges provided financial assistance to undocumented students in the form of small scholarships. For students attending school in states where they were allowed to pay resident in-state tuition fees, as opposed to the international student fees they would otherwise have had to pay, the lower tuition rate was a significant form of financial support, as Jacinto describes: "I got a scholarship here for $200 just because of my high GPA, so they do help out a little. The waiver that we don't have to pay international tuition is a great help. It makes it possible for us to attend."

Institutional Challenges

Even though the community college is the most financially viable option for undocumented students, it still remains a significant challenge. Students not only have to pay for all tuition costs, but they also are less likely to receive financial support from their low-income parents. In fact, many students also help their parents financially in addition to paying for school costs. Difficulty balancing school with other obligations and responsibilities was a theme most salient for community college students. Students were constantly concerned about not being able to pay for their tuition or apply to the school of their choice due to cost, as was the case for Beatriz:

> When I was in high school I had applied to a private school. But being undocumented, and it's so expensive, I couldn't get scholarships or financial aid. And I didn't want my dad to be paying $60,000 for something that I may not like. So I decided to go to a community college and this is where I am. And it has been a long 4 years because stuff happens. Like with money, or you have to go to work, somehow it delays itself, but I am going to finish hopefully in 1 year. Now I am taking a year off of school to work and save up.

Beatriz was working 40 hours per week at the time of the interview. Nailea, a second-year student, has also had a very difficult time paying for all her college expenses. Like Beatriz, she has also had to take time off from school: "It's been rough. I have been having to pay everything on my own. I have had to take off a couple of quarters because of no money."

In addition to financial concerns, and balancing work with school, some undocumented students at the community college faced other institutional challenges. Daniella spent a lot of time researching the school she attended because many of the schools she visited did not support undocumented students:

> I have done my research, and the college that I attend is one of the best colleges because I went to other colleges and I tried to find out what they offer for undocumented students and a lot of schools didn't even know what that meant. They had very little information and I just felt very disappointed. That's why I chose this college. It's kind of far for me but I think I have made a good choice just because they have a lot of resources. They're the college that I know is more informed about people in my situation. They have scholarships for us. I was actually given a scholarship and that helped me a lot.

Isabel also describes a lack of support for undocumented students at her community college: "I don't think they do as much as they probably could do. You're on your own. If there was a way of getting maybe the word out or getting some more help, that would be great." Esperanza has not been able to complete some of the requirements of her program because she worries that they will ask her for a social security number, which she does not have:

> I get scared of applying to scholarships. I still haven't done my internship in broadcasting because I'm scared that whenever I get to go to a radio station, they might ask me for a social security card. The only scholarship I have applied to is at the community college that I go to, but I haven't applied to any other ones because I don't think they're going to be able to help me.

She also worries about the rising cost of school and the various friends who have dropped out because they can no longer afford to pay their tuition:

> When I started going to school, the units were $11, so I was happy, but when they got to $18, I was like, "Oh, my God, what am I going to do now?" I'm going to work more or am I going to stop going? I can afford $11, anybody can afford that, but $18, and then it went up to $26. When it got to $18, a lot of my classmates that are undocumented dropped out. They stopped attending, they started working, and I would be like, "When are you going back to school?" They're like, "Oh, I need to save money," and it's bad because they haven't come back and I'm afraid that they're not going to do it anymore.

Social and Academic Support

Faculty support. An important source of support for undocumented students at the community college was the faculty. Beatriz's faculty advisor, for example, was one of the most influential people in her life: "She has always been there for me. I could always go up to her and tell her anything. She understands where I come from and she knows my situation." Jacqueline also found a mentor at her community college: "My mentor was very important because she would tell me, 'We will find a solution. Don't worry, we will find a way.' She talked to some people, asked around, always looking out for me. She was very important." Juana's history professor had a profound influence on her because he came from a socioeconomic background that was similar to hers:

My history professor is very down to earth. He's real. He grew up in
the same areas that I did and he was very open about things that
were going on. . . . I would say that he's one of the professors that
really inspired me because he started from the ghetto, too. He started
from scratch and he worked his way up and he's working on his Ph.D.
degree. . . . It's awesome to see that.

Academic support programs. Due to their high grades, many of the
students we interviewed were invited to participate in academic enrichment programs, like Puente (Spanish for "bridge"), which provides rigorous coursework, sustained academic counseling, and mentoring. These programs were an important resource for undocumented students like Thalia,
who joined the Puente program that provided access to caring counselors
and professors. Linda also enjoyed the extensive support of the Puente program on her campus:

My first year, I met an English instructor that introduced me to the
Puente program, which helps minority students who want to go to a
4-year college, who want to transfer. We visit universities, UC Santa
Barbara, Berkeley, private schools. They also gave me a $1,000
scholarship, which paid for my tuition. My Puente counselor has been
helping me with letters of recommendation for scholarships.

Lisa and Jairo also credit the Puente program for their academic success at
the community college. Jairo states:

I got into the Puente program and that has helped me tremendously.
They're always on top of you, in a good way because they want you
to do well. And they will stay after class and talk to you. And we will
have discussions and take trips to other universities. And we always
talk about social issues dealing with Latinos and Hispanics. They really
keep you on top of your game.

Paulina applied to the Honors program at her community college because
she felt she was not being challenged intellectually in her regular class:

I felt like community college was high school part two. I wasn't being
challenged. And then a friend of mine whom I had met in one of my
classes told me about the Honors track. And I said, "What is so good
about it?" And he's like, "It's just like a lot of more rigorous work. It's not
just one piece of paper and then you're done." So I went and I checked
it out. And it was work, work, work. So I applied for it.

Campus climate. Although much of the literature on community colleges cites the lack of supportive resources, undocumented students like Thalia reported positive views of their campus: "Everybody thinks it's a bad college because it is in the ghetto but I am there and I am succeeding. I think it is a good college with some really good professors." Isabel also reports a similar positive experience at her community college, even though she has to travel a long distance to get to campus:

> Distance-wise it's pretty far and I could easily just stay at my local community college, but I really like the environment here. I had teachers that really worked with you to get things done and if you have trouble they'll help you out.

Jacqueline also reported a variety of opportunities at her community college: "They offered lots of good things for undocumented students. They guided me very well and made me feel like I had an opportunity in my life and I wasn't just stuck there." Karen also had positive things to say about her community college:

> It's been absolutely wonderful. I think I've learned a lot more things. I never thought it'd be this great. I've met new people. I have more communications with teachers than I thought I would have and it's a great environment, too.

Paulina used nothing but superlatives to describe her community college:

> The English department is the best. It's also very racially diverse. I only have good things to say about it. Although it might not be seen as one of the best junior colleges anywhere, I think it is. I have learned so much. And the people there are interested in me getting out of there and doing something with my life. Not just being there forever and ever.

Community college and university students also did not differ in their sense of distress, discrimination, or sense of rejection due to their undocumented status, although they reported slightly higher rates than the high school students. All three groups reported similarly high levels of bilingualism. The only significant difference between community college and university students was in their sense of relative well-being compared with others in their country of origin. Only 69% of community college students felt that their conditions in the United States were better than in their country of origin, compared with 82% of university students (see Table 5.1).

Drive and Determination

A prevalent theme in the interviews with the community college students was their sense of drive and determination. Even though for many the community college route was not their first choice, they were intent on continuing and doing well. For example, Beatriz was motivated to prove people wrong about undocumented students: "I probably have more motivation because of my status. It makes it so much harder that I think I have to prove people wrong. And is not only that, I also want to do it for myself." Carla concurred when I asked if her status made her reconsider her college plans: "No, not at all. It's actually enforcing that. It's such a challenge that I want to complete it." Carla saw a college degree as an accomplishment that transcends her legal marginality:

> I want to be educated because that's something that no one can take away from me. I'm the first one in my family to come here and to actually pursue something, like have a dream for this and work. I want to make my family very, very proud.

A second source of motivation for community college undocumented students was the hardships encountered by their parents in their physically demanding jobs. Daniella was inspired by her parents' work ethic:

> What motivates me is seeing my parents work. My parents work really, really hard. I've seen my parents work so hard in sweatshops, restaurants. Just seeing my parents work so hard and coming home complaining about how hard they had worked, their pain and their suffering, that keeps me going. I feel like, "Wow, I'm not doing that." What they have to do every day, wake up early in the morning and come back home at night, is way worse. I just feel that I have been given a little bit more than they have, so that to me just makes me think, "Well, I just got to work with what I got to make my parents' situation a little bit better."

Karen was also motivated by her parents; she wanted them to be proud of her: "I want to feel good about myself. I want people, my family especially, to feel good about me, to know that I was doing it, that I wanted to do it." Esperanza was similarly motivated by her mother's and sister's hardship:

> I saw what my mom was going through with my father and saw my sister at a young age getting married, already having a kid, and I'm like, "I don't want this for me. I want something better because I know that if

they brought me here for something better, I'm going to have to find it myself." And we were already struggling, so . . . and my mom . . . this is one thing that mom always tells me, "Struggle right now and later you will get something back," and that's what she tells me right now.

Community college students also demonstrated perseverance in their attitudes about coursework. Isabel was very strategic in how she approached her school work: "So I guess in order to really get through it you have to want it badly, to say, 'Okay, you know what? I'm passing this class. I'm going to do my best and stay committed to it.'" One of the most compelling stories of determination and perseverance was shared by Esperanza:

It doesn't matter if I have to repeat my class, it doesn't matter if I have to work more hours at work to pay the money, to pay again for that math class. I also know that if I put more effort and work for it, I am going to pass it and I am going to be able to go to a higher level. . . . I don't see myself dropping out of school. Even if it takes me longer to finish my career, but as long as I keep on going to school, I'm happy and I know that I'll be making my mom happy, too.

CONCLUSION

Although a few key differences arose between the academic profiles of community college students and university students, despite higher levels of employment, community college students were similar to their university and college-going high school counterparts, particularly in their civic engagement and extracurricular participation. Forty-six percent of college students interviewed were either currently community college students or began their higher education studies at the community college level. Working long hours outside of school seems to impact their academic performance somewhat and may also affect their educational goals, possibly as a result of increased hardship they experience managing work and school. This may also be reflected by their lower level of optimism compared with high school and university students.

One of the highlights for students at the community college was the level of support they receive from caring faculty, who again, based on student reports, not only reached out and supported students, but also went above and beyond their formal roles as professors. Several students described these professors as "mentors." Students also benefited from the support they received from academic outreach programs. These programs not only became important sources of information on how to navigate the institutional bureaucracy, but also helped students develop concrete plans to transfer to the university. Through these programs, students also met other students who shared not only their educational goals but also some of the same hardships. The programs were often one of the few sources of scholarship money to pay for college. Finally, academic outreach programs provided students with more rigorous academic courses. Despite their initial disappointment at not being able to enroll directly in 4-year universities, once they began attending, students reported an overall positive experience at the community college. As noted in previous chapters, undocumented students reframed their experience in a positive way by highlighting opportunities to meet new and diverse friends, positive experiences with professors, and access to resources specifically for undocumented students. They also referred to the affordability of the community college.

Notwithstanding these important sources of support, information, and scholarships, and low tuition rates, community college students still struggled to balance their school work with their jobs. Students experienced various interruptions in their schooling because they had to take a leave from school due to a lack of funds to pay tuition. They expressed disappointment at having to stay longer at the community college because they could not remain enrolled continuously, despite their long work hours. Various students reported working in excess of 40 hours per week. Students also reported some institutional barriers. Not all students felt that their community college was supportive of undocumented students. Some students reported that their community college had no idea who undocumented students were and had no resources in place to help them. The various forms and paperwork they had to fill out to attend and requests for their social security number or driver's license were frequent reminders of their stigma. Students were also not able to join various academic support programs or complete required internships because they required proof of legal status or a social security number. Finally, students constantly worried about the ever-increasing cost of tuition. Many described friends who dropped out and did not return because they could not afford the increasing tuition rates.

Although undocumented students face an uncertain future, the most striking theme from the interviews was their tenacious optimism. Rather than become dejected, some students derived their motivation to continue in school from being undocumented. They reframed it as a challenge they were intent on overcoming. Even when faced with the prospect of earning a college degree and not being able to use it, community college students highlighted the sense of accomplishment from just becoming "educated," regardless of their prospects for employment. Their valuing of a college degree as seminal milestone was reinforced by their working-class parents who modeled a strong work ethic despite the hardship they endure in their physically demanding low-wage jobs. Students wanted to earn a college degree, even if they don't get to use it, because they wanted to make their parents proud. They saw their accomplishment as a way to repay their parents for all the sacrifices they have made to provide a better life and educational opportunities.

6

Undocumented College Graduates and the Impact of Legal Status

At a time when 3.2 million undocumented children and young adults are making their homes in the United States, what does it mean to grow up acculturating to the norms and standards of a culture that eventually puts legal limitations on your potential? How do families, schools, and community institutions mediate the effects of the law? The case for undocumented students is arguably even more contradictory than that of adult undocumented immigrants. Since many arrived in the United States as young children, they learned the language and absorbed the customs and culture in ways not possible for those who migrate as adults (Abrego, 2006; Fernández-Kelly & Curran, 2001). Undocumented students dress and speak English in ways that make them largely indistinguishable from their U.S.-born peers (Olivas, 1995). Since undocumented students do not conform to social assumptions, they are often able to avoid questions about their legal status (Abrego, 2006; Gonzales, 2008). In this sense, undocumented students are simultaneously included and excluded from U.S. society.

LIMINAL LEGALITY

Since undocumented youths have legal access to public education through high school, the educational system plays a central role in the development of their identity and understanding of American social norms—forces that, along with the law, powerfully determine legal consciousness (Carrera, 1989; Lopez, 2003). Straddling between legal and illegal categories, and between inclusion and exclusion, these students' liminal status, criminalized for being undocumented, yet legitimated for their successful student status, magnifies the role of the law in their lives (Gonzales, 2007, 2008; Menjivar, 2006). What are the consequences of growing up "American," yet living with only partial access to the mechanisms that promote social mobility? Unlike their parents, most undocumented students do not migrate with the understanding of toiling in low-wage jobs. They have grown up in the United States and have aspirations and expectations similar to those of their native-born and legal immigrant peers (Gans, 1992). Their legal status, however, separates them from their peers, and their aspirations cannot be fully realized without significant changes to the immigration laws that currently prevent their full participation.

Liminality

According to the liminal legality framework (Abrego, 2008; Gonzales, 2008; Menjivar, 2006), as children, undocumented students experience a liminal "illegality" during childhood, whereby most of the limitations of unauthorized status are dormant, and a reanimated "illegality" as they move into adulthood. Although undocumented status, or "illegality," undoubtedly limits the options of young adults, it is mediated by institutions such as schools. Those who develop networks of support and information during high school, for example, are able to mobilize resources that allow them successful transitions into adulthood. As they move into college, they enjoy the protection provided by higher education institutions to develop positive identities and important skills that allow them to successfully negotiate college barriers. Those youngsters who are not provided the opportunity to develop skills and build relationships with adult mentors may have difficulty moving on to college, and as a result, confront greater limitations, dangers, and stress of "illegality" without the legal protections of school.

Thus, the period that spans from childhood to early adolescence, marked as one of liminality, or suspended "illegality," is an important buffer stage whereby young people are incorporated into important dimensions of society. Most of the dimensions of their own "illegality" are, for the most part, dormant. Undocumented children move through their own development and participate in the school system that shelters them from the constraints and effects of "illegality." During this stage of liminality, many of these young people exhibit more positive aspirations about their futures and are more resilient. Most of them have not experienced the full brunt of the condition of illegality, and their expectations for the future are shaped in a parallel fashion with their legal peers (Gonzales, 2008). The better and longer the buffer that suspends the effects of their "illegality" is preserved, the stronger the opportunity to successfully compete in school, develop a positive self-image, and prepare themselves for full and active participation in the legal world. By the time they reach adulthood, the impediments and opportunities they faced as adolescents play strong determining roles in how their adult lives will unfold (Gonzales, 2008).

Entry into "Illegality"

An important characteristic of liminal "illegality" is that what has been suspended eventually becomes manifest. Whereas undocumented status does
not pose too many obstacles in childhood, it is a salient feature beginning
in adolescence when the limits imposed by "illegality" begin to emerge. At
every turn, undocumented youth face constraints on their ability to participate. While certain avenues are closed, others are restricted. Although
various turning points mark and define successful transitions from childhood to adolescence to adulthood, many of these important stages require
state-issued forms of identification and legal status. Unable to obtain forms
of identification such as a driver's license or library card, buy a cell phone,
apply for a work permit, or receive financial aid to attend college, undocumented young adults are shut out of these important activities and distanced
from their peers. Accomplishing these tasks often means having to take difficult risks that involve embarrassment on an ongoing basis (Gonzales, 2008;
Menjivar, 2006).

Because the entry into adulthood is practically an entry into "illegality," undocumented young adults find themselves contending with blocked
opportunities, stigma, and fear. Even though many of these young people
have to contribute to their families and take care of themselves, mundane
acts of day-to-day adult life are outside of the legal realm. They spend much
of their time looking over their shoulders and worrying about what might
happen to them and their family if they come into contact with the police
or immigration officials. If they have legal peers, they see the ways in which
their "illegality" blocks their progress as their friends surge ahead. Forced
to make difficult choices about revealing or concealing their status, they
alternate between two worlds, one that knows their status and another that
does not (Gonzales, 2008; Menjivar, 2006).

To make matters worse, the routes toward legalization are few and entail
long waits. Family sponsorship and marriage to U.S. citizens can allow these
young people opportunities to transition into the legal world, but the number
of eligible visas per year is small and legalization through family sponsorship
can take an inordinately long period of time. Waiting years for visas to be processed can leave these youngsters in prolonged states of liminality, as the fear
of taking jobs or doing anything to jeopardize their standing leaves them with
few options and restricts their ability to be self-sufficient.

Undocumented youngsters, however, do not experience these transitions
uniformly. The protective buffer that suspends "illegality" in childhood is
either preserved or eroded by the particularities of high school and family
lives. If undocumented youth are able to seamlessly move from high school
to postsecondary institutions, they can preserve the buffer and continue to
experience fewer restrictions. They can carry out their day-to-day lives with-

out having to test their legal limits (drive or work), and can focus on educational pursuits. But what happens to those fortunate few who are able to enjoy the buffering effects of schooling and, despite the odds, graduate from college? As they exit the protective environments of schooling and aspire to enter the labor market and other activities that require legal status, they face increasingly risky and precarious situations that expose them to their legal limitations and the daunting realities and conditions of "illegality."

UNDOCUMENTED COLLEGE GRADUATES

In addition to undocumented students, in this study I also surveyed and interviewed several undocumented college graduates. Table 6.1 indicates that overall undocumented college graduates have very similar demographic characteristics to undocumented high school and undergraduate students. On average, they are in their mid-20s in age, have parents with less than a high school education, and have above average academic achievement in high school. In fact, their overall college GPA was higher than the GPAs of both community college and university undocumented students. This is particularly remarkable since they also worked longer hours in their part-time jobs compared with university students.

Table 6.1. Academic Engagement Comparisons of Undocumented Students and Undocumented College Graduates

	High School (*n* = 20)	Community College (*n* = 37)	University (*n* = 53)	Graduate (*n* = 20)
Age at time of study	18.11	20.54	20.71	24.71
Immigration age	5.74	7.14	7.61	9.18
Mother's education	8.17	8.15	8.57	7.59
Father's education	8.89	9.29	10.33	10.94
High school GPA	3.61	3.14	3.67	3.5
College GPA	--	3.13	3.08	3.43
AP/Honors courses	6.3	2.14	5.26	3.8
High school hours worked/week	7.44	15.19	11.98	21.23
College hours worked/ week	--	30.52	21.65	28.06

Table 6.2 indicates that undocumented college graduates also have high civic engagement rates, similar to those of undocumented high school and college students. They have slightly higher rates of activism, particularly compared with high school students. The cross-sectional data show an increase toward higher rates of activism as students move higher in their educational attainment. Their rates of tutoring, functionary work, extracurricular participation, and leadership roles were high, comparable to those of undocumented students. In all, undocumented college graduates have developed the same academic and leadership talents as current undocumented students at the high school, community college, and university level. Like these students, they demonstrate great potential that remains to be recognized under current immigration laws.

Alba

A good example of unrecognized talent is Alba. Despite having a college degree, Alba's status has forced her to alter her career plans: "I already finished college and I know I want to be a high school math teacher, but I can't teach. Initially, I was doing nothing, I was frustrated, I was depressed, I was sad, and I didn't know what to do next. Now, I started going to school again, but I am going to be a dental assistant." Even though Alba now has a teaching credential, she cannot pursue her desired career because of her status: "I have a bachelor's in math and a teaching credential. I was about to get a master's, but I needed to teach full-time and I

Table 6.2. Civic Engagement Comparisons of Undocumented Students and Undocumented College Graduates (in percentages)

	High School (n = 20)	Community College (n = 37)	University (n = 53)	Graduate (n = 20)
Civic engagement	85	89	89	90
Social service	5	16	16	16
Activism	5	14	13	22
Tutoring	55	46	46	55
Functionary work	60	81	81	78
Extracurricular participation	85	95	94	96
Leadership position	75	76	81	77

can't because of my status." If Alba's status was not preventing her from pursuing her career goals, she would go back to school and earn a Ph.D. and teach at the community college level.

Dulce

Similar to the undocumented students profiled in previous chapters, Dulce excelled academically in high school and graduated as the valedictorian of her senior class. She first realized that her status would hinder her educational opportunities when she began applying to college: "I was offered the Presidential Scholarship at a public university, but when they learned of my status, they said I couldn't get it." Although Dulce's legal status limited her college options, she received strong support from various educators who helped her fund her education: "The assistant principal at my high school would call his friends and ask for funding . . . he would just encourage me to continue and not to give up. And then there was this other teacher, she contacted one of her friends and her friend gave me a scholarship, which I received all throughout my undergraduate career, for 5 years. . . . " Like Alba, Dulce feels that her legal status has not allowed her to move forward with her career: "I received my bachelor's degree and I can't really pursue my career. . . ." She is currently applying to law school and in the future wants to become an immigration attorney because she feels this career will allow her to "continue to be a contributing member of society."

Lucia

Another undocumented college graduate, Lucia, was also ranked in the top 50 of her graduating class of 1,000 and graduated with a 3.89 GPA. Although Lucia had college aspirations in high school, she recounted being discouraged by her college counselor from pursuing those plans:

> She said, "Let me tell you something. Your people do great things."
> I remember this word-for-word . . . . she said, "You're great mothers, you're great housekeepers, I mean, my nanny was a wonderful woman. She was Mexican and I loved her very much, so you don't have to do all those things. I mean, I don't really know if you can do all those things, so why don't you focus on something you can do?" And I just looked at her and I thought, "Well, what do you mean? What do you mean what I can do?" And she was like, "We have some great woodshop classes. You could be a florist. Could you imagine yourself? You could do flowers," and I just looked at her and I said, "Thank you very much. This is not what I'm looking for," and I grabbed my sheet of paper and I went next door to the other counselor.

Despite her counselor's advice, Lucia applied to college and was initially accepted to UC Berkeley. When she could not provide them with a social security number, however, they withdrew her acceptance and she instead attended a local public 4-year university. Paying her tuition each quarter was a challenge, so Lucia worked a variety of different jobs. As she explained, "I would clean houses, I would take care of people's kids, I would mow lawns, I would do anything just to make sure I got that money to pay for the classes every quarter." In addition to working, Lucia was extremely involved in local politics: "I volunteered in every political campaign in my area . . . any chance there was to help a Democratic party candidate of some sort, I would help them." Despite all the hardships she endured to earn both a B.A. and M.A. degree, the American Dream continues to elude Lucia: "I got this great education and then I went back to working fast-food, taking care of people's kids and cleaning homes. . . . For my parents, it was heartbreaking to see me go through all this only to go back and do what they did." For Lucia, the hardest part of being an undocumented college graduate is "Knowing that it doesn't matter how many degrees you get, it doesn't matter . . . at the end of my degree, there was no job for me. . . . There was no way of me putting all this education to use. . . ."

Michael

Although undocumented college graduates demonstrate tenacity and perseverance, they remain marginalized despite their high potential to contribute to American society. Michael, for example, who was 8 years old when he came to the United States, always wanted to be a doctor and intended to serve low-income communities. Although he was accepted to many prestigious universities his senior year of high school, he could not attend: "I remember out of high school I had been accepted to seven different universities and I had already picked UC Berkeley but my situation wouldn't let me go. All the universities sent documents saying you can't go." Michael ended up attending the local community college and eventually transferred to UCLA, where he earned his B.A. degree. Since he could not afford to attend medical school despite his stellar college GPA, Michael enrolled in a master's degree program in public health. In the future, he still hopes to become a medical doctor, but he also has ambitions to run for political office to effect systematic change:

> I want to be able to give back to my community and create programs. Maybe create a nonprofit organization. But the most important thing to me is to create policy change. Helping someone, tutoring someone is important but I think the biggest change you can make is at the policy level.

LEGALIZATION AND INTEGRATION

Overall, comparing the educational experiences of undocumented students and college graduates, the frustrations due to their status were the most palpable among college graduates. According to Lucia:

> I feel like it's a punishment. I did everything you told me to. I stayed out of trouble. I stayed out of gangs. I didn't get pregnant at 16. I'm a great member of society. I know more of civic duty . . . more about politics than most U.S.-born citizens. So why do I feel punished?

In the same vein as most of the research literature that examines the economic and social benefits of legalization, Alba makes the same argument. When I asked her what she would tell members of Congress regarding undocumented students, she stated:

> To have a way for students to legalize their status in the country so we can contribute because most of us are studying to be teachers, doctors, and lawyers. Even if we're finished with our education, it is a waste of talent because we can't really participate in society.

The ongoing challenges faced by undocumented college graduates in this study have begun to surface elsewhere in the research literature. A recent study, for example, described the story of an undocumented student who was admitted to several highly selective 4-year colleges and universities, but due to her legal status and limited financial resources, could not afford to enroll (Rogers et al., 2008). She began taking classes part-time at the local community college while working full-time to support herself. On campus, she led other students in efforts to clean the local beaches and volunteered at a homeless shelter. Combining a full-time work schedule with college studies, she eventually transferred to a 4-year university, where she studied political science, graduating with her bachelor's degree. However, because she still lacked legal residency, she took a job as a waitress at a local restaurant. In the meantime, she continues to hope that she will one day gain legal residency, as she would like to pursue becoming an immigration attorney. She frequently draws on her understanding of the legal and political system to help neighbors and colleagues at work (Rogers et al., 2008).

The experiences of undocumented college graduates highlight the link between legal status and access to the U.S. educational system, and social and economic integration. Although legal status does not trump other factors that have been found to influence immigrants' educational aspirations and achievement, such as individual traits, family, and community factors, it plays a central role in shaping the benefits they can reap from their educational accomplishments. What are the implications for broader society when a significant number of its residents remain marginalized despite public educational investment in developing their academic, civic, and leadership talents? What would happen if immigration laws changed and everyone who was in the country now without legal status was given a pathway to legalization? Would legalization bring high levels of integration and upward mobility? Would it help in reducing poverty? And lastly, would it provide better job opportunities?

Insights from IRCA

Many news reports and commentators in the United States link unauthorized immigration to negative economic effects, cultural fragmentation, and issues of national security. As a result of these perceived negative consequences, resistance to unauthorized immigrants appears to have increased, as demonstrated by Arizona's SB1070 anti-immigrant law and the proliferation of similar copycat laws being introduced in state legislatures across the country. Studies that have examined the impact of legalization on economic outcomes suggest that the effects of immigration are not negative. For example, most of the undocumented immigrants who obtained legal status in the United States under the 1986 Immigration Reform and Control Act (IRCA) found better jobs by 1992 than the ones they secured when they arrived (Powers, Kraly, & Seltzer, 2004). As a group, most of the undocumented immigrants who legalized through IRCA arrived with relatively low skill levels and found low-skill, low-wage jobs. Yet by 1992, 5 years after legalization, most had jobs that were better than the first jobs they reported, and for many, much better than the jobs they had held in their homeland.

The study focused primarily on the employment situation and occupations of a sample of undocumented individuals who legalized their status under IRCA and who responded to two detailed surveys conducted by Westat, Inc., for the Department of Labor. The Legalized Population Survey (LPS-1) conducted in 1989 included a sample of 6,193 legalized immigrants and the Legalized Population Follow-Up Survey (LPS-2) conducted in 1992 included a sample of about 4,000 people who had participated in the first survey. About 70% of the unauthorized immigrants within the sample came from Mexico, with the next largest groups from other developing countries. On average, the immigrants were 22–24 years old when they came to the United States and reported a 7th- to 8th-grade education at the date of the first survey (Powers, Kraly, & Seltzer, 2004). About 48% of men and 38% of women experienced a gain in their occupational status between their first job and their job in 1992. Once they became part of the U.S. labor force, the immigrants on average showed movement from occupations at the lowest status levels in their first job in the United States to occupations in 1992 that approached and sometimes exceeded the jobs they reported in their countries of origin (Powers, Kraly, & Seltzer, 2004).

One of the more careful IRCA studies suggests that after 4 years, the wages of legalized men increased 9% more than would be expected absent legalization (Kossoudji & Cobb-Clark, 2002). The impact on women was even greater (Rivera-Batiz, 1998). Bernstein and Blazer (2008) estimates that if the 7.1 million undocumented families received a 9% raise, their collective annual income would increase by over $18 billion, an amount comparable to some of the largest government antipoverty programs. But these figures understate anticipated economic gains from legalization because conditions for undocumented workers are much worse today than when IRCA was passed (Kossoudji & Cobb-Clark, 2002). Moreover, the income gains would increase year by year because undocumented status suppresses wage growth (Bratsberg, Ragan, & Nasir, 2002). For example, according to 2004 Current Population Survey data, lawful permanent residents who had been in the United States for more than 10 years had incomes 31% higher than those who have been here a shorter time; the comparable increase for undocumented immigrants was only 16% (Fix, 2006).

These studies suggest that, when given an opportunity to regularize their status, undocumented immigrants experience significant upward mobility. It is, therefore, likely that if currently undocumented students and college graduates were granted legal status, they would not only improve their own circumstances, but would make greater contributions to the U.S. economy. For example, estimates suggest that legalization efforts would provide 360,000 current undocumented high school graduates in the United States with a legal means to work, and could provide incentives for another 715,000 youngsters between the ages of 5 and 17 to finish high school. If undocumented immigrants are given the opportunity to receive additional education and training, and move into better-paying jobs, they will pay more in taxes and have more money to spend and invest.

Economic Impact of Legalization

Results from studies that examine the economic impact of legalization coincide with numerous national-level empirical studies that have been conducted on the economic costs and returns of immigrant populations, both documented and undocumented. Using various methodologies and scenarios, researchers have examined the public fiscal costs and returns of immigrants in terms of social services used relative to taxes paid and their effects on employment and wages, the growth rate of the economy, and prices of goods and services, among other variables (Edmonston & Smith, 1997). Such studies have generally illuminated some important points. First, recent immigrants generally have low incomes, lower than those of native residents. This is significant because, typically, lower-income families contribute less to public revenue. Second, research indicates that, although children and elderly immigrants consume more tax revenues than they contribute (as is also the case with U.S. citizens who are children or elderly), immigrants are net taxpayers during their working-age years. Finally, the long-term fiscal impact of an immigrant depends upon the level of education achieved. In particular, immigrants with more education have more positive long-term fiscal impacts (Edmonston & Smith, 1997). Putting these together, it is reasonable to expect that providing access to legalization and higher education for undocumented children and young adults would ensure a higher positive fiscal impact on the U.S. economy.

The finding that immigrants with more education have greater long-term fiscal impact on a receiving society echoes much of the literature surrounding human capital theory and the investment concept of education—investing in education generally increases individuals' lifetime earnings and makes them more productive members of the labor force, which itself translates into higher levels of output, income, and economic return at the local, state, and national levels (Hearn, 2001). Along with the quantifiable economic benefits of investing in education, scholars have also pointed to the broader societal impacts of higher levels of educational attainment. Education has value beyond direct economic benefits because it contributes to enriching individuals' lives and the societies in which they live (Bowen, 1971). In addition, researchers have found significantly lower incarceration rates and higher volunteerism among those with some college (Baum & Payea, 2005).

Are there benefits to be had both to the individual and to the country for improving undocumented immigrants' postsecondary educational attainment levels? Four sets of benefits for higher education have been commonly identified, these being public economic benefits, private economic benefits, public social benefits, and private social benefits. Without legalization, undocumented college graduates may end up working in lower-paying, under-the-table jobs that require limited skills. Upon graduation, these undocumented students may not see the private economic benefits of lower unemployment, higher salaries, improved working conditions, higher savings, and professional mobility. They also may not reap the private social benefit of increased personal status or improved quality of life for their children. This is significant, for in choosing to pursue postsecondary education, undocumented students will, in effect, forego the earnings they could have accrued by working those 4 years (albeit without authorization and, most likely, in a low-paying position) even though their net returns to postsecondary education are uncertain.

What is needed for undocumented students, then, beyond greater access to higher education, is the full enfranchisement that results from documented status, thus leading to higher-paying jobs that can improve their individual socioeconomic status. There is a policy disconnect between providing tuition benefits to undocumented students while not providing a mechanism that allows either the students themselves or the public to gain the returns of this investment. This policy disconnect takes on greater or lesser proportions depending on predictions of future workforce needs. For example, it is estimated that by 2015, the United States will have increased its college participation rates by only 13%, a growth rate that will cause it to lag further behind other developed nations, including Canada, Korea, and Sweden, in levels of postsecondary attainment (Ruppert, 2003). Estimates suggest that by 2020, the United States will have created 15 million new jobs that require some college education, but will face a shortfall of 12 million workers with qualifications to fill the new positions (Carnevale & Fry, 2001). Although economic growth in the United States has traditionally been facilitated by growth in the numbers of native-born workers of prime working age, from now until 2021, there will be no net increase in the numbers of native-born workers aged 25–54, so any growth in the labor supply must come from immigrants or older workers (Aspen Institute, 2002). These two trends mean that the projected worker and skills gap could threaten U.S. productivity, growth, and international competitiveness and, most important, widen the socioeconomic divide (Aspen Institute, 2002).

FORMERLY UNDOCUMENTED
COLLEGE GRADUATES

Can undocumented college graduates help the U.S. economy to fill the need for a college-educated workforce if provided a path to legalization? How would legalization impact the college-going rates of currently undocumented youths? What happens when young adults who have lived most of their life undocumented are able to legalize their status? Do they accomplish the educational and professional goals they aspire to but were uncertain they could attain when they were undocumented? Do they continue to be motivated and driven to succeed as well as remain civically engaged? Rogers and colleagues (2008) describe an undocumented student in their study who became a legal resident during her senior year and subsequently enrolled in a California public university the next fall. In college, she was elected as a student senator, served on the national Coordinating Committee for MEChA, and participated in a variety of other campus clubs and organizations. As a sophomore, she was active in a campaign to save a local hospital clinic that serves a largely immigrant population. As she neared graduation, she planned to pursue work as a community organizer. Another student was admitted to several universities, but due to his lack of legal status, he could not access state or federal financial support for college. Fortunately, a Jesuit university offered him a private scholarship, which he accepted. During his sophomore year of college, the student was able to secure legal resident status. He provided academic guidance and tutored high school students throughout his 4 years in college. Active in the university's outreach efforts to the immigrant community, he often visited schools to talk about his high school experience. After graduating from college, he began a career as a high school counselor. Seif (2004) also describes an undocumented high school graduate who despaired about the lack of access to higher education. As an undocumented student, he worked alongside concerned educators and community activists who founded the Leticia A. Network to support undocumented student access to higher education in California. As a student activist, he attended various press conferences and court hearings. After legalizing his status through IRCA, he continued his political activity as citizenship director of a national nonprofit organization.

These studies suggest that universal access to public school matters to the overall health of American democracy. By attending U.S. public schools, undocumented youth develop civic capacity and a commitment to civic engagement. Using survey and interview data from 20 participants who can attest to the life-changing impact of legalization, I also examined the educational and professional attainments and civic contributions of college graduates who had lived most of their life undocumented but were able to legalize their status during high school or college.

Table 6.3 shows a comparison between undocumented students, undocumented college graduates, and formerly undocumented college graduates. Undocumented college students who had been able to legalize their status had demographic profiles similar to those of undocumented students and college graduates in that they were raised in homes with parents that had less than a high school education, they excelled academically in both high school and college, and they also worked long hours in their part-time jobs during high school and college.

Table 6.4 reveals few differences between undocumented students, undocumented college graduates, and formerly undocumented college graduates in their civic engagement patterns. All three groups demonstrated high levels of civic engagement. A key difference between formerly undocumented students and undocumented students and graduates is their rates of providing social services and activism. Formerly undocumented college graduates were more likely to have provided social services but were less likely to have been involved in activism. Whereas legal marginality often drives activism among undocumented youth, this was not the case with young adults who had legalized their status, which no longer had any bearing on their everyday experiences.

Table 6.3. Demographic and Academic Engagement Comparisons of Undocumented Students, Undocumented College Graduates, and Formerly Undocumented College Graduates

	Undocumented Students (*n* = 110)	Undocumented College Graduates (*n* = 20)	Formerly Undocumented College Graduates (*n* = 34)
Age at time of study	19.97	24.71	25.8
Immigration age	6.97	9.18	8.0
Mother's education	8.35	7.59	8.03
Father's education	9.71	10.94	8.85
High school GPA	3.48	3.5	3.48
College GPA	3.10	3.43	3.15
AP/Honors courses	4.4	3.8	3.29
High school hours worked/week	12.74	21.23	18.54
College hours worked/week	25.22	28.06	25.48

Table 6.4. Civic Engagement Comparisons of Undocumented Students, Undocumented College Graduates, and Formerly Undocumented College Graduates

	Undocumented Students (*n* = 110)	Undocumented College Graduates (*n* = 20)	Formerly Undocumented College Graduates (*n* = 34)
Civic engagement	90%	90%	88%
Social service	16%	16%	32%
Activism	21%	22%	12%
Tutoring	57%	55%	53%
Functionary work	78%	78%	73%
Extracurricular participation	95%	96%	94%
Leadership position	78%	77%	76%

Sofia

One of the formerly undocumented young adults I interviewed was Sofia. She was 3 years old when she came to the United States. The first educational obstacle she faced due to her undocumented status occurred early in her schooling:

> In elementary school I received a savings bond as a reward for participating in a reading program that was going to be placed in a bank account in order to gain interest for my college fund. That was something that I couldn't do because I didn't have a social security number under which it could be placed. After that, it became scholarships that I couldn't claim because I didn't have a social security number. I had many incidents like that leading up to high school.

In high school, the number of challenges she faced continued to increase: "For a long time I didn't even think that I would be able to continue my education after high school. . . . One of the hardest times for me was the application process. Funding was always an issue." It was especially difficult for Sofia to see the educational opportunities that her friends had that were not available to her:

> The most challenging was not having the same opportunities that other students around me had who had done just as well. . . . For me, it was very contradictory. . . . I had always been taught the principles of this country are always that if you work hard you will get what you work for and that everybody is equal in this country. . . . I had done everything that I could to be able to go to college and to be able to attend a college of my choice, but it was something I just couldn't control.

After coping with the challenges of being undocumented for most of her life, she experienced a dramatic change during her second year of college, when she finally was able to legalize her status:

> One of the things that really changed my experience in college was getting my legal residency. My outlook on life has completely changed because a lot of doors that were closed to me are now open. I can apply for internships. I can consider studying abroad. Those were all things that were out of the question before.

Currently, Sofia is deciding between two career paths:

> I am deciding whether I want to pursue education because education has changed my life and I could potentially change the lives of others, but I am leaning a little more toward immigration law because I think there is a lack of immigration lawyers who are successful at helping people.

Juana

Juana is a future teacher. She was about 1 and a half when she came to the United States. She became a legal temporary resident during 10th grade in high school. She was not eligible for any type of financial aid until she became a permanent resident. For that reason, she had to wait a semester after she graduated from high school to start college: "I was one of the lucky ones. I was fortunate enough to get my legalization and actually be able to attend college." At the time of the interview, Juana worked part-time as a teacher's assistant while attending community college. She plans to transfer to a 4-year university the following year to get her teaching credential and major in Chicano studies. After she graduates, she wants to become a teacher: "I want to teach. I definitely see the need for bilingual teachers. I think that becoming a teacher would help me get kids to think for themselves and question what's going on so they'll have the power and ability to make change for themselves."

Miriam

Miriam is a future professor. She was 17 years old when she came to the United States. After graduating from high school, Miriam got married. She wanted to go to college, but her status made it difficult. Eventually, she enrolled in community college and transferred to a top public university. During the summer, she would do research for professors. While in college, she worked washing dishes on the weekends to pay her tuition and expenses. Miriam got legal residency during her last year of college. Toward the end of college, she also had a professor who encouraged her to apply to graduate school: "He pushed me so hard to apply to grad school but I was 100% sure that they would not by any means accept me." Her professor's insistence worked. When I interviewed her, Miriam was in her second year of graduate school, working on her Ph.D.

Julia

Julia is also a future professor. She came to the United States when she was 13 years old. In high school, she was discouraged by various educators from pursuing her higher education goals:

> I wanted to go to a UC school and that's when I started talking to the counselors and then that's when they started telling me, "No, you should go to community college. It's really hard to go there and the requirements are really high," but I took the SATs. . . . When I graduated from high school, I was ranked number 7 out of 300 students so I applied to college, I applied to UC schools, and got accepted.

Julia legalized her status her sophomore year in high school. Before then, her future seemed uncertain: "I didn't know when I was going to get it and I didn't think I was going to get it before going to college." Julia attended college and graduated with a degree in chemical engineering. As she neared college graduation, Julia realized she enjoyed doing research: "I really wanted to start working, but then the more I started doing research the more I started liking it . . . so I started thinking about graduate school." Julia decided to apply and was accepted into a Ph.D. program right after college. At the time of the interview, Julia was in her third year of the Ph.D. program. When she graduates she plans to:

> Be a teacher, a professor, at either a community college level or private college. I would really like to teach college students, be involved in the educational system here in California. I know that if I decide to do that, I'll find different ways to encourage people. Also, since one of the reasons I went to grad school is because I like doing research, I'd like to go into the biotech industry.

Jessica

Jessica is a public interest lawyer. She was 13 years old when she came to the United States. After high school, due to her undocumented status, she attended community college for a total of 6 years before transferring to a 4-year university. She excelled academically in community college and had a 3.8 GPA. She had been accepted to prestigious public universities after 2 years at the community college, but she could not afford to attend due to her status. Jessica felt her community college experience had a very strong impact on her personal long-term career goals:

> My whole time at community college was influential because it was when I became aware of the limitations that my status had, and obviously that changed me. It made me realize that it wasn't just me, it was a bunch of people. So that was very powerful and led me to immigration type of work.

When she finally adjusted her status, Jessica was able to transfer to a public university and graduate. After college, Jessica was accepted into one of the top law schools in the country, UC Berkeley's Boalt School. When she graduated, she received the school's public interest award and received a post-graduate fellowship to work with several national immigrant rights organizations. Jessica pursued law school to become a public interest lawyer:

> I wanted to be a public interest lawyer, the one that helps the community. I want to do immigrants' rights obviously because of my

experiences and friends and family members who have gone through similar situations. . . . This was just the ultimate way for me to give back. And what better way than through law, which is so powerful.

Reflecting on the challenges she faced as an undocumented student, Jessica noted, "Before, the biggest frustration was school. Not being able to transfer, not being able to do what everyone else does and takes for granted; going to school, moving on." Jessica plans to continue working as a lawyer advocating for the rights of immigrants. She exclaimed, "If I could do this for the rest of my life, I would be happy."

Monica

Monica is a mental health professional. She was 12 years old when she came to the United States. As she reflected on her educational experiences as an undocumented student in community college, she noted, "It was limiting because I couldn't transfer even though I got my degree in 2 years and I was an honor student." Monica's strategy when she was undocumented was to not stick out: "I just didn't want to be noticed. You don't want to be noticed even though you want to excel." After completing undergraduate and graduate degrees, Monica embarked on a career as a mental health professional: "I work with mentally ill people. So I guess I do social work. I work for the government. . . . Eventually, after doing this job for a little while, I would love to join a federal agency and go from there."

Ignacio

Ignacio is a public school teacher and a future community college professor. He legalized his status when he was in 10th grade. He graduated from high school in the top 10% of his class with a 3.9 GPA. He also received the student athlete of the year award for the county. He attended college on an athletic scholarship and graduated with a major in liberal arts and bilingual education. His senior year, Ignacio decided he wanted to become a teacher, so he enrolled in a teaching credential program. He continued with his education and enrolled in a master's in multilingual education program: "Then I started applying for full-time jobs. They hired me right away. So I started working as an elementary school teacher." During his years as an elementary and later a middle school teacher, Ignacio has held several leadership positions on his school campus: "I was the GATE coordinator in elementary school for 2 years. Right now this is my third year as a bilingual coordinator at the middle school." After Ignacio completed his master's degree, he stated, "I was missing going to school. I was missing reading books. I enjoyed that. At the same time, my school principal was applying to a Ph.D. program. She encouraged me to apply with her." At the time of the interview, Ignacio had recently graduated with a Ph.D. in education. He wants to become a community college professor: "I feel like I can make an impact in the community college. I think it's a difficult place because you have to make a decision about either going to work or continuing with your education." As he reflects on how his life would be different if he was still undocumented, Ignacio notes, "I would probably be working as a truck driver or working at a low paying job getting minimum wage."

Nicole

Nicole is also an educator. She was 4 years old when she came to the United States with her mother, father, and four siblings. It was in her junior year of high school, as she started planning for college, when she first found out about her legal status: "I remember talking to my parents about it and I remember my mom expressing some concern about it. And then I remember her telling me that it wasn't possible that I could go to college because I didn't have papers." Nicole ended up attending a community college for 2 years. During community college, she always had to work to pay for her tuition and books because she was not eligible for financial aid. She was never able to participate in extracurricular activities because she was always working. Nicole applied and was accepted to UC Berkeley and UC Davis after she and her family received legal status. After college, Nicole went on to graduate school and now holds a doctorate in education. Her future professional goals include:

> To work with districts or with programs that target low-performing schools and low-performing students. Working with the students who are the most underserved. The teachers and the principals and districts that serve the students that are most underserved. That kind of work is very meaningful to me.

Degree Completion and Professional Attainment

Table 6.5 provides a summary of the highest educational attainment and professional endeavors of college graduates in this study who lived a significant portion of their lives as undocumented youth, but were able to legalize their status during high school or college. Not only did these individuals earn a college degree, but 63% also completed a graduate degree, including 31% who earned a J.D. or Ph.D. The findings also reveal that almost all these respondents pursued or are pursuing service careers as teachers, professors, civil rights lawyers, social workers, and counselors. These data not only provide a sense of the types of accomplishments that would not

Table 6.5. Formerly Undocumented College Graduate Educational and Professional Attainment

Pseudonym	Highest Degree Attained	Current Profession
Ramon	Ph.D.	College professor
Nicole	Ph.D.	K–12 educator
Jessica	J.D.	Civil rights lawyer
Ignacio	Ph.D.	K–12 educator
Isidro	Ph.D.	College professor
Jocelyn	M.A.	Spanish & cultural studies Ph.D. student
Luz	M.A.	Elementary school teacher/education Ph.D. student
Monica	MSW	Social worker
Mabel	M.A.	Counseling psychology Ph.D. student
Nadia	M.A.	Teacher
Julia	B.A.	Engineering Ph.D. student
Silvia	B.A.	Clinical psychology Ph.D. student
Miriam	B.A.	Ph.D. student
Raquel	B.A.	Ph.D. student
Moises	B.A.	Law school student
Natalia	B.A.	Training specialist

have been possible without legalization, but also give a preview of the types of educational attainment and professional endeavors that current undocumented students and college graduates can also pursue if they are provided with a path to legalization.

CONCLUSION

Since the *Plyler* ruling requires undocumented students to be educated at least through the end of high school, this means that today there are thousands of undocumented students graduating from high school each year, many of whom have lived in the United States for nearly 2 decades and who are unlikely to return to their country of origin after graduation. Even if the U.S. border were hermetically sealed today, the immigration patterns of the past 20 years mean that U.S. high schools will be graduating undocumented students for at least the next 15 to 20 years, which raises the policy question of what to do with such students when they do finish high school or college. Irrespective of whether we may agree with the moral argument that allowing such students access to college would be rewarding the illegal behavior of their parents, from an economic policy point of view, the major question would seem to be whether allowing them to graduate from college and work would serve as a means to begin to recoup some of the social and economic investment already made in them.

Opponents of enacting either federal or state legislation to provide tuition benefits to undocumented immigrants argue that doing so condones illegal immigration and will be an incentive for more people to enter the United States illegally in search of education benefits, which will further increase costs. This interpretation of the migration process—that immigrants are attracted to the United States by high social benefits (health, education, and welfare)—fails to appreciate the complexity of international migration. Factors including the role of migrant networks and family connections, the migration industry (labor recruiters, brokers, interpreters, smugglers, and so on), structural dependence on immigrant labor on the part of the host country and structural dependence on exporting labor on the part of sending nations all impact the migratory process (Castles, 2004). Although the empirical evidence suggests that undocumented workers do not come to the United States to take advantage of its welfare system, and conversely are not likely to leave because the state denies certain benefits, the dominance of this discourse has been significant; it has served to structure the political thinking and rhetoric of those who oppose giving undocumented students access to higher education and legalization.

Both formerly undocumented college graduates and undocumented college graduates believe in the meritocratic notion that education is a key to success, but the reality is that undocumented graduates cannot reap these perceived benefits from their marginally legal positions. Thus, even when immigrants participate in and contribute to society (e.g., working, earning a college degree), they are excluded from full membership if they lack full (permanent) legal recognition. As a result, legal status becomes an important axis of stratification that shapes immigrants' assimilation in critical ways (Menjívar, 2006). Thus, in line with the theory of segmented assimilation, the data on undocumented and formerly undocumented college graduates presented in this chapter demonstrate that immigration policies matter a great deal for mobility across generations (Portes & Rumbaut, 2001).

7

Conclusion

This is the only home we know. We are ready to contribute.
We are ready to be a part of American society.
—Sasha (undocumented college student)

Since undocumented students have no legal or legitimate paths to secure residency or citizenship under current U.S. immigration law, they are arguably a disenfranchised group. At first glance, there is much evidence to assume that their immigrant status would serve to keep them politically detached and away from civic activity. Most of these young adults are well aware of the anti-immigrant climate in the United States, and the consequences of their organizing, which frequently includes the threat of deportation. Their status puts them in close contact and conflict with the laws of the state, and this significantly limits their options for participation. The high levels of civic engagement and activism by undocumented students in this study run contrary to conventional wisdom and much of the scholarly literature regarding youth participation. In contrast to theoretical frameworks that predict marginalized groups feeling trapped and powerless, college-going undocumented students work to socially and legally reposition themselves in broader society (Abrego, 2008; Bumiller, 1988; Engel & Munger, 1996; Nielsen, 2000), managing their stigmatized social identity while underscoring their merits as a means to claim their rights (Abrego, 2008; Gonzales, 2008; Seif, 2004). The contexts of their lives provide important clues about why these young people are engaged at such high levels.

OVERVIEW OF MAIN FINDINGS

Working-class, college-eligible undocumented Latino students are distinct in various ways. Their academic profile is very different from the academic profile of most Latino students in the United States. They have higher than average GPAs, higher participation rates in Gifted and Talented Education programs, take a higher number of Advanced Placement courses, and receive various academic and extracurricular awards. Their strong psychosocial orientation toward schooling is quite possibly an important factor in their academic success and high educational aspirations. Like most immigrants, they struggled when they first learned English. Many students describe various experiences with unsupportive teachers, counselors, and insensitive classmates who questioned their academic talents. Despite these challenges, this book describes how students draw on their inner strength, social support networks, and their strong commitment to education to succeed.

It is easy to forget the precarious legal status of undocumented students if one merely glances at their long list of academic accomplishments. Chapter 2 noted that although these students dedicate themselves to school and doing well academically, they soon learn that the opportunities promised to them as a result of their dedication preclude them. Despite meeting the eligibility criteria, undocumented students are not able to participate in a variety of programs that require proof of legal status. Although their academic credentials make them eligible for summer jobs, internships, study abroad programs, academic enrichment programs, and scholarships, they are not able to reap the rewards of their educational investments. At the college level, the challenges further increase, as they are ineligible for any form of public funding to pay for college. Undocumented students not only have to forego attending the universities to which they are admitted—often the most selective and prestigious universities in the country—but instead are forced to begin their higher education studies at the local community college and must work long hours to afford the tuition. Since they are not eligible to apply for a driver's license, they often depend on unreliable public transportation to get to school. These challenges are constant reminders of the numerous limitations they face daily due to their legal status. Additionally, students see their U.S.-born classmates, who, despite inferior academic records, are able to pursue a college education, having access to full financial resources not available to them. Despite moments of despair, undocumented students find ways to reframe their circumstances in positive terms. They compare their opportunities with what they might have had in their country of origin and use that perspective to remain committed to their educational goals. Supportive teachers, counselors, and parents often play a key role in helping them maintain a positive outlook.

The undocumented Latino students in this study are not only stellar students academically, but they are also "model citizens." Chapter 3 demonstrated that in addition to their afterschool jobs, their responsibilities at home, and their volunteer work, undocumented students are involved in sports, student council, the band, and the school newspaper, among many other activities. Once students reach college, however, the increasing number of hours they must work to pay for tuition costs negatively affects their extracurricular participation rates. Beginning in elementary school, students begin to take on various leadership positions. Students are motivated to get involved to expand their horizons, develop leadership skills, contribute to their communities, and ultimately, develop a sense of belonging. Chapter 4 examined the civic activities in which students participate, such as providing social services, working for a cause, political activism, tutoring, and functionary work. It also elaborated on the various ways in which undocumented Latino youth are participating in American civic life at very high rates, which are often higher than their U.S.-born counterparts (Kleiner & Chapman, 1999; National Center for Education Statistics, 1999; Torney-Purta, 2002). This is a remarkable finding, given the numerous obstacles that undocumented students face due to their legal status, including working long hours per week to pay for school and personal expenses, and in many cases, difficulty finding reliable transportation to their volunteer activities.

The findings suggest that, in addition to ideals such as duty and helpfulness to others, undocumented students are motivated to volunteer not only because it is psychically rewarding, but also because it makes them feel empowered to work on social issues that directly affect them, such as educational access, poverty, and legal rights for immigrants. For undocumented students, civic engagement may be an attractive alternative to the frustrating impediments due to their legal marginality and is one of the few public acts they can do to feel like contributing members of society. The undocumented Latino youth in this study appear to embrace their role as civic participants despite their social marginalization. Rather than become completely dejected, hopeless, and apathetic, they invest time and effort in community service, volunteerism, political mobilization, activism, and advocacy. A significant body of research suggests that these civically engaged young adults are on a path to become the leaders of tomorrow (Fendrich, 1993; Hanks & Eckland, 1978; Ladewig & Thomas, 1987; McAdam, 1988; Otto, 1976; Verba, Schlozman, & Brady, 1995). Since service has been a formative experience for undocumented youth in this study, they will most likely continue to assume leadership positions in their community and remain civically active throughout their lives. The extent of that leadership, however, remains uncertain as long as their legal status remains unchanged.

Although it is not always their first choice, armed with a sense of optimism, most college-eligible undocumented students enroll at their local community college. As Chapter 5 demonstrated, these institutions often serve as their de facto gateway to higher education due to their low cost and close proximity to their homes. At the community college, students often find supportive and nurturing faculty, and enroll in academic outreach programs that provide rigorous academic courses and are important sources of information on how to transfer to a 4-year university. The community college experience, however, is not without its tribulations. Even with low tuition rates, students still struggle to make their tuition payments and balance school with long hours working at minimum-wage jobs. Many students are forced to take frequent leaves of absence from college due to a lack of money, prolonging their stay at the community college. Although some students are fortunate enough to attend community colleges that provide various forms of support, others are not so lucky. Some community colleges have no idea that undocumented students are a part of their student body, and thus, have no resources in place to help them.

Although undocumented students face an uncertain future, the most striking theme from the interviews was the students' tenacious optimism. Rather than become dejected, some students derive their motivation to continue with their struggle from their undocumented status. They reframe it as a positive influence and a challenge that they are intent on overcoming. Even at the prospect of earning a college degree and not being able to use it, community college students highlight the sense of accomplishment from just becoming "educated," regardless of their prospects for employment in the future, because they want to make their parents proud and because they see it as a way to repay them for all the sacrifices they made to provide a better life.

IMMIGRANT PARADOX

The results from this study coincide with previous "immigrant paradox" research, which posits that first-generation immigrants have better health and educational outcomes than individuals born in the United States, despite similarly disadvantaged circumstances (Fuligni, 1997; Hummer, Powers, Pullum, Gossman, & Frisbie, 2007; Kao, 1999; Kao & Tienda, 1995; Palloni & Morenoff, 2001; Portes, 1995; Portes & Rumbaut, 1990). Explanations for this immigrant advantage include selection bias (individuals with greater psychological and physical robustness may be more likely to embark on the immigrant journey), social and kinship networks (Palloni & Morenoff, 2001), cultural norms and values transported from the home country, and the interplay between immigrants' characteristics and the context of reception within the United States (Portes, 1995).

These studies also suggest that immigrant youth appear to have a more optimistic view than their U.S.-born counterparts of succeeding in U.S. society and have been shown to have greater academic motivation (Frome & Eccles, 1998; Kao & Tienda, 1995; Ogbu & Simmons, 1998; Suarez-Orozco & Suarez-Orozco, 1995). For example, in a study of the effects of the attitudes and behaviors of immigrant children and their families on academic achievement, Fuligni (1997) found that even after controlling for ethnicity, immigrant students emphasized educational success more than their native-born peers. Family can also have an indirect role in academic motivation.

Some immigrant groups tend to have a stronger sense of family obligation and responsibility, which may motivate them academically (Berry, Phinney, Sam, & Vedder, 2006; Fuligni, 1997). Immigrant children are also more likely than children from non-immigrant families to have parents who are married, which can provide greater overall stability and parental support for development (Brandon, 2002; Leventhal, Xue, & Brooks-Gunn, 2006).

Qualitative research has also shown that Mexican immigrant parents place primary importance on raising children who are "*bien educado*" (well-behaved), above all else (Valdés, 1996). These parents place great emphasis on children's respect for authority figures, which may promote increased adherence to classroom rules and more respectful behavior toward teachers (Keefe & Padilla, 1987). These parental values are communicated to youth directly, and they are likely to influence specific parenting behaviors that support these socialization goals. Resilience and self-affirmation may also play a central role. Those in the first generation may also be more likely to draw on the inoculating effects of the dual frame of reference between the country of origin and the new setting ("my life is much better here than there") as well as hope (Suárez-Orozco & Suárez-Orozco, 1995, 2001).

NEXT STEPS

Thirty-five years ago, in 1975, the state of Texas passed a law to deny undocumented immigrant students access to public education. Civil rights organizations challenged the Texas law and in 1982, the United States Supreme Court ruled in the case of *Plyler v. Doe* that undocumented children had the right to attend school K–12 regardless of their immigration status, a right guaranteed by the equal protection clause of the Fourteenth Amendment. Most recently, Rincon (2008) has argued for an expansion of undocumented students' educational rights to include higher education in the same way that other researchers have drawn on the principle of equality and equity guaranteed under the U.S. constitution to argue against school practices such as academic tracking (Oakes, 1985; Rincón, 2008; Wells & Serna, 1996). Equal access to higher education by undocumented immigrants is all the more salient given the economic contributions to the U.S. economy made by their parents and many of these youth themselves, who must also find employment while attending school. The lack of legal status, poverty, and difficulty speaking English have determined that many foreign-born laborers and their immigrant children are limited to jobs that pay low wages, coupled with difficult working conditions. In its ruling in the *Plyler v. Doe* case over 28 years ago, the Supreme Court referred to this fact. The majority decision pointed out that "without an education, these undocumented children, already disadvantaged as a result of poverty, lack of English speaking ability and undeniable racial prejudices . . . will become permanently locked into the lowest socioeconomic class" (p. 208). In this respect, the argument that the denial of education creates a permanent underclass still holds, even for high school graduates, as it is widely accepted that a high school diploma is not sufficient to acquire most jobs that allow individuals to earn a "living wage."

Who Deserves Citizenship? Moving Beyond Simplistic Discourse

What is our responsibility to undocumented children when they leave childhood and come of age as adults? Do our responsibilities for undocumented children end when they graduate high school and become undocumented adults? What does it mean to provide children with certain rights and protections that ultimately expire? Growing numbers of undocumented children moving into adulthood represent a critical problem and policy dilemma. The post-IRCA undocumented children are now beginning to come of age and face limited options for adjusting their status. A child who came to the United States at age 5 in 1990, for example, is now 23 years old, and a child who came to the United States at age 5 in 1995 is now 18 years old. These undocumented young adults are just now experiencing the transitions from high school to uncertain adult lives. Indeed, restrictions on their ability to receive financial aid, coupled with family poverty, have limited their post–high school options. As 65,000 undocumented students graduate from high school each year, they do so with uncertain futures and limited means through which to make successful transitions to adulthood.

Among the undocumented population are some 3.2 million children and young adults who entered the United States as minors and are guilty of nothing more than obeying their parents. The overwhelming majority have grown up in the United States, attended U.S. schools, and stayed out of trouble. They deserve legal status so that they can pursue their lives in the United States as Americans. Undocumented status constitutes an impermeable barrier to mobility, blocking access to good jobs and higher education for youth who have grown up American.

To fully rectify the flaws in our ineffective immigration system, we must move beyond current overly simplistic notions of "illegality." The American economy asked for workers, and with them came families and children who now call cities across the country their home. Socially, undocumented youth are indisputably full-fledged members of U.S. society— even if only at the lower rungs of the economic ladder. After having been educated in our schools, they speak English (often with more ease than Spanish), envision their futures here, and powerfully internalize U.S. values and expectations of merit. However, there are no available structural paths, even for those who excel academically. Paradoxically, their efforts to adapt and contribute economically are met with legal obstacles. Rather than valuing these youth as important societal resources, current policies restrict their options and curb the transformative potential that undocumented youth have in their communities.

For most of these promising students, their birthplace was literally a "geographic accident of birth," as they were brought to the United States by their parents when they were very young, and have resided and lived in the country for virtually all their lives. Since they were raised in the United States during their formative years, they consider themselves Americans. In fact, most know no other culture other than that of the United States, as their ties with their native countries were severed years ago when they immigrated to the United States with their parents. Most students do not even become aware of their lack of legal status until their final years in high school. Without full legal rights, undocumented youth will continue to be barred from the traditional paths of upward mobility that are available to other immigrants throughout U.S. history.

Perry's (2004, 2006) framework on membership provides a compelling approach that moves beyond simplistic notions of illegality by exploring the social integration of undocumented persons. In his research, Perry notes that citizens and noncitizens, Republicans and Democrats, students and nonstudents all agreed that substantive membership in American society included various criteria not recognized in the legal/illegal dichotomy currently used in policy discussions regarding the merits of providing a path to legalization for undocumented students and their families. According to Perry, a wide spectrum of Americans, both immigrants and U.S.-born alike, describe getting an education and working in the United States, and leaving countries of origin to come to the United States, as examples of an individual's *investment* in this country, and thus substantial membership. Aspirations to pursue higher education and eventual employment in the United States, as expressed by undocumented students, is also an indicator of substantial membership.

Perry (2006) argues that undocumented individuals meet Americans' notion of societal membership and, therefore, should be legally incorporated. In interviews with various stakeholders in Texas, such as public officials and undocumented individuals, he notes that residency in a community was a key component in membership. Undocumented individuals meet that criteria by their sustained time living in their respective communities, which has led to various forms of cultural and material exchanges, strengthened their sense of belonging to that community, and thus fostered community recognition of membership by social exchange and reciprocity.

Undocumented students also meet substantial membership criteria due to the civic knowledge they acquire in their schooling, which allows them to participate in the sociopolitical, cultural, and legal environments of the political community. Successful completion of high school is an important indicator of the basic skills involved in verbal communication, quantitative literacy, civic matters, history, and culture acquired by undocumented students. Participation in the workforce and school systems are also factors that contribute to membership and are evidenced by undocumented youths' school attendance and employment history (Perry, 2004, 2006).

Community service and extracurricular activities are also indicators of substantial membership (Perry, 2004, 2006). Community service is also indicative of substantial membership because it is an altruistic investment of time that demonstrates ethical and moral character. Participation in organizations that reflect American values and beliefs, and thus, denote an "American" identity, is another indicator. Participation in these activities demonstrates patriotism, another indicator of substantial membership, which also includes a shared sense of destiny with other Americans. For undocumented students, applying to college is a good indicator that they envision a future connection to the United States, one that has already been shaped by their school attendance at the primary and secondary levels. Finally, law abidingness and the low incarceration rates of undocumented persons further serve to illustrate their substantive membership.

Perry's definition of membership, informed by the convergent view of both legal citizens and undocumented persons, suggests that a comprehensive framework should be used to determine eligibility for legal status, rather than simply public opinion or political rhetoric (Perry, 2004, 2006). The principles of substantive membership signify a priori conditions that substantiate people's rights to social benefits in the United States. Democratic nations cannot entice workers to the country, benefit from their labor, neglect employment and immigration law enforcement, permit and encourage substantive membership, and then deny benefits to undocumented members. This "Potential Citizen" framework should be considered as a policy tool to demarcate levels of membership that are not considered in current administrative or legal structures that fail to recognize undocumented persons as substantive members. In *Plyler v. Doe*, the Court granted undocumented children various educational provisions because their futures were deemed personal investments and were viewed as connected to the political community.

In-State Tuition Legislation

Until now, this battle for undocumented youth has been fought almost exclusively in the realm of higher education. Growing numbers of undocumented children are moving into adulthood, while only about 5% to 10% of all undocumented high school graduates goes on to college (Passel, 2003). In 2001, almost 20 years after the *Plyler* ruling, Texas became the first state to allow the same population of undocumented students access to college at in-state tuition rates. As of 2011, 12 other states have also passed similar laws. With few funding sources available, in-state tuition laws for undocumented students have been found to have a significant effect. Undocumented students are 1.54 times more likely to enroll in a postsecondary institution if a state offers in-state tuition rather than out-of-state tuition charge (Flores, 2010). Undocumented students are also 69% more likely to enroll in college if they reside in a metropolitan area within a state that offers in-state tuition than if they live in one that does not (Flores, 2010). For college-ready undocumented students to achieve their dream of a college education, practices must be implemented to inform them of their eligibility for in-state tuition as well as policies to provide them with financial aid. Yet, in order to change practices and policies around financial aid and college access for undocumented students, educational practitioners and policymakers must possess an understanding of the unique experiences of the college-ready undocumented student (Chavez et al., 2007; Oliverez, 2006).

Educational Practice Reform

As undocumented students become more represented on college campuses, there is a growing concern among higher education practitioners about their responses to the needs of these students. Undocumented students are far less likely to know the requirements necessary or the process of applying to college due to their lack of familiarity with the U.S. education system (Contreras et al., 2008). To this end, research and practical resources have emerged to begin to address these issues (Miksch, 2005). It remains to be seen how these research efforts will translate (or not) into greater inroads on issues such as the availability of public financial aid for undocumented students—a challenge that nearly all recent studies of undocumented students' experiences in higher education have discussed as a key barrier to their transition to and persistence in college (Chavez et al., 2007). Undocumented students who are savvy enough to navigate high school and complete the requirements for college are still left with the considerable challenge of financing their college education.

Staff members are responsible for conveying the most up-to-date and accurate information to their students. Advisors, college counselors, financial aid staff, and outreach personnel are all on the front line of interacting with college students, and a critical element of their position is to assist students with navigating college. Undocumented Latino students are the most vulnerable within the Latino college population because of their status and often are the most in need of these services (Gandara & Contreras, 2009). From admissions and residency to making tuition payments, students find little coordination across administrative units and find themselves having to make multiple trips to offices in order to get their questions answered and their problems resolved. As increasing numbers of undocumented students make it to college, many develop an interest in specialized programs that bestow credentials but require state exams, background checks, and direct services with clients. Many campuses, however, do not offer clearly defined parameters for permissible participation on campus. Some students stumble across information on the Internet, often risking being misinformed. Although small numbers of students have found their way through these administrative barriers, several other students have been denied entry.

Among the 13 states that provide in-state tuition rights to undocumented students, there is a need to ensure institutional adherence to state laws through audits of the implementation of these laws (Contreras, 2009). Many secondary and postsecondary staff in educational institutions are not fully aware of the state's in-state tuition laws. Many institutional officials are unaware of the in-state tuition laws and, as a result, do not know that undocumented students can attend college. Students are often given misinformation in high school that continues into community college and university contexts (Gonzales, 2008). Previous studies also reveal that not all college staff are willing to provide information to undocumented students (Contreras, 2009; Gonzales, 2008). Some have political differences with the current laws that provide access to admission and in-state tuition. These staff either behave in a discriminatory manner or discourage undocumented students from finding the answers they need regarding financial aid, programs, or courses, thus undermining their higher education access (Contreras, 2009).

The pervasive anti-immigrant climate in the nation today highlights the need for greater oversight in all institutions to ensure that Latino students in K–12 and higher education receive proper information about all the educational options available to undocumented Latino students. Previous findings strongly suggest that professional development is needed for college and university staff who routinely conduct outreach and recruitment and work in critical offices dealing directly with undocumented students. Moreover, it is important to devise early intervention strategies that target undocumented students and their families to provide them with important information and resources. Without networks of information, many of these students miss existing opportunities. These interventions may prevent adults from discouraging undocumented students from realizing their dreams or giving them inaccurate information. Furthermore, routine audits by state entities or oversight from state offices for civil rights would help ensure that in-state tuition laws are fully implemented (Contreras, 2009).

As undocumented students arrive on college campuses in larger numbers, with advanced skills levels and greater experience in leadership activities, they are demonstrating higher levels of resiliency and organization, asserting claims to an equal education and pushing through administrative barriers. Over the course of my research, I witnessed many students bounce back from obstacles only to find ways to come up with tuition, gain acceptance into a program, or mobilize others to aid in their cause. Recognizing the general lack of information among families and even school officials about the rights that undocumented students and families have to pursue higher education, undocumented student-led support groups have begun providing information about higher education access to students, parents, teachers, and counselors. In California, student information sharing and advocacy within the university setting are moving an increasing number of students through California's public college and university system, being less dependent on the actions of front-line workers by drawing on the resources in their student networks (Chavez et al., 2007; Gonzales, 2008).

Education Policy Reform

Although the 13 states that have passed laws to extend resident tuition to undocumented students are clearly attempting to improve their postsecondary opportunities, such laws do not address the limitations inherent in having undocumented status. They do not remedy the fact that under current federal law, undocumented students are not eligible for any of the $129 billion annually distributed in federal financial aid and loans for postsecondary education (Baum & Payea, 2005). The lack of access to federal funds for postsecondary education represents a financial barrier to college for undocumented students that even resident tuition cannot offset. For example, over the last 5 years, the average advertised tuition and fees at U.S. public institutions has increased 40% at 4-year institutions, and 19% at 2-year institutions. For the lowest-income families, such sharp increases mean that without access to student aid, the average price of public 4-year colleges and universities would comprise nearly 29% of their total household income and the price of 2-year institutions would make up about 11%. Because undocumented students are not eligible for federal financial aid and in all but two states are not eligible for state aid, even with in-state tuition rates, college—particularly 4-year institutions—may still be out of reach. Thus, although many lower-income, undocumented students have high expectations that they will attend college, these expectations do not match reality (Hearn, 2001). For example, a 2003 study of the undocumented and legal immigrant high school population in Chicago found that while more undocumented students surveyed had college aspirations (80%) than did their legal immigrant counterparts (77%), 43% of undocumented students indicated that they did not know how they would pay for college, compared with 17% of immigrant students with legal status (Mehta & Ali, 2003).

Immigration Policy Reform

During the past 4 years that I have studied the educational experiences of college-going undocumented students, I have come to learn that in fact, despite the countless newspaper articles, news features, and blogs that claim Americans do not support providing a path to legalization to undocumented immigrants, readily available poll data do not support that assertion. Despite America's ambivalence about undocumented immigrants, support for legalization has steadily increased across all sectors of American society. Over the past 5 years, poll data indicate that no less than two-thirds of Americans have expressed their support across several public opinion polls (*Immigration*, 2010). As recently as December 2009, when the unemployment rate was at its highest and everyone was concerned about healthcare reform, a BSG poll found that 66% of Americans support comprehensive immigration reform (CIR). Support was consistent across the political spectrum, with 69% of Democrats, 67% of Independents, and 62% of Republicans supporting CIR. Furthermore, 55% agreed that the economic crisis makes it more crucial than ever that we solve immigration problems. A comparison of previous BSG polls highlights the consistently high support for legalization. In May 2009, 68% supported legalization; in November 2008, support was 67%. The BSG poll data are consistent with other national polls conducted over the past 5 years. A May 2009 poll by the Pew Research Center for the People & the Press found that support for a pathway to citizenship for undocumented immigrants has risen from 58% in 2007 to 63% in 2009 (Pew Research Center for the People & the Press, 2009). In May 2009, a Washington Post/ABC News poll showed that 61% of respondents supported legalization. Similarly, an April 2009 poll by the New York Times/CBS News found that 65% of respondents supported a path to citizenship for undocumented immigrants. In December 2007, the same poll found 66% support. Table 7.1 provides a chronological snapshot of the poll data across 5 years and 11 different nationally representative polls (*Immigration*, 2010).

As increasing numbers of undocumented students graduate from college, they remain undocumented and unable to make use of their training upon completion, highlighting the need to allow this population to adjust their immigration status. From a public policy perspective, increased educational attainment levels of undocumented immigrants are less than effective if they are not accompanied by federal legislation that provides a path to legalization to fully maximize the personal and societal benefits of their increased skills. Many of these young people aim to be public servants because their lived experiences have created a desire to give back to their communities. These students are aspiring doctors, lawyers, and teachers, all professions for which bilingual and culturally representative candidates are greatly needed. Until

**Table 7.1. Percentage of Respondents Who Support Providing a Path to
Legalization for Undocumented Immigrants on Public Opinion Polls,
2005–2009**

Poll	2005	2006	2007	2008	2009
BSG				67	66–68
Pew Research Center			58		63
Washington Post/ABC News			58		61
New York Times/CBS News		74–77	67		65
Los Angeles Times/Bloomberg		67	60–63		
CNN/Opinion Research Corp.		79	77–80		
NBC News/Wall Street Journal		61			
USA Today/Gallup		61–66	59		
Quinnipiac University		69			
Fox News/Opinion Dynamics	62	63–69			
Time		76–78			

Source: Immigration, 2010

current immigration policies are reformed, these young people will continue
to be unable to fulfill their aspirations and contribute to society. Without the
ability to actualize their education in the legal workforce, their situation represents wasted talent. Recently—due in large part to high-profile cases such as
that of Dan-el Padilla Peralta, the Princeton 2006 graduate and salutatorian
who was offered a scholarship to attend Oxford but was unable to return to
the United States—the plight of undocumented college students has entered
into the larger immigration debate and public discourse (Dwosh & Epstein,
2006). The stories of dozens of young people like Dan-el Padilla Peralta have
come to represent undocumented students as high achievers in school, sports,
and in their communities who have been denied the opportunity to move
forward and contribute to the society and the economy.

The DREAM Act

The size of the undocumented population, along with its dispersal to non-
traditional destinations (states other than California, Florida, Illinois,
New Jersey, New York, and Texas), has made immigrant students' lack
of access to higher education a national issue. The fact that states such as

Kansas, Oklahoma, Utah, and Washington have passed legislation to allow in-state tuition for undocumented students underscores the need for national legislation to ensure nationwide college access and legalization opportunities for this population.

Olivas (2004) argues that the issue of undocumented college students is an admissions case, an immigration matter, a taxpayer suit, a state civil procedure issue, a question of higher education tuition, a civil rights case, and a political issue. Essentially, it is a story about college-age young adults who have lived virtually all their lives in the United States and who want to attend college and enjoy the upward mobility that a college degree provides (Olivas, 1995). In that respect, while the in-state tuition laws allow these students the opportunity to obtain a postsecondary degree, current immigration federal law keeps them from being employed, thus thwarting the possibility to enjoy the upward mobility conferred by their college diplomas.

The DREAM Act represents a powerful imperative for recipients of conditional status to either pursue a college education or join the military. It also provides a strong incentive for undocumented students now in U.S. schools to finish high school, and it may provide a strong incentive to recent undocumented dropouts to complete their schooling or obtain a GED. Making legal status conditional on young adults' educational and military choices has no precedent in U.S. immigration policy. The DREAM Act does not guarantee any undocumented student the right to remain in the United States, and does not grant automatic or blanket amnesty to its potential beneficiaries. However, it does give some who have been acculturated in the United States the opportunity of earning the right to remain.

Widespread support. In chronicling the struggles of bright, hardworking, and dedicated undocumented college students, I came to learn that more than 100 national and 800 local and regional organizations publicly support the DREAM Act and CIR (*List of Dream Act Endorsements*, 2010). Many have written to members of Congress to urge the passage of legislation (Redden, 2007). These not only include pro-immigrant activist groups, but mainstream organizations such as AFL-CIO, American Federation of Teachers, National Association for College Admissions Counseling, National Education Association, National PTA, American Council on Education, and the College Board. Support also includes letters written to Congress urging the passage of the DREAM Act by presidents of the most influential and prestigious universities such as Harvard University and Stanford University (Faust & Hennessy, 2010). Corporate America has also expressed support for the DREAM Act. On April 3, 2009, Microsoft was one of the first Fortunate 500 companies to publicly declare support. The following month, New York mayor Michael Bloomberg and Wall Street companies, including Macy's, Morgan Stanley, Citigroup, American Express, JP Morgan Chase, and Pfizer, also announced their support (Riley, 2009). Religious groups have also increased their advocacy for immigration reform. Although initially the Catholic Church was the most visible group, many Protestant denominations, including Evangelicals, have joined the call for immigration reform. Legalization for undocumented immigrants is supported by the leadership of various Protestant groups, including Baptist, Pentecostal, Episcopal, Lutheran, and Presbyterian congregations (Fulwood, 2009). In fact, the National Association of Evangelicals (NAE) issued a resolution in October 2009 advocating for comprehensive immigration reform (Carey, 2010).

State governments have also indicated their support for their undocumented residents, particularly college-going undocumented students, through in-state tuition laws. Charged with the task of educating all children regardless of their legal status, states have been frustrated by the federal government's failure to address immigration reform. For over a decade, California, Texas, and eleven other states have struggled to provide access to higher education to college-going undocumented students because federal law prohibits most forms of financial aid. Tired of waiting, these states have taken matters into their own hands by passing state laws that allow undocumented student residents to be eligible for lower in-state tuition rates. In addition to Texas and California, the other states are New York, Illinois, Utah, Washington, Oklahoma, Kansas, New Mexico, Nebraska, and most recently, Wisconsin, Maryland, and Connecticut. Texas and New Mexico have gone a step further by also providing access to state funds to pay for tuition costs. These states, in which 77% of the estimated 12 million undocumented immigrants reside (Passel & Cohn, 2009) and which are the most affected by the legal limbo of these residents, officially recognize the potential economic and social contributions of undocumented college students and have decided to invest in nurturing their academic talent through state laws.

In summary, over the past 5 years, at least two-thirds of Americans have indicated their support for legalization for undocumented immigrants, along with increasing numbers of national organizations, Fortunate 500 companies, religious organizations, and states governments. The president and congressional elected officials must recognize that their fear of losing reelection for supporting immigration reform is not supported by the facts presented here. They must not allow the minority voice of anti-immigrant groups to dictate immigration policy. Despite their ambivalence about their immigrant neighbors, the majority of Americans agree that the most pragmatic solution is legalization.

Economic impact. The continuing neglect of immigration reform not only ignores the hardship endured by millions who live in American society as de facto second-class citizens, it also ignores the ongoing intellectual loss of thousands of talented college-going undocumented students. In the newly born undocumented youth activist movement, they are referred to as DREAMers, whose hopes and aspirations are tied to the passage of the DREAM Act. They have been waiting for 10 years for the opportunity to gain legalization and contribute to the economic vitality of American society. Many of these DREAMers exhibit the same drive and determination that led recent famous immigrants to this country, such as Jerry Yang, the co-founder of Yahoo, or Sergei Brin, the co-founder of Google, to create Fortune 500 companies that employ thousands of American workers and donate millions of dollars to social causes. Several recent studies highlight the economic benefits of providing a path to legalization for undocumented immigrants (Hill, Lofstrom, & Hayes, 2010; Hinojosa-Ojeda, 2010; Pastor, Scoggins, Tran, & Ortiz, 2010).

Passage of the DREAM Act would allow undocumented young adults to apply for jobs that are commensurate with their education as opposed to the minimum-wage jobs currently held by most undocumented college graduates. Their economic output, and the amount we can tax, would double. We would all be able to get a higher economic return from our investment in their education, which current immigration laws prevent. Research also suggests that young adults who are highly civically engaged, like the activist undocumented youth advocating for the DREAM Act, continue to do so throughout their adult lives. Thus, we can reasonably expect that the thousands of activist undocumented students across the country will benefit American society in another way if the DREAM Act is passed: They will apply their leadership skills to become leaders in city councils, school boards, state legislatures, and nonprofit and business sectors. Our rigid immigration laws deny these students any means to gain legal status, and deprive communities of the use of their talents and ambition. Shouldn't we stop wasting and rejecting that energy and ability, and instead nurture it for the good of American society by passing the DREAM Act?

Impact on higher education access. The DREAM Act would immediately make 726,000 undocumented young adults eligible for conditional legal status, while another 934,000 would be potential future beneficiaries (Batalova & McHugh, 2010). The DREAM Act would lead more immigrants to graduate from high school and college, it would also increase tax revenues and reduce government expenses. The increased fiscal contribution would repay the required educational investment within a few years and thereafter would provide a profit to taxpayers for several decades. The impact of the DREAM Act would not be limited to increased earnings, tax revenues, and social services savings. Freeing thousands of young immigrants to join the legal workforce would also help business and the economy fill crucial needs. Under current law, most undocumented youth are unable to complete their education and are forced to work illegally in the cash economy. Many settle for work as domestic servants, day laborers, ambulatory sellers, and sweatshop factory workers (Hill, Lofstrom, & Hayes, 2010; Hinojosa-Ojeda, 2010; Pastor, Scoggins, Tran, & Ortiz, 2010).

One particular concern that has been voiced about the DREAM Act is that it could take away seats in colleges and universities, as well as financial aid, from native-born students who want to pursue postsecondary education. However, this fear is not borne out by the experiences of the states that, since 2001, have passed laws allowing undocumented students who attend and graduate from in-state high schools to qualify for in-state college tuition. Such legislation has not precipitated a large influx of undocumented students, displaced native-born students, or been a financial drain on the educational system. In fact, these measures tend to increase school revenues by bringing in tuition from students who otherwise would not be in college (Gonzales, 2007).

Educational access for all undocumented students. Like *Plyler v. Doe,* the DREAM Act is only a *partial* solution. School experiences have a strong bearing on future success or failure. As the literature on educational achievement has consistently stated, Latino students continue to lag behind their peers in educational achievement. Confronted with very large schools and inadequate resources to meet their needs, many of these students are left to fall through the cracks. In order to ensure the success of legislation such as the DREAM Act, it is of the utmost importance to increase the number of potential beneficiaries. Ultimately, this means addressing existing inequalities within the school system. In order for the DREAM Act to have a larger impact, school reform needs to happen simultaneously.

Some argue that while stories of high-achieving undocumented students may compel the public to scrutinize current immigration laws, the use of superstar students who have been denied opportunity because of their undocumented status as the poster kids for legalization forces the debate into a question of deservedness that pits superstar students against their lesser-achieving peers, who for a variety of potential reasons—including family circumstances, school tracking, and poverty—do not have the right combination to excel academically (Gonzales, 2008, 2009). Whereas students who have a favorable position within the school (i.e., they have high levels of achievement, benefit from the support of teachers, and are able to mobilize some resources in their favor) are more readily able to reveal the details of their status in order to gain further resources, their less academically achieving counterparts receive few rewards from the school for disclosing their status, and for many of them, this is simply not an option.

For those undocumented students on the other side of school advantage, the negative effects of large classes, lack of individualized attention, and stigmatizing labels are several. Without support from teachers and other school staff, many students have difficulty improving their circumstances and getting through school. Further, sitting in large classrooms and standing in a very long line to see counselors pushes them further away from getting the help they critically need. As they approach the end of high school, many of the limitations of their "legality" begin to emerge. Students without a trusting and supportive relationship with adult mentors choose to conceal their immigrant status and related problems and, as a result, the school setting is not the safe cocoon it is for other students who can reveal their status and receive help. Rather, it is yet another environment where they must keep hidden most of the details of their daily lives. Because of this, many of these students are either weeded out or fall through the cracks (Gonzales, 2008, 2009, 2010).

Students who are not able to develop important relationships with teachers in their general track classes are shut out of many opportunities (Gonzales, 2008, 2010). They are not able to get help when they need it, and they do not have relationships to draw on for assistance with personal and family problems. Undocumented students in negatively tracked classes face potentially disastrous consequences since they lack relationships with adults to help guide them through the most important and daunting transition in their lives. Without special attention and support, because they are not able to get into college—either because of dropping out, lacking the necessary information, or simply not being on track to go to college—they are thrust into the world of "illegality" that awaits them after high school. For these undocumented youth, the buffer that has protected them from the dramatic consequences of their illegality begins to erode as they near high school graduation. As the low high school graduation statistics show, many lose faith in their education as the challenges they face become too great (Gonzales, 2008; Passel & Cohn, 2009). As part of the policy discussions on the merits of the DREAM Act and comprehensive immigration reform, we must not forget about the undocumented students who have not excelled academically due to poor schooling experiences and other social and economic hardships. They are equally deserving of legalization and the opportunity to better provide for their families and contribute to the economic and civic vitality of the United States.

FINAL THOUGHTS

If we are to take seriously our national commitment to create greater access to higher education, it is important to move away from conceptualizations of immigrant students as taking up resources, and toward a view that they are deserving of an investment of resources. In light of their significant presence in our public schools, our future as a nation is likely better served by the view that it is in our interest to invest in the development of these students' strengths and remove current educational barriers (Rodriguez, 2007).

Given that U.S. schools are required to provide access to public education to children regardless of their immigration status, it is logical to ensure that those resources invested early in their educational process are followed with resources that ensure the full realization of their potential as they prepare for entry into higher education.

Baseless Anti-Immigrant Rhetoric

Political science researchers have argued that language has been strategically used to frame the immigration debate, constructing "illegal" immigrants as criminal and deviant, thus justifying efforts to exclude them from U.S. society (Lakoff, 2006). The framing of immigrants as "illegal" often serves to hide our shared humanity and allows anti-immigrant sentiment, policies, and practices to become normalized ways of responding to undocumented immigration (Perez-Huber, 2009). The constructions of Latino/a immigrants as criminal, dangerous, and threatening to an "American" way of life reiterated in the media, saturating public discourse with negative images of Latino/a immigrants, reinforce the "illegal" frame (Chávez, 2001, 2008; Santa Ana, 2002). These negative portrayals of undocumented Latino/a immigrants have become so prevalent within immigration discourse that they have become "common sense" in how we understand immigration issues and subsequently inform institutional policies that deny undocumented immigrants the same rights and treatment as their U.S.-born and "legalized" counterparts (Lakoff, 2006; Perez-Huber, 2009).

Expedite Reform Efforts

During the last decade, a resurgent immigrant rights movement, arguing that current immigration policy is a human rights and pragmatic disaster, has elevated legalization onto the national political agenda. The nation simply cannot live indefinitely with immigration policies driven by demagoguery and gridlock—policies that are both impractical and inconsistent with democracy. Contemporary policies regarding the control of undocumented migration have had deleterious effects on undocumented children and their access to basic social rights. The tension between the needs to protect children and the needs for security is currently tilted toward the need for security at the expense of undocumented children. Recent waves of deportations have separated children from their parents.

Migrant "illegality" has risen in global importance as a chief immigration policy dilemma (De Genova, 2002; Inda, 2006). In the United States today, undocumented youth have taken up the mantle of mobilizing others like them to fight for their own position in society. With their backs against the wall and too much to lose, they engage in organizing and advocacy using various skills developed through leadership and civic engagement activities in school, thanks to the *Plyler* case. Despite their increasing activism, their legislative battle for increased educational access and societal participation has so far yielded a few significant victories. With each denial, students regroup to push forward once again, making their voices heard on college campuses and becoming increasingly visible in their communities. More and more, they are being sought out by schools and civic organizations to give presentations, speak at conferences, train staff members, and mobilize other activists (Gonzales, 2008). Preventing undocumented high school graduates from obtaining higher education is bad public policy. Following Brennan's argument in *Plyler v. Doe*, the future social and economic benefits of allowing these students to be educated would far outweigh any current incentive to save money. Hindering these students' ability to obtain higher education hurts the United States both economically and socially, particularly because many of these undocumented students do not plan to return to their countries of origin and will likely remain in the United States throughout their lives. From an economic standpoint, the obstacles presented by current laws are merely creating a subclass of citizens who otherwise are fully capable of becoming skilled professionals, and significant taxpayers. From a social standpoint, these impediments permanently lock these immigrants into the lowest socioeconomic class, perpetuating poverty among Latino immigrant communities.

Two-thirds of all immigrants live in six states: California, Florida, Illinois, New Jersey, New York, and Texas. These states in particular have much to gain from their population of undocumented students. Per the federal mandate of *Plyler v. Doe*, they have invested state resources into educating these students up to the high school level, and have nurtured them into becoming self-sustaining individuals. These states should receive federal support in the form of legislation to legalize undocumented students. The unwelcome but inescapable reality for undocumented students is that, without the prospect of adjusting their immigration status, the education they receive is useful individually for personal growth, but is of no consequence for the betterment of the overall condition of Latino immigrants in the United States because the undocumented remain unable to fully participate in society.

The United States was founded upon the notion that achievement should trump status. These students have worked hard to overcome the hardship of poverty to become valedictorians, athletes, artists, and academic champions. They attend schools that often lack books and other educational supplies, Advanced Placement classes and functional bathrooms, yet they manage to earn stellar grades and gain acceptance to top universities. The better policy is to view them as the valuable resource they are for our nation's future. Undocumented children do not have the independent ability to conform to federal law. Laws that punish children due to the actions of their parents who were just trying to provide a better future for them do not comport with fundamental conceptions of justice.

Some characterize undocumented students as an additional burden on the educational system. This argument assumes that undocumented students are the cause of the problems in the educational system. The problems of the United States' educational system are far more complex than those involving undocumented youth. Therefore, the additional burden of educating undocumented children is not the root of the problem, and thus, it is not a good reason to deprive undocumented children of an education. The solution is not to deprive children of the means by which they can improve their lives, and thereby improve society. The progressive approach is one that accepts the reality of the undocumented population and demands that the federal government afford them the ability to become productive members of society.

The research presented in this book suggests that undocumented students are substantive members of American society and should receive legal status. Our current immigration laws fail to recognize the multitude of ways in which undocumented students contribute to the health and vitality of our social institutions and communities. Only federal legislation has the power to revise immigration law to allow these students to adjust their status and end the burden of discrimination and dehumanizing branding of *illegals* and *aliens*. The message sent by federal, state, and local governments, and echoed in the media, is that these students and their families — among the most impoverished groups who are locked in the lowest-paying, dead-end jobs —are a threat to U.S.-born citizens. The debate, however, must consider the condition of their presence. Legal incorporation of undocumented youths and their families is a question of dignity and fundamental human rights.

As a nation, we must do the right thing when it comes to undocumented students. Whereas the United States has sought to be a champion of human rights throughout the world, when it comes to undocumented youth living among us, we have forsaken this policy of humanity. Instead, we have instituted immigration laws that criminalize and punish them. Millions of children and young adults are disenfranchised because they cannot become citizens in their country of residence. If democracy is to be maintained and enhanced, all members of society must have a political voice as a citizen. Citizenship must take into account not only residence within a nation's territory, but also other significant links such as family bonds, economic involvement, or cultural participation, as demonstrated by the students described in this book. Undocumented youth live among us and often have formed family and strong community connections. Lack of legal status renders immigrants not simply foreigners, but brands them as criminals, subject to expulsion—as no less than complete outcasts. Under the current system, length of residence is irrelevant. Family ties are meaningless. Hardship is immaterial. We should welcome undocumented students who have already become part of the social fabric of our nation. Like newcomers of the past, they are here to seek a better life through hard work and dedication to school and family.

This book presents compelling evidence that suggests that Congress must address the tentative situation of millions of young people who are hostages of a confusing and contradictory immigration system. In school, we encourage these students to aspire to greatness, yet we deny them the opportunity to share in the "American Dream." Can we really afford to pass up such a valuable resource? The undocumented students in this study have "played by the rules" their entire lives. They have been model citizens in every sense of the word, as evidenced by numerous awards from their schools and communities in recognition of their academic talent and civic virtues. In essence, they are at the very least, Americans by heart. Their civic and academic dedication and model citizen behavior should be officially recognized by the United States and rewarded with the rights and privileges of American citizenship.

References

Abrego, L. J. (2006). "I can't go to college because I don't have papers": Incorporation patterns of Latino undocumented youth, *Latino Studies, 4*(3), 212–231.

Abrego, L. J. (2008). Legitimacy, social identity, and the mobilization of law: The effects of Assembly Bill 540 on undocumented students in California. *Law & Social Inquiry, 33*(3), 709–734.

Aleinikoff, T. A., & Rumbaut, R. G. (1998). Terms of belonging: Are models of membership self-fulfilling prophecies? *Georgetown Immigration Law Journal, 13*(1), 1–24.

Alva, S. A. (1991). Academic invulnerability among Mexican-American students: The importance of protective resources and appraisals. *Hispanic Journal of Behavioral Sciences, 13*, 18–34.

Altschuler, D. (2011, March 18). The DREAM is Not Dead. *America's Quarterly.* Retrieved from http://www.americasquarterly.com

Andolina, M. W., Jenkins, K., Zukin, C., & Keeter, S. (2003). Habits from home, lessons from school: Influences on youth civic engagement. *Political Science and Politics, 36*(2), 275–280.

Arellano, A. R., & Padilla, A. M. (1996). Academic invulnerability among a select group of Latino students. *Hispanic Journal of Behavioral Sciences, 18*(4), 485–507.

Ask Senator Scott Brown to meet with immigrant youth from Massachusetts (2010, April). Retrieved from http://www.change.org

Associated Press. (2011, February 23). Men avoid life in prison for role in illegal immigrant's beating death. *WFMZ.* Retrieved from http://www.wfmz.com

The Aspen Institute. (2002). *Grow faster together, or grow slowly apart: How will America work in the 21st century?* Washington, DC: Author.

Bada, X., Fox, J., & Selee, A. (2006). *Invisible no more.* Washington, DC: Woodrow Wilson International Center for Scholars.

Bailey, T., & Weininger, E. B. (2002). Performance, graduation and transfer of immigrants and natives in City University of New York community colleges. *Educational Evaluation and Policy Analysis, 24*(4), 359–377.

Balsano, A. (2005). Youth civic engagement in the United States: Understanding and addressing the impact of social impediments on positive youth and community development. *Applied Development Science, 9*(4), 188–201.

Barber, B. L., Eccles, J. S., & Stone, M. R. (2001). Whatever happened to the "Jock," the "Brain," and the "Princess"?: Young adult pathways linked to adolescent activity involvement and social identity. *Journal of Adolescent Research, 16,* 429–455.

Barnes, S. L. (2006). Black church culture and community action. *Social Forces, 84,* 967–994.

Barrera, M. (1979). *Race and class in the Southwest: A theory of racial inequality.* Notre Dame, IN: University of Notre Dame Press.

Barry, R., & Barry, P. (1992). Establishing equality in the articulation process. *New Directions for Community Colleges, 78*(2), 35–44.

Batalova, J., & McHugh, M. (2010). *DREAM vs. reality: An analysis of potential DREAM Act beneficiaries.* Washington, DC: Migration Policy Institute.

Bauer, P. F. (1994). The community college as an academic bridge. *College and University, 69*(3), 116–122.

Baum, S., & Payea, K. (2005). *The benefits of Higher Education for Individuals and Society.* New York: The College Board.

Bean, J. P., & Eaton, S. B. (2000). A psychological model of college student retention. In J. M. Braxton (Ed.), *Reworking the student departure puzzle.* Nashville, TN: Vanderbilt University Press.

Bean, J. P., & Metzner, B. S. (1985). Interaction effects based on class level in an explanatory model of college student dropout syndrome. *American Educational Research Journal, 22,* 35–64.

Benard, B. (1995). *Fostering resiliency in kids: Protective factors in the family school and community.* San Francisco: West Ed Regional Educational Laboratory.

Bernstein, A. (1986). The devaluation of transfer: Current explanations and possible causes. *New Directions for Community Colleges, 54,* 31–40.

Bernstein, J., & Blazer, J. (2008). Legalizing undocumented immigrants: An essential tool in fighting poverty. *Journal of Poverty Law & Policy, 42*(7–8), 408–415.

Berry, J.W., Phinney, J. S., Sam, D. L., & Vedder, P. (2006). *Immigrant youth in cultural transition.* Mahwah, NJ: Erlbaum.

Bobo, L., & Gilliam, F. D., Jr. (1990). Race, sociopolitical participation, and black empowerment. *The American Political Science Review, 84,* 377–393.

Bohrman, R., & Murakawa, N. (2005). Remaking big government: Immigration and crime control in the United States. In J. Sudbury (Ed.), *Global lockdown: Gender, race, and the rise of the prison industrial complex* (pp. 112–120). New York: Routledge.

Bowen, H. R. (1971). Society, students, and parents—A joint responsibility: Finance and the aims of American higher education. In D. W. Breneman, L. L. Leslie, & R. E. Anderson (Eds.), *ASHE readers on finance in higher education* (pp. 25–35). Needham Heights, MA: Simon & Schuster.

Bowen, W. G., & Bok, D. (1998). *The shape of the river: Long-term consequences of considering race in college and university admissions.* Princeton, NJ: Princeton University Press.

Bowles, S., & Gintis, H. (1976). *Schooling in capitalist America*. New York: Basic Books.

Bragg, D. D. (2001). Community college access, mission, and outcomes: Considering intriguing intersections, and challenges. *Peabody Journal of Education, 76*(1), 93–116.

Brandon, P. D. (2002). The living arrangements of children in immigrant families in the United States. *International Migration Review, 36*(2), 416–436.

Bratsberg, B., Ragan, Jr., J. F., & Nasir, J. M. (2002). The effect of naturalization on wage growth: A panel study of young male immigrants. *Journal of Labor Economics, 20*(3), 568–597.

Brint, S., & Karabel, J. (1989). *The diverted dream: Community colleges and the promise of educational opportunity in America, 1900–1985*. New York: Oxford University Press.

Brown, R. K. (2006). Racial differences in congregation-based political activism. *Social Forces, 84,*1581–1604.

Brown Professors, Simmons rally for the DREAM Act. (2010, November 30). *The Associated Press*. Retrieved from http://www.boston.com

Bumiller, K. (1988). *The civil rights society: The social construction of victims*. Baltimore: Johns Hopkins University Press.

California Community Colleges. (1994). *Transfer: Preparing for the year 2000*. Sacramento: California Community Colleges. (ERIC Document Reproduction Service No. ED371810)

California Department of Education. (2009). Dataquest. Retrieved from: http://dq.cde.ca.gov/dataquest/

Camarillo, A. (1979). *Chicanos in a changing society*. Cambridge, MA: Harvard University Press.

Campbell, A., Gurin, G., & Miller, W. (1954). *The voter decides*. Evanston, IL: Row & Peterson.

Caputo, A. (2010, February 2). D.C. Immigration march planned: "We won't be taken for granted." Progress Illinois. Retrieved from http://www.progressillinois.com

Carey, G. (2010, January 28). Why Evangelicals want immigration reform this year. *The Washington Post*. Retrieved from www.newsweek.washingtonpost.com

Carmines, E. G. (1978). A competence theory versus need theory of political involvement. *Journal of Political and Military Sociology, 6,* 17–28.

Carnegie Corporation. (1992). *A matter of time: Risk and opportunity in the nonschool hours*. New York: Author.

Carnevale, A., & Fry, R. (2001). *Economics, demographics, and the future of higher education policy* (No. 15). Washington, DC: National Governors' Association.

Carpini, M. X., & Keeter, S. (1996). *What Americans know about politics and why it matters*. New Haven, CT: Yale University Press.

Carrera, J. W. (1989). *Educating undocumented children: A review of practices and policies. A Trends and Issues Paper*. Charleston, WV: ERIC Clearinghouse on Rural Education and Small Schools (ED319585).

Castles, S. (2004). Why migration policies fail. *Ethnic and Racial Studies, 27* (2), 205–227.

Cervantes, R. C., & Castro, F. G. (1985). Stress, coping, and Mexican American mental health: A systematic review. *Hispanic Journal of Behavioral Sciences, 1*, 1–73.

Chavez, E. I. (2009). *Closed doors, open windows: Legal status in the lives of undocumented youth.* Unpublished senior thesis, Stanford University.

Chavez, L. R. (1998). *Shadowed lives: Undocumented immigrants in American society.* Fort Worth, TX: Harcourt Brace College Publishers.

Chávez, L. R. (2001). *Covering immigration: Popular images and the politics of the nation.* Berkeley: University of California Press.

Chávez, L. R. (2008). *The Latino threat: Constructing immigrants, citizens and the nation.* Palo Alto, CA: Stanford University Press.

Chavez, M. L., Soriano, M., & Oliverez, P. (2007). Undocumented students' access to college: The American dream denied. *Latino Studies, 5*, 254–263.

Chronicle of Higher Education. (2001, August 21). *Almanac Issue.*

City University of New York. (1995). *Immigration/migration and the CUNY student of the future.* New York: Author.

Cohen, A. M., & Brawer, F. B. (2003). *The American community college.* San Francisco: Jossey-Bass.

Community leaders and residents gather at event in support of 1,500 mile 'Trail of Dreams' walk for immigration reform. (2010, January 18). *Saint Augustine Florida News.* Retrieved from http://www.staugnews.com

Contreras, F. (2009). *Sin papeles and rompiendo barreras*: Latino college students and the challenges in persisting in college. *Harvard Educational Review, 79*, 610–632.

Contreras, F., Stritikus, T., O'Reilly-Diaz, K., Torres, K., Sanchez, I., Esqueda, M., Ortega, L., & Sepulveda, A. (2008). Understanding opportunities to learn for Latino students in Washington State. Report prepared for the Washington State Commission on Hispanic Affairs and the Washington State Legislature. Retrieved from http://www.kcts9.org

Corrigan, P. W., & Lundin, R. (2001). *Don't call me nuts!: Coping with the stigma of mental illness.* Tinley Park, IL: Recovery Press.

Crocker, J., Major, B., & Steele, C. (1998). Social stigma. In D. Gilbert, S. T. Fiske, & G. Lindzey (Eds.), *The handbook of social psychology* (4th ed., Vol. 2, pp. 504–553). New York: McGraw-Hill.

Crystal, D. S., & DeBell, M. (2002). Sources of civic orientation among American youth: Trust, religious valuation, and attributions of responsibility. *Political Psychology, 23*(1), 113–132.

Daniels, A. K. (1988). *Invisible careers: Women civic leaders from the volunteer world.* Chicago: University of Chicago Press.

Dauber, S. L., Alexander, K. L., & Entwisle, D. R. (1996). Tracking and transitions through the middle grades: Channeling educational trajectories. *Sociology of Education, 69*, 290–307.

De Genova, N. (2002). Migrant "illegality" and deportability in everyday life. *Annual Review of Anthropology, 31*, 419–447.

De Genova, N. (2004). The legal production of Mexican/migrant "illegality." *Latino Studies, 2*(2), 160–185.

De Leon, S. (2005). *Assimilation and ambiguous experience of the resilient male Mexican immigrants that successfully navigate American higher education.* Doctoral dissertation, University of Texas Austin.

DeMartini, J. (1983). Social movements participation. *Youth and Society, 15*, 195–223.

DeSipio, L. (1996). *Counting on the Latino vote: Latinos as a new electorate.* Charlottesville: University of Virginia Press.

de Tocqueville, A. (1848). *Democracy in America.* New York: Harper & Row.

Diaz-Strong, D., & Meiners, E. (2007). Residents, alien policies, and resistances: Experiences of undocumented Latina/o students in Chicago's colleges and universities. *InterActions: UCLA Journal of Education and Information Studies, 3*, 1–20.

Dixson, A. D. (2003). "Let's do this!" Black women teachers' politics and pedagogy. *Urban Education, 38*, 217–235.

Dougherty, K. J. (1992). Community colleges and baccalaureate attainment. *Journal of Higher Education, 63*(2), 188–214.

Dougherty, K. J. (1994). *The contradictory college: The conflicting origins, impacts, and futures of the community college.* Albany: State University of New York Press.

Dougherty, K. J. (2002). The evolving role of the community college: Policy issues and research questions. In J. C. Smart & W. G. Tierney (Eds.), *Higher education: Handbook of theory and research* (pp. 295–348). New York: Agathon.

Dowd, A. C., Bensimon, E. M., Gabbard, G., Singleton, S., Macias, E., Dee, J., & Giles, D. (2006). *Transfer access to elite colleges and universities in the United States: Threading the needle of the American dream.* Retrieved from www.jackkentcookefoundation.org

Dozier, S. B. (1993). Emotional concerns of undocumented and out-of-status foreign students. *Community Review, 13*, 33–29.

Dozier, S. B. (2001). Undocumented and documented international students: A comparative study of their academic profile. *Community College Review, 29*(2), 45–53.

Drachman, E. (2006). Access to higher education for undocumented students. *Peace Review: A Journal of Social Justice, 18*, 91–100.

Dweck, C. S., & Licht, B. G. (1980). Learned helplessness and intellectual development. In J. Garber & M. E. P. Seligman (Eds.), *Human helplessness: Theory and application,* (pp. 197–221). New York: Academic Press.

Dweck, C. S., & Wortman, C. B. (1982). Learned helplessness, anxiety, and achievement motivation: Neglected parallels in cognitive, affective, and coping responses. In H. W. Krohne & L. Laux (Eds.), *Achievement, stress, and anxiety* (pp. 93–125). Washington, DC: Hemisphere.

Dwosh, A. E., & Epstein, J. (2006). American Dream. *The Daily Princetonian*. Retrieved from http://www.dailyprincetonian.com

Eccles, J. S., & Barber, B. L. (1999). Student council, volunteering, basketball, or marching band: What kind of extracurricular involvement matters? *Journal of Adolescent Research, 14*, 10–43.

Eccles, J. S., Barber, B. L., Stone, M., & Hunt, J. (2003). Extracurricular activities and adolescent development. *Journal of Social Issues, 59*, 865–889.

Eccles, J. S., & Gootman, J. A. (2002). *Community programs to promote youth development*. Washington, DC: National Academy Press.

Edmonston, B., & Smith, J. P. (Eds.). (1997). *The new Americans: Economic, demographic, and fiscal effects of immigration*. Washington, DC: National Academy Press.

Engel, D. M., & Munger, F. W. (1996). Rights, remembrance, and the reconciliation of difference. *Law & Society Review, 30*(1), 7–54.

Entwisle, D. R., Alexander, K. L., & Olson, L. S. (1997). *Children, schools, and inequality*. Boulder, CO: Westview.

Faust, D., & Hennessy, J. (2010, December 8). Deserving of the DREAM. *Politico*. Retrieved from http://www.politico.com

Feingold, A. (1994). Gender differences in personality: A meta-analysis. *Psychological Bulletin, 116*, 429–456.

Feldman, A. F., & Matjasko, J. L. (2005). The role of school-based extracurricular activities in adolescent development: A comprehensive review and future directions. *Review of Educational Research, 75*, 159–210.

Fendrich, J. (1993). *Ideal citizens*. Albany: State University of New York Press.

Fernández-Kelly, P., & Curran, S. (2001). Nicaraguans: Voices lost, voices found. In R. G. Rumbaut & A. Portes (Eds.), *Ethnicities: Children of immigrants in America* (pp. 127–155). Berkeley: University of California Press and Russell Sage Foundation.

Fields, R. R. (1962). *The community college movement*. New York: McGraw-Hill.

Finch, R. T. (1987). Characteristics and motivations of college students volunteering for community service. *Journal of College Student Personnel, 28*, 424–431.

Finkel, S. E. (1985). Reciprocal effects of participation and political efficacy: A panel analysis. *American Journal of Political Science, 29*, 891–913.

Finn, J. D. (1989). Withdrawing from school. *Review of Educational Research, 59*, 117–142.

Fitch, T. (1987). Characteristics and motivations of college students volunteering for community service. *Journal of College Student Personnel, 28*(5), 424–431.

Fix, M. (2006). *Testimony prepared for the Committee on Ways and Means, U.S. House of Representatives hearing on the impacts of border security and immigration on ways and means programs, July 26, 2006*. Washington, DC: Migration Policy Institute.

Flanagan, C., & Gallay, L. S. (1995). Reframing the meaning of "political" in research with adolescents. *Perspectives on Political Science, 24*, 34–41.

Flores, S. M. (2010). State "Dream Acts": The effect of in-state resident tuition policies on the college enrollment of undocumented Latino students in the United States. *The Review of Higher Education, 33*, 239–283.

Flores, S. M., & Chapa, J. (2009). Latino immigrant access to higher education in a bipolar context of reception. *Journal of Hispanic Higher Education, 8*(1), 90–101.

Fortuny, K., Capps, R., & Passel, J. S. (2007). *The characteristics of unauthorized immigrants in California, Los Angeles County, and the United States.* Washington, DC: The Urban Institute.

Fredricks, J. A., & Eccles, J. S. (2005). Developmental benefits of extracurricular involvement: Do peer characteristics mediate the link between activities and youth outcomes? *Journal of Youth and Adolescence, 6,* 507–520.

Fredricks, J. A., & Eccles, J. S. (2006a). Is extracurricular participation associated with beneficial outcomes: Concurrent and longitudinal relations? *Developmental Psychology, 42,* 698–713.

Fredricks, J. A., & Eccles, J. S. (2006b). Extracurricular involvement and adolescent adjustment: Impact of duration, number of activities, and breadth of participation. *Applied Developmental Science, 10,* 132–146.

Fredricks, J. A., & Eccles, J. S. (2008). Participation in extracurricular activities in the middle school years: Are there developmental benefits for African American and European American youth? *Journal of Youth and Adolescence, 37,* 1029–1043.

Frome, P., & Eccles, J. (1998). Parents' influence on children's achievement-related perceptions. *Journal of Personality and Social Psychology, 74*(2), 435–452.

Frum, J. L. (2007). Postsecondary educational access for undocumented students: Opportunities and constraints. *American Academic Journal, 3,* 81–107.

Fry, R. (2002). *Latinos in higher education: Many enroll, too few graduate.* Washington, DC: Pew Hispanic Center.

Fry, R. (2004). *Latino youth finishing college: The role of selective pathways.* Washington, DC: Pew Hispanic Center.

Fuligni, A. (1997). The academic achievement of adolescents from immigrant families: The roles of family background, attitudes, and behavior. *Child Development, 69*(2), 351–363.

Fulwood, S. (2009). *Loving thy neighbor: Immigration reform and communities of faith.* Washington, D.C.: Center for American Progress.

Galarza, E. (1977). *Farm workers and agri-business in California, 1947–1960.* Notre Dame: University of Notre Dame Press.

Galston, W. A. (2004). Civic education and political participation. *Political Science and Politics, 37,* 263–266.

Gandara, P. (1982). Passing through the eye of the needle: High achieving Chicanas. *Hispanic Journal of Behavioral Sciences, 4,* 167–180.

Gandara, P., & Contreras, F. (2009). *The Latino education crisis: The consequences of failed social policies.* Cambridge, MA: Harvard University Press.

Gans, H. (1992). Second generation decline: Scenarios for the economic and ethnic futures of the post-1965 American immigrants. *Ethnic and Racial Studies, 15*(2), 173–192.

Garcia, S. R., & Marquez, M. (2001). Motivational and attitudinal factors amongst Latinas in U.S. electoral politics. *NWSA Journal, 13,* 112–122.

Garmezy, N. (1981). Children under stress: Perspectives on antecedents and correlates of vulnerability and resistance to psychopathology. In A. I. Rabin, J. Arongy, A. M. Baverlay, & R. A. Zucker (Eds.), *Future explorations in personality* (pp. 196–269). New York: Wiley Interscience.

Garmezy, N. (1983). Stressors on childhood. In N. Garmezy & M. Rutter (Eds.), *Stress, coping and development in childhood* (pp. 43–84). New York: McGraw-Hill.

Garmezy, N., & Rutter, M. (Eds.). (1983). *Stress, coping, and development in children*. New York: McGraw-Hill.

Garmezy, N., Masten, A. S., & Tellegen, A. (1984). The study of stress and competence in children: A building block for developmental psychopathology. *Child Development, 55*, 97–111.

Garza, E., Reyes, P., & Trueba, E. (2004). *Resiliency and success: Migrant children in the United States*. Boulder, CO: Paradigm Publishers.

Geertz, C. (1973). Thick description: Toward an interpretive theory of culture. In C. Geertz (Ed.), *The interpretation of cultures* (pp. 3–30). New York: Basic Books.

Glanville, J. L. (1999). Political socialization or selection? Adolescent extracurricular participation and political activity in early adulthood. *Social Science Quarterly, 2*, 279–291.

Goffman, E. (1963). *Stigma: On the management of spoiled identity*. Englewood Cliffs, NJ: Prentice-Hall.

Gonzales, R. G. (2007). Wasted talent and broken dreams: The lost potential of undocumented students. *Immigration Policy in Focus, 5*(13), 1–11.

Gonzales, R. G. (2008). Left out but not shut down: Political activism and the undocumented student movement. *Northwestern Journal of Law and Social Policy, 3*, 219–245.

Gonzales, R. G. (2009). On the rights of undocumented children. *Society, 46*(5), 419–422.

Gonzales, R. G. (2010). On the wrong side of the tracks: Understanding the effects of school structure and social capital in the educational pursuits of undocumented immigrant students. *Peabody Journal of Education, 85*, 469–485.

Gonzalez, G. G., & Fernandez, R. A. (2003). *A century of Chicano history: Empire, nations, and migration*. New York: Routledge.

Gonzalez, M. S., Plata, O., Garcia, E., Torres, M., & Urrieta, L. (2003). Testimonios de Immigrantes: Students educating future teachers. *Journal of Latinos and Education, 2*(4), 233–243.

Gordon, K. (1996). Resilient Hispanic youths' self-concept and motivational patterns. *Hispanic Journal of Behavioral Sciences, 18*(1), 63–73.

Gray, M. J., Rolph, E., & Melamid, E. (1996). *Immigration and higher education*. Santa Monica, CA: RAND.

Greene, R. R. (2002). Human behavior theory: A resilience orientation. In R. R. Greene (Ed.), *Resiliency: An integrated approach to practice. policy, and research* (pp. 1–27). Washington, DC: NASW Press.

Grubb, W. N. (1991). The decline of community college transfer rates: Evidence from national longitudinal surveys. *Journal of Higher Education, 62*(2),194–222.

Gurak, L. J. (1999). The promise and the peril of social actions in cyberspace. In M. Smith & P. Kollock (Eds.), *Communities in cyberspace* (pp. 243–263). London: Routledge.

Hagedorn, L., Maxwell, W., Chen, A., Cypers, S., & Moon, H. S. (2002). *A community college model of student immigration, language, GPA, and course completion.* Los Angeles: University of Southern California School of Education.

Hamilton, D., & Fauri, D. (2001). Social workers' political participation: Strengthening the political confidence of social work students. *Journal of Social Work Education, 37*, 321–332.

Hamilton, N., & Chinchilla, N. S. (2001). *Seeking community in a global city: Guatemalans and Salvadorans in Los Angeles.* Philadelphia: Temple University Press.

Hanks, M., & Eckland, B. K. (1978). Adult voluntary associations and adolescent socialization. *Sociological Quarterly, 19*, 481–490.

Hart, D., Donnelly, T. M., Youniss, J., & Atkins, R. (2007). High school community service as a predictor of adult voting and volunteering. *American Educational Research Journal, 44*(1), 197–219.

Harvey, W. B. (2003). *Minorities in higher education: Twentieth annual status report, 2002–2003.* Washington, DC: American Council on Education.

Hearn, J. (2001). Access to postsecondary education: Financing equity in an evolving context. In M. B. Paulsen & J. C. Smart (Eds.), *The Finance of Higher Education: Theory, Research, Policy and Practice* (pp. 439–460). New York: Agathon Press.

Herman, N. J. (1993). Return to sender: Reintegrative stigma-management strategies of ex psychiatric patients. *Journal of Contemporary Ethnography, 22*, 295–330.

Hess, D. E. (2005). How do teachers' political views influence teaching about controversial issues? *Social Education, 69*(1), 47–48.

The high-quality learning conditions needed to support students of color and immigrants at California community colleges: Policy report. (2002). San Francisco: California Tomorrow.

Hill, L. E., Loftsrom, M., & Hayes, J. M. (2010). *Immigrant legalization: Assessing the labor market effects.* San Francisco: Public Policy Institute of California.

Hinojosa-Ojeda, R. (2010). *Raising the floor for American workers: The economic benefits of comprehensive immigration reform.* Washington, DC: Center for American Progress.

Hoachlander, G., Sikora, A. C., Horn, L., & Carroll, C. D. (2003). *Community college students: Goals, academic preparation, and outcomes (NCES 2003–164).* Washington, DC: U.S. Department of Education, National Center for Education Statistics.

Hochschild, J. (1995). *Facing up to the American Dream: Race, class, and the soul of the nation.* Princeton, NJ: Princeton University Press.

Hodgkinson, V. A., & Weitzman, M. S. (1997). *Volunteering and giving among American teenagers 14 to 17 years of age.* Washington, DC: Independent Sector.

Hoefer, M., Rytina, N., & Baker, B. C. (2009). *Estimates of the unauthorized immigrant population residing in the United States: January 2008.* Washington, DC: Department of Homeland Security Office of Immigration Statistics.

Holland, A., & Andre, T. (1987). Participation in extracurricular activities in secondary school: What is known, what needs to be known? *Review of Educational Research, 57,* 437–466.

Horn, L., & Nevill, S. (2006). *Profile of undergraduates in U.S. postsecondary education institutions: 2003–04, with a special analysis of community college students* (No. 2006-184). Washington, DC: U.S. Department of Education, National Center for Education Statistics.

Horn, L., Nevill, S., & Griffith, J. (2006). *Profile of undergraduates in U.S. postsecondary education institutions, 2003–2004, with special analysis of community college students* (Report No. 2006-184). Washington, DC: NCES Institute of Education Sciences.

Hummer, R. A., Powers, D. A., Pullum, S. G., Gossman, G. L., & Frisbie, W. P. (2007). Paradox found (again): Infant mortality among the Mexican-origin population in the United States. *Demography, 44,* 441–457.

Hurtado, S. H., Saenz, V. B., Santos, J. L., & Cabrera, N. L. (2008). *Advancing in higher education: A portrait of Latina/o College Freshmen at four year institutions, 1975–2006.* Los Angeles: Higher Education Research Institute, UCLA.

Igoa, C. (1995). *The inner world of the immigrant child.* Mahwah, NJ: Lawrence Erlbaum Associates.

Immigration. (2010, October 21). Retrieved from http://www. pollingreport.com/immigration

Inda, J. I. (2006). *Targeting immigrants: Government, technology, and ethic.* Oxford, UK: Blackwell.

Jarvis, S. E., Montoya, L., & Mulvoy, E. (2005). *The political participation of working youth and college students.* Austin, TX: The Center for Information and Research on Civic Learning and Engagement.

Jauregui, J. A., Slate, J. R., & Stallone, M. (2008). Texas community colleges and characteristics of a growing undocumented student population. *Journal of Hispanic Higher Education, 7*(4), 346–355.

Jensen, L. A. (2008). Immigrants' cultural identities as sources of civic engagement. *Applied Developmental Science, 12*(2), 74–83.

Jimerson, S., Egeland, B., & Teo, A. (1999). A longitudinal study of achievement trajectories: Factors associated with change. *Journal of Educational Psychology, 91,* 116–126.

Johnston, R. C. (2000, May 31). Guidance counselors often struggle to help undocumented students. *Education Week.* Retrieved from http://www.edweek.org

Jones, E. E., Farina, A., Hastorf, A. H., Markus, H., Miller, D. T., & Scott, R. A. (1984). *Social stigma: The psychology of marked relationships.* Hillsdale, NJ: Lawrence Erlbaum Associates.

Jozefowicz-Simbeni, D.M.H., & Allen-Meares, P. (2002). Poverty and schools: Intervention and resource building through school-linked services. *Children & Schools, 24,* 123–136.

Juan. (2010, February 20). *Contradictions.* Retrieved from http://www.trail2010.org/blog/2010/feb/20/contradictions

Jun, A. (2001). *From here to university: Access, mobility, and resilience among urban Latino youth.* New York: Routledge Falmer.

Kahne, J., & Westheimer, J., (2003). Teaching democracy: What schools need to do. *Phi Delta Kappan, 85*(1), 57–66.

Kaiser, C. R., & Major, B. (2006). A social psychological perspective on perceiving and reporting discrimination. *Law & Social Inquiry, 31*(4), 801–830.

Kao, G. (1999). Psychological well-being and education achievement among immigrant youth. In D. J. Hernandez (Ed.), *Children of immigrant: Health, adjustment and public assistance* (pp. 410–477). Washington, DC: National Academy Press.

Kao, G., & Tienda, M. (1995). Optimism and achievement: The educational performance of immigrant youth. *Social Science Quarterly, 76,*1–19.

Karabel, J. (1972). Community college and social stratification. *Harvard Educational Review, 41,* 521–562.

Karen, D. (1991). The politics of class, race, and gender: Access to higher education in the United States, 1960–1986. *American Journal of Education, 99*(2), 208–237.

Kedzie, C. R. (1997). A brave new world or a new world order? In S. Kiesler (Ed.), *Culture of the Internet* (pp. 209–232). Mahwah, NJ: Erlbaum.

Keefe, S. E., & Padilla, A. M. (1987). *Chicano ethnicity.* Albuquerque: University of New Mexico Press.

Kelly, D. C. (2004). *Civic views of young adult minorities: Exploring the influences of kinship on communities and youth mentoring communities on prosocial behaviors.* College Park, MD: The Center for Information & Research on Civic Learning & Engagement (CIRCLE).

Kintzer, F. C. (1970). *Nationwide pilot study on articulation.* Los Angeles: University of California. (ERIC Document Reproduction Service No. ED045065)

Kintzer, F. C. (1973). *Middleman in higher education.* San Francisco: Jossey-Bass.

Kintzer, F. C. (1996). *An historical and futuristic perspective of articulation and transfer in the United States.* Los Angeles: University of California. (ERIC Document Reproduction Service No. ED389380)

Kintzer, F. C., & Wattenbarger, J. L. (1985). *The articulation/transfer phenomenon: Patterns and directions.* Washington, DC: American Association of Community and Junior Colleges.

Kirby, L. D., & Fraser, M. W. (1997). Risk and resilience in childhood. In M. W. Fraser (Ed.), *Risk and resilience in childhood: An ecological perspective* (pp. 10–33). Washington, DC: NASW Press.

Kleiner, B., & Chapman, C. (1999). *Youth service-learning and community service among 6th- through 12th-grade students in the United States: 1996 and 1999.* National Center for Education Statistics, U. S. Department of Education: Office of Educational Research and Improvement. Retrieved from: http://nces.ed.gov/programs

Knoell, D. M. (1966). *Toward educational opportunity for all.* Albany: State University of New York.

Knoell, D. M., & Medsker, L. L. (1965). *From junior to senior college: A national study of the transfer student.* Washington, DC: American Council on Education.

Koltai, L. (1981). *The state of the district, 1981.* Los Angeles: Los Angeles Community College District. (ERIC Document Reproduction Service No. ED207654)

Kossoudji, S., & Cobb-Clark, D. (2002). Coming out of the shadows: Learning about legal status and wages from the legalized population. *Journal of Labor Economics, 20*(3), 598–628.

Laanan, F. S. (2001). Transfer student adjustment. *New Directions for Community Colleges, 114,* 5–13.

Ladewig, H., & Thomas, J. K. (1987). *Assessing the impact of 4H on former members.* College Station: Texas A & M University.

Lake, R. L., & Huckfeldt, R. (1998). Social capital, social networks, and political participation. *Political Psychology, 19*(3), 567–584.

Lakoff, G. (2006). *Thinking points: Communicating our American values and vision.* New York: Rockridge Institute.

Larson, R. W., & Verma, S. (1999). How children and adolescents spend time across the world: Work, play, and developmental opportunities. *Psychological Bulletin, 125,* 701–736.

Latinos in education: Early childhood, elementary, secondary, undergraduate, graduate. (1999). Washington, DC: White House Initiative on Educational Excellence for Hispanic Americans.

Leary, M. R., & Schreindorfer, L. S. (1998). The stigmatization of HIV and AIDS: Rubbing salt in the wound. In V. J. Derlaga, & A. P. Barbee (Eds.), *HIV and Social Interaction* (pp. 12–29). Thousand Oaks, CA: Sage Publications.

Lee, W. Y. (2001). Toward a more perfect union: Reflecting on trends and issues for enhancing the academic performance of minority transfer students. *New Directions for Community Colleges, 30*(2), 39–44.

Leovy, J. (2001, March 24). When no green card means no college. *Los Angeles Times,* p. A–1.

Lerner, R. M., & Steinberg, L. (Eds.). (2004). *Handbook of adolescent psychology.* Hoboken, NJ: Wiley.

Leventhal, T., Xue, Y., & Brooks-Gunn, J. (2006). Immigrant differences in school-age children's verbal trajectories: A look at four racial/ethnic groups. *Child Development, 77,* 1359–1374.

Link, B. G., Mirotznik, J., & Cullen, F. T. (1991). The effectiveness of stigma coping orientations: Can negative consequences of mental illness labeling be avoided? *Journal of Health and Social Behavior, 32,* 302–320.

List of Dream Act Endorsements. (2010). Retrieved from http://salsa.democracyin action.org

Lombardi, J. (1979). *The decline of transfer education.* Washington, DC: National Institute of Education. (ERIC Document Reproduction Service No. ED179273)

Lopez, M. H. (2003). Volunteering among young people (CIRCLE working paper). Retrieved from http://www.civicyouth.org

Lopez, M. H., & Marcelo, K. B. (2008). The civic engagement of immigrant youth: New evidence from the 2006 civic and political health of the nation survey. *Applied Developmental Science, 12*(2), 66–73.

Luthar, S. S., Cicchetti, D., & Becker, B. (2000). The construct of resilience: A critical evaluation and guidelines for future work. *Child Development, 71,* 543–562.

Luthar, S. S., & Zelazo, L. B. (2003). Research on resilience: An integrative view. In S. S. Luthar (Ed.), *Resilience and vulnerability: Adaptation in the context of childhood adversities* (pp. 510–549). New York: Cambridge University Press.

MacQueen, K. M., McLellan, E., Kay, K., & Millstein, B. (1998). Codebook development for team-based qualitative analysis. *Cultural Anthropology Methods, 10*(2), 31–36.

Mahoney, J. L., & Cairns, R. B. (1997). Do extracurricular activities protect against early school dropout? *Developmental Psychology, 33,* 241–253.

Mahoney, J. L., & Cairns, R. B., & Farmer, T.W. (2003). Promoting interpersonal competence and educational success through extracurricular activity participation. *Journal of Educational Psychology, 95*(2), 409–418.

Mahoney, J. L., Larson, R. W., & Eccles, J. S. (Eds.). (2005). *Organized activities as contexts of development: Extracurricular activities, after-school and community programs.* Mahwah, NJ: Lawrence Erlbaum Associates, Inc.

Mahoney, J. L., Larson, R. W., Eccles, J. S., & Lord, H. (2005). Organized activities as developmental contexts for children and adolescents. In J. L. Mahoney, R. W. Larson, & J. S. Eccles (Eds.), *Organized activities as contexts of development: Extracurricular activities, after-school and community programs* (pp. 3–22). Mahwah, NJ: Erlbaum.

Mahoney, J. L., Schweder, A. E., & Stattin, H. (2002). Structured after-school activities as a moderator of depressed mood for adolescents with detached relations to their parents. *Journal of Community Psychology, 30,* 69–86.

Mahoney, J. L., & Stattin, H. (2000). Leisure activities and adolescent antisocial behavior: The role of structure and social context. *Journal of Adolescence, 23*(2), 113–127.

Marsh, H. W. (1992). Extracurricular activities: Beneficial extension of the traditional curriculum or subversion of academic goals? *Journal of Educational Psychology, 84*(4), 553–562.

Marsh, H. W., & Kleitman, S. (2002). Extracurricular school activities: The good, the bad, and the non-linear. *Harvard Educational Review, 72*(4), 464–514.

Martin, S. A. (1999). *Early intervention program and college partnerships.* Washington, DC: George Washington University, School of Education and Human Development.

Martinez, L. M. (2005). Yes we can: Latino participation in unconventional politics. *Social Forces, 84,* 135–155.

Mascaro, L., & Muskal, M. (2010). Dream Act fails to advance in Senate. *Los Angeles Times.* Retrieved from http://www.latimes.com

Massey, D. S., Durand, J., & Malone, N. J. (2002). *Beyond smoke and mirrors: Mexican immigration in an era of economic integration.* New York: Russell Sage Foundation.

Masten, A. S. (1994). Resilience in individual development: Successful adaptation despite risk and adversity. In M. C. Wang & E.W. Gordon (Eds.), *Educational resilience in inner-city America: Challenges and prospects* (pp. 3–25). Hillsdale, NJ: Lawrence Erlbaum.

Masten, A. S., & Powell, J. L. (2003). A resilience framework for research, policy, and practice. In S. S. Luthar (Ed.), *Resilience and vulnerability: Adaptation in the context of childhood adversities* (pp. 1–28). New York: Cambridge University Press.

McAdam, D. (1988). *Freedom summer.* New York: Oxford University Press.

McDonough, P. M. (1997). *Choosing colleges: How social class and schools structure opportunity.* Albany: State University of New York Press.

McNamee, S. J., & Miller, R. K. (2004). *The Meritocracy myth.* Lanham, MD: Rowman & Littlefield.

McNeal, R. B. (1995). Extracurricular activities and high school dropouts. *Sociology of Education, 68,* 62–81.

McNeal, R. B. (1998). High school extracurricular activities: Closed structures and stratifying patterns of participation. *Journal of Education Research, 91,* 183–191.

Mehta, C., & Ali, A. (2003). *Education for all: Chicago's undocumented immigrants and their access to higher education.* Chicago: Center for Urban Economic Development at the University of Illinois.

Mena, J. (2004, September 19). *"DREAM Act"* Offers Hope to Immigrant Students. *Los Angeles Times.* Retrieved from http://www.latimes.com

Menjívar, C. (2006). Liminal legality: Salvadoran and Guatemalan immigrants' lives in the United States. *The American Journal of Sociology, 111*(4), 999–1037.

Metz, E., & Youniss, J. (2003). A demonstration that school-based required service does not deter—but heightens—volunteerism. *Political Science and Politics, 36(2),* 281–286.

Metz, E. C., & Youniss, J. (2005). Longitudinal gains in civic development through school-based required service. *Political Psychology, 26*(3), 413–437.

Miksch, K. L. (2005). Legal issues in developmental education: Immigrant students and the DREAM Act. *Research and Teaching in Developmental Education, 22*(1), 59–65.

Miles, M. B., & Huberman, A. M. (1994). *Qualitative data analysis*. San Francisco: Sage.

Morales, A., Herrera, S., & Murry, K. (2009). Navigating the waves of social and political capriciousness: Inspiring perspectives from DREAM-eligible immigrant students. *Journal of Hispanic Higher Education, 10*(3), 266–283.

Moulds, C. (2011, March 17). State committee passes new version of DREAM Act. *The Daily Californian*. Retrieved from http://www.thedailycalifornian.com

Munoz, S. M. (2008). *Understanding issues of college persistence for undocumented Mexican immigrant women from the new Latino Diaspora: A case study*. Doctoral dissertation, Iowa State University.

National Center for Education Statistics. (1999). *NAEP 1998: Civics*. Retrieved from http://nces.ed.gov/nationsreportcard/naepdata

National Center for Education Statistics. (2006). *Digest of Education Statistics, 2005*. Retrieved from http://www.nces.ed.gov/programs/digest/d05/tables/

Nie, N. H., Junn, J., & Stehlik-Barry. (1996). *Education and democratic citizenship in America*. Chicago: University of Chicago Press.

Niemi, R. G., & Junn, J. (1998). *Civic education: What makes students learn*. New Haven, CT: Yale University Press.

Nielsen, L. B. (2000). Situating legal consciousness: Experiences and attitudes of ordinary citizens about law and street harassment. *Law & Society Review, 34*(4), 1055-1090.

Nolin, M. J., Chaney, B., Chapman, C., & Chandler, K. (1997). *Student participation in community service*. Washington, DC: U.S. Department of Education.

Nora, A., & Rendón, L. (1990). Determinants of predisposition to transfer among community college students: A structural model. *Research in Higher Education, 31*, 235–255.

Nora, A., Rendón, L., & Cuadraz, G. (1999). Access, choice, and outcomes: A profile of Hispanic students in higher education. In A. Tashakkori & S. H. Ochoa (Eds.), *Education of Hispanics in the United States: Politics, policies, and outcomes* (Readings on equal education, vol. 16, pp. 175–199). New York: AMS Press.

Norrid-Lacey, B., & Spencer, D. A. (1999). *Dreams I wanted to be reality: Experiences of Hispanic immigrant students at an urban high school*. (ERIC Document Reproduction Service No. ED 434 527).

Oakes, J. (1985). *Keeping track: How schools structure inequality*. Binghamton, NY: Vail Ballou Press.

Ochoa-Becker, A. S. (1996). Building a rationale for issues-centered education. In P. W. Evans & D. W Saxe (Eds.), *Handbook on teaching social studies issues: NCSS Bulletin 93* (pp. 6–13). Washington, DC: National Council for the Social Studies.

Ogbu, J., & Simmons, H. D. (1998). Voluntary and involuntary minorities: A cultural-ecological theory of school performance with some implications for education. *Anthropology & Education Quarterly, 29*, 155–188.

Oliner, P., & Oliner, P. M. (1988). *The altruistic personality: Rescuers of Jews in Nazi Europe*. New York: Free Press.

Olsen, M. E. (1982). *Participatory pluralism: Political participation and influence in the United States and Sweden.* Chicago: Nelson Hall.

Olivas, M. (2004). IIRIRA, the Dream Act and Undocumented College Residency. *The Journal of College and University Law, 30*(2), 435–464.

Olivas, M. (1995). Storytelling out of school: Undocumented college residency, race, and reaction. *Hastings Constitutional Law Quarterly, 22*(4), 1019–1086.

Oliverez, P. M. (2006). *Ready but restricted: An examination of the challenges of college access and financial aid for college-ready undocumented students in the U.S.* Doctoral dissertation, University of Southern California.

Olsson, C. A., Bond, L., Burns, J. M., Vella-Brodrick, D. A., & Sawyer, S. M. (2003). Adolescent resilience: A concept analysis. *Journal of Adolescence, 26*, 1–11.

Otto, L. B. (1976). Social integration and the status attainment process. *American Journal of Sociology, 81*, 1360–1383.

Padilla, A. M. (1986). Acculturation and stress among immigrants and later generation individuals. In D. Frick, H. Hoefert, H. Legewie, R. Mackensen, & R. K. Silbereisen (Eds.), *The quality of urban life: Social, psychological, and physical conditions* (pp. 100–120). Berlin, Germany: de Gruyter.

Padilla, A. M., Cervantes, R. C., Maldonado, M., & Garcia R. E. (1988). Coping responses to psychosocial stressors in Mexican and Central American immigrants. *Journal of Community Psychology, 16*, 418–427.

Palloni, A., & Morenoff, J. D. (2001). Interpreting the paradoxical in the Hispanic paradox: Demographic and epidemiologic approaches. *Annals of the New York Academy of Sciences, USA, 954*, 140–174.

Pascarella, E., & Terenzini, P. T. (1991). *How college affects students.* San Francisco: Jossey-Bass.

Passel, J. S. (2003). *Further demographic information relating to the DREAM Act.* Washington, DC: The Urban Institute.

Passel, J. S. (2005). *Estimates of the Size and Characteristics of the Undocumented Population.* Washington, DC: Pew Hispanic Center.

Passel, J. S. (2006). *The size and characteristics of the unauthorized migration population in the U.S.: Estimates based on the March 2005 Current Population Survey.* Washington, DC: Pew Hispanic Center.

Passel, J. S., & Cohn, D. (2009). *A portrait of unauthorized immigrants in the United States.* Washington, DC: Pew Hispanic Center.

Passel, J. S., & Cohn, D. (2011). *Unauthorized immigrant population: National and state trends, 2010.* Washington, DC: Pew Hispanic Center.

Pastor, M., Scoggins, J., Tran, J., & Ortiz, R. (2010). *The economic benefits of immigrant authorization in California.* Los Angeles: Center for the Study of Immigrant Integration.

Patrick, H., Ryan, A. M., Alfeld-Liro, C., Fredricks, J. A., Hruda, L. Z., & Eccles, J. S. (1999). Adolescents' commitment to developing talent: The role of peers in continuing motivation for sports and the arts. *Journal of Youth and Adolescence, 28*, 741–763.

Peck, S. C., Roeser, R. W., Zarrett, N., & Eccles, J. S. (2008). Exploring the roles of extracurricular activity quantity and quality in the educational resilience of vulnerable adolescents: Variable- and pattern-centered approaches. *Journal of Social Issues, 64*(1), 135–155.

Perez, P. (1999). *Development of a mentor program for Latino students at Borough of Manhattan Community College.* Ed.D. Practicum Paper, Nova Southeastern University, Ft. Lauderdale, FL.

Perez, W. (2009). *We ARE Americans: Undocumented students pursuing the American Dream.* Sterling, VA: Stylus Publishing.

Perez, W., Espinoza, R., Ramos, K., Coronado, H., & Cortés, R. (2009). Academic resilience among undocumented Latino students. *Hispanic Journal of Behavioral Sciences, 31*(2), 149–181.

Perez, W., Espinoza, R., Ramos, K., Coronado, H., & Cortés, R. (2010). Civic engagement patterns of undocumented Mexican students. *Journal of Hispanic Higher Education, 9*(3), 245–265.

Perez-Huber, L. (2009). Challenging racist nativist framing: Acknowledging the community cultural wealth of undocumented Chicana college students to reframe the immigration debate. *Harvard Educational Review, 79*(4), 704–729.

Perry, A. M. (2004). *Philosophical arguments of membership: The case of undocumented immigrants and financial aid for postsecondary education.* Unpublished doctoral dissertation, University of Maryland, College Park.

Perry, A. M. (2006). Substantive members should receive financial aid. *Journal of Hispanic Higher Education, 5*(4), 1–25.

Pew Research Center for the People & the Press. (2009). *Trends in Political Values and Core Attitudes: 1987–2009.* Washington, DC: Author.

Phillippe, K. A., & Sullivan, L. G. (2005). *National profile of community colleges: Trends and statistics* (4th ed.). Washington, DC: Community College Press.

Pincus, F. L. (1980). The false promises of community colleges: Class conflict and vocational education. *Harvard Educational Review, 50,* 332–361.

Pincus, F. L., & Archer, E. (1989). *Bridges to opportunity? Are community colleges meeting the transfer needs of minority students?* New York: College Board.

Plyler, Superintendent, Tyler Independent School District, et al. v. Doe, Guargian, et al., 457 202 (1982).

Portes, A. (1995). Children of immigrants: Segmented assimilation and its determinants. In A. Portes (Ed.), *The economic sociology of immigration: Essays on networks, ethnicity, and entrepreneurship* (pp. 248–279). New York: Russell Sage.

Portes, A., & Rumbaut, R. G. (1990). *Immigrant America: A portrait.* Berkeley: University of California Press.

Portes, A., & Rumbaut, R. G. (2001). *Legacies: The story of the immigrant second generation.* Berkeley, CA: University of California Press.

Portes, A., & Rumbaut, R. G. (2006). *Immigration America* (3rd ed.). Berkeley: University of California Press.

Potochnick, S. R., & Perreira, K. M. (2010). Depression and anxiety among first-generation immigrant Latino youth: Key correlates and implications for future research. *The Journal of Nervous and Mental Disease, 198*(7), 470–477.

Powers, M. G., Kraly, E. P., & Seltzer, W. (2004). *IRCA: Lessons of the last U.S. legalization program.* Washington, DC: Migration Policy Institute.

Preston, J. (2010, January 1). To overhaul immigration, advocates alter tactics. *New York Times.* Retrieved from http://www.nytimes.com

Ramakrishnan, K., & Espenshade, T. (2001). Immigrant incorporation and political participation in the United States. *International Migration Review, 35*(3), 870–909.

Rangel, Y. T. (2001). *College immigrant students: How undocumented female Mexican immigrant students transition into higher education.* Unpublished doctoral dissertation, University of California, Los Angeles.

Redden, E. (2007, July 19). A new tack for the DREAM Act. *Inside Higher Ed.* Retrieved from http://www.insidehighered.com

Richman, J. M., & Fraser, M. W. (2001). Resilience in childhood: The role of risk and protection. In J. M. Richman & M.W. Fraser (Eds.), *The context of youth violence: Resilience, risk, and protection* (pp. 1–12). Westport, CT: Praeger.

Rifkin, T. (1996). Transfer and articulation policies: Implications for practice. *New Directions for Community Colleges, 96*, 35–43.

Riley, K. (2009, June 4). Time for undocumented students' DREAM to be realized. *The Seattle Times.* Retrieved from http://www.seattletimes.nwsource.com

Rincon, A. (2008). *Undocumented immigrants and higher education: Sí se puede!* New York: LFB Scholarly Publishing.

Rivera-Batiz, F. L. (1998). Undocumented workers in the labor market: An analysis of the earnings of legal and illegal immigrants in the United States. *Journal of Population Economics, 12*(1), 91–116.

Rodriguez, G. M. (2007). Cycling on in cultural deficit thinking: California school finance and the possibilities of critical policy analysis. In G. M. Rodriguez & R. A. Rolle (Eds.), *To what ends and by what means? The social justice implications of contemporary school finance theory and policy* (pp. 107–143). New York: Routledge.

Roeser, R. W., & Peck, S. C. (2003). Patterns and pathways of educational achievement across adolescence: A holistic-developmental perspective. In W. Damon (Series Ed.) & S. C. Peck & R. W. Roeser (Vol. Eds.), *New directions for child and adolescent development: Vol. 101. Person-centered approaches to studying human development in context* (pp. 39–62). San Francisco: Jossey-Bass.

Rogers, J., Saunders, M., Terriquez, V., & Velez, V. (2008). Civic lessons: Public schools and the civic development of undocumented students and parents. *Northwestern Journal of Law and Social Policy, 3*, 201–218.

Romo, R. (1979). *East Los Angeles: History of a Barrio.* Austin: University of Texas Press.

Ruiz, V. (1998). *From Out of the Shadows: Mexican Women in Twentieth Century America.* New York: Oxford University Press.

Rumbaut, R. G. (2005). Turning points in the transition to adulthood: Determinants of educational attainment, incarceration, and early childbearing among children of immigrants. *Ethnic and Racial Studies, 28,* 1041–1086.

Ruppert, S. S. (2003). *Closing the participation gap: A national summary.* Denver: Education Commission of the States.

Rutter, M. (1985). Resilience in the face of adversity. Protective factors and resistance to psychiatric disorder. *British Journal of Psychiatry, 147,* 598–611.

Sacchetti, M. (2010, April 17). Brown will meet with immigrants' advocates. *The Boston Globe.* Retrieved from http://www.boston.com

Sacchetti, M. (2009, May 21). Harvard's Faust backs path to legal residency. *The Boston Globe.* Retrieved from http://www.boston.com

Salinas, A., & Llanes, J. R. (2003). Student attrition, retention, and persistence: The case of the University of Texas–Pan American. *Journal of Hispanic Higher Education, 2,* 73–97.

Santa Ana, O. (2002). *Brown tide rising: Metaphors of Latinos in contemporary American public discourse.* Austin: University of Texas Press.

Santiago, T. (2010, April 16). WDAC helps to mobilize over 10,000 people. *WDAC.* Retrieved from http://www.wdac.info

Sax, L. J., Lindholm, J. A., Astin, A. W., Korn, W. S., & Mahoney, K. M. (2001). *The American freshman: National norms for fall 2001.* Los Angeles: Higher Education Research Institute, UCLA Graduate School of Education & Information Studies.

Scaturo, D. J., & Smalley, N. S. (1980). Locus of control as a multidimensional personality correlate of political involvement. *Journal of Psychology: Interdisciplinary and Applied, 105,* 83–92.

Schussman, A., & Soule, S. A. (2006). Process and protest: Accounting for individual protest participation. *Social Forces, 84,* 1083–1108.

Schwartzman, K. C. (1998). Globalization and Democracy. *Annual Review of Sociology, 24,* 159–181.

Seif, H. (2004). Wise up!: Undocumented Latino youth, Mexican-American legislators and the struggle for higher education access. *Latino Studies, 2*(2), 210–230.

Serow, R. C. (1991). Students and voluntarism: Looking into the motives of community service participants. *American Educational Research Journal, 28*(3), 543–556.

Shaw, K. M., & London, H. B. (2001). Culture and ideology in keeping transfer commitment: Three community colleges. *Review of Higher Education, 25*(1), 91–114.

Siantz, M. (1997). Factors that impact developmental outcomes of immigrant children. In A. Booth, A. C. Crouter, & N. Landale (Eds.), *Immigration and the family: Research and policy on U.S. immigrants* (pp. 149–161). Hillsdale, NJ: Lawrence Erlbaum Associates.

Siegel, K., Lune, H., & Meyer, I. H. (1998). Stigma management among gay/bisexual men with HIV/AIDS. *Qualitative Sociology, 21*(1), 3–24.

Sierra, C. M., Carrillo, T., DeSipio, L., & Jones-Correa, M. (2000). Latino immigration and citizenship. *PS: Political Science and Politics, 33*, 523–534.

Sigel, R. S. (1975). Psychological antecedents and political involvement: The utility of the concept of locus-of-control. *Social Science Quarterly, 56*, 315–323.

Sills, D. L. (1957). *The volunteers: Means and ends in a national organization.* Glencoe, IL: Free Press.

S.I.N. Collective. (2007). Students informing now (S.I.N.) challenge the racial state in California without shame . . . SIN verguenza! *Educational Foundations, 21*(1–2), 71–90.

Solorio, D. (2009). *Undocumented student access to higher education: Funding tuition.* Unpublished thesis, Stanford University.

Stanton-Salazar, R. (2001). *Manufacturing hope and despair: The school and kin support networks of U.S.-Mexican youth.* New York: Teachers College Press.

Steele, C. (1988). The psychology of self-affirmation: Sustaining the integrity of the self. *Advances in Experimental Social Psychology, 21*, 261–302.

Stepik, A., Stepik, C. D., & Labissiere, Y. (2008). South Florida's immigrant youth and civic engagement: Major engagement: Minor differences. *Applied Developmental Science, 12*(2), 57–65.

Stipek, D., & Weisz, J. (1981). Perceived personal control and academic achievement. *Review of Educational Research, 51*, 101–137.

Strauss, A., & Corbin, J. M. (1990). *Basics of qualitative research: Grounded theory procedures and techniques.* Newbury Park, CA: Sage.

Suarez-Orozco, M. M. (1989). *Central American refugees and U.S. high schools: A psychosocial study of motivation and achievement.* Palo Alto, CA: Stanford University Press.

Suarez-Orozco, M. M. (1996). California dreaming: Proposition 187 and the cultural psychology of racial and ethnic exclusion. *Anthropology and Education Quarterly, 27*(2), 151–167.

Suarez-Orozco, M., & Suarez-Orozco, C. (1995). *Transformations: Immigration, family life, and achievement motivation among Latino adolescents.* Stanford, CA: Stanford University Press.

Suarez-Orozco, C., & Suarez-Orozco, M. (2001). *Children of immigration.* Cambridge, MA: Harvard University Press.

Suárez-Orozco, C., Suárez-Orozco, M., & Todorova, I. (2008). *Learning a new land: Immigrant students in American society.* Cambridge, MA: Harvard University Press.

Swail, W. S., Cabrera, A. F., & Lee, C. (2004). *Latino youth and the pathway to college.* Washington, DC: Pew Hispanic Center.

Taylor, S. E. (1983). Adjustment to threatening events: A theory of cognitive adaptation. *American Psychologist, 38*, 1161–1173.

Thornton, S. J. (1991). Teacher as curricular-instructional gatekeeper in social studies. In J. P. Shaver (Ed.), *Handbook of research on social studies teaching and learning* (pp. 237–248). New York: MacMillan Publishing Company.

Tornatzky, L. G., Cutler, R., & Lee, J. (2002). *College knowledge: What Latino parents need to know and why they don't know it.* Los Angeles: Tomás Rivera Policy Institute at the University of Southern California.

Torney-Purta, J. (2002). The school's role in developing civic engagement: A study of adolescents in twenty-eight countries. *Applied Developmental Science, 6(4)*, 203–212.

U.S. Department of Education. (1995). *The condition of education, 1995.* Washington, DC: National Center for Educational Statistics.

U.S. Department of Education. (2003). *The condition of education, 2003* (NCES 2003-067). Washington, DC: Author.

Valdés, G. (1996). *Con respeto: Bridging the distances between culturally diverse families and schools: An ethnographic portrait.* New York: Teachers College Press.

Verba, S., Schlozman, K. L., & Brady, H. E. (1995). *Voice and equality: Civic volunteerism in American politics.* Cambridge, MA: Harvard University Press.

Wang, M. C., Haertel, G. D., & Walberg, H. J. (1994). Educational resilience in inner cities. In M. C. Wang & E. W. Gordon (Eds.), *Educational resilience in inner-city America: Challenges and prospects* (pp. 45–72). Hillsdale, NJ: Erlbaum.

Wassmer, R., Moore, C., & Shulock, N. (2004). Effect of racial/ethnic composition on transfer rates in community colleges: Implications for policy and practice. *Research in Higher Education, 45,* 651–672.

Waters, M. C. (1999). *Black identities: West Indian immigrant dreams and American realities.* New York: Russell Sage Press.

Wellman, J. V. (2002). *State policy and community college-baccalaureate* (National Center Report, No. 02-6). Washington, DC: National Center for Public Policy and Higher Education and the Institute for Higher Education Policy.

Wells, A. S., & Serna, I. (1996). The politics of culture: Understanding local political resistance to detracking in racially mixed schools. *Harvard Educational Review, 66*(1), 93–118.

Werner, E. E. (1989). High-risk children in young adulthood: A longitudinal study from birth to 32 years. *American Journal of Orthopsychiatry, 59,* 72–81.

Werner, E. E., Bierman, J. M., & French, F. E. (1971). *The children of Kauai: A longitudinal study from the prenatal period to age ten.* Honolulu: University of Hawaii Press.

Werner, E. E., & Smith, R. S. (1982). *Vulnerable but invincible: A longitudinal study of resilient children and youth.* New York: McGraw-Hill.

Werner, E. E., & Smith, R. S. (1992). *Overcoming the odds: High-risk children from birth to adulthood.* New York: Cornell University Press.

Wiehe, V. R., & Isenhour, L. (1977). Motivation of volunteers. *Journal of Social Welfare, 4,* 73–79.

Willig, A. C., Harnisch, D. L., Hill, K. J., & Maehr, M. L. (1983). Sociocultural and educational correlates of success-failure attributions and evaluation anxiety in the school setting for Black, Hispanic, and Anglo children. *American Educational Research Journal, 20,* 385–410.

Witt, A. A., Wattenbarger, J. L., Gollanttscheck, J. F., & Suppiger, J. E. (1994). *America's community colleges: The first century.* Washington, DC: American Association of Community Colleges.

Wylie, R. (1979). *The self-concept: Theory and research on selected topics* (Vol. 2). Lincoln: University of Nebraska.

Yale-Loehr, S., & Koehler, S. (2005). *Overview of U.S. immigration law.* Retrieved from http://www.twmlaw.com/site/resources/general20cont.html

Yates, L. S. (2004). *Plyer v. Doe* and the rights of undocumented immigrants to higher education: Should undocumented students be eligible for in-state college tuition rates? *Washington University Law Quarterly, 82,* 585–609.

Young Illegal Immigrants "Coming Out" in Illinois. (2010, March 11). *The Associated Press.* Retrieved from http://www.dailyhelard.com

Youniss, J., Bales, S., Christmas-Best, V., Diversi, M., McLaughlin, M., & Silbereisen, R. (2002). Youth civic engagement in the twenty-first century. *Journal of Research on Adolescence, 12*(1), 121–148.

Youniss, J., McLellan, J. A., & Mazer, B. (2001). Voluntary service, peer group orientation, and civic engagement. *Journal of Adolescent Research, 16*(5), 456–468.

Youniss, J., McLellan, J. A., & Yates, M. (1997). What we know about generating civic identity. *American Behavioral Scientist, 40,* 620–631.

Youniss, J., & Yates, M. (1997). *Community service and social responsibility in youth.* Chicago: University of Chicago Press.

Youniss, J., Yates, M., & Su, Y. (1997). Social integration: Community service and marijuana use in high school seniors. *Journal of Adolescent Research, 12,* 245–262.

Zamani, E. M. (2001). Institutional responses to barriers to the transfer process. *New Directions for Community Colleges, 114,* 15–24.

Zarya, V. (2010, February 12). Gutmann supports the DREAM Act. *The Daily Pennsylvanian.* Retrieved from http://www.dailypennsylvanian.com

Zhou, M. (1997). Growing up American: The challenge of immigrant children and children of immigrants. *Annual Review of Sociology, 23,* 63–95.

Index

Note: Page numbers followed by an "f" or "t" indicate figures or tables, respectively; the letter "n" refers to a note number.

About the Author

William Pérez is an associate professor of education at Claremont Graduate University (CGU). Born in San Salvador, El Salvador, he immigrated to the United States at the age of 10 to escape the civil war. He spent his remaining childhood in Pomona, California, attended Pomona College, and later earned a Ph.D. in child and adolescent development from Stanford University. Before joining CGU, Perez worked at various research institutes, including the RAND Corporation, the Stanford Institute for Higher Education Research, the UCLA Neuropsychiatric Institute, and the Tomas Rivera Policy Institute.

Perez's research focuses on the social and psychological development of immigrant adolescents. He also studies the academic achievement and higher education access of Latino students. His current research examines the achievement motivation and civic engagement of undocumented students. Perez's recent works include, *Undocumented Latino College Students: Their Socioemotional and Academic Experiences* (2011), "Civic Engagement Patterns of Undocumented Mexican Students" (*Journal of Hispanic Higher Education,* 2010), "Cursed and Blessed: Examining the Socioemotional and Academic Experiences of Undocumented Latino/A College Students" (*New Directions for Student Services,* 2010), "Supporting College-Eligible Undocumented Students: The Role of College Counselors" (*Journal of College Admission,* 2010), "Extending Our Investments: Higher Education Access for Undocumented Students" (*Diversity & Democracy,* 2009), "Academic Resilience Among Undocumented Latino Students" (*Hispanic Journal of Behavioral Sciences,* 2009), and *We Are Americans: Undocumented Students Pursuing the American Dream* (2009).